Whispers from the Past

Advance Praise for *Whispers from the Past*

'This wonderfully written book by Subhash Kak offers a captivating journey into the richness, depth, and breadth of Kashmir's history and culture. The author seamlessly weaves together threads of art, philosophy, literature, and spirituality, unveiling the profound contributions of Kashmir to the world over a millennium. Through the exploration of luminaries like Patañjali and Abhinavagupta, the book delves into the interpretation of Yoga and consciousness science, showcasing Kashmir's status as a creative hub.

The narrative skilfully blends scholarly insights with the enchanting fables of *Panchatantra*, creating a scenario that not only educates but also resonates with the reader's imagination. The book not only caters to the general reader but also incorporates recent research, providing, with authenticity, a holistic view of Kashmir's intellectual and cultural currents.

I am amazed at the simplicity with which Subhash Kak explores the unity in Kashmir's approach to art and aesthetics as a means to inspire and transform! He emphasizes that great art goes beyond mere cleverness, aiming to connect the audience with their own wellspring of creativity. The inclusion of diverse topics from drama and Ayurveda to military campaigns and representations of divinity enriches the narrative, reflecting the multifaceted nature of Kashmiri tradition.

I found *Whispers from the Past* an enlightening narrative that uncovers the profound lessons embedded in Kashmir's art and wisdom, drawing parallels with contemporary sensibilities. This book has not only broadened my understanding of Kashmir's heritage but has also kindled a desire to further explore the timeless lessons it holds for our contemporary world. Subhash Kak's ability to bridge the scholarly with the accessible makes this exploration both enlightening and enjoyable.'

Sampadananda Mishra

Director, Centre for Human Sciences,
Rishihood University, Sonipat

'*Whispers from the Past* fills a lacuna in the growing scholarship and general reader's interest in Kashmir's civilization. In a simple and easily understandable language, Kak gives the reader a tour of the highlights of Kashmir's outpouring in the sciences and the arts. It is a paean to what the beautiful Kashmiri mind achieved in all the variegated facets of life. For the Kashmiris, the purpose of art was to enliven life. This it did through the triggering of the "juice of life" within oneself. Art had to have a radiant splendour demonstrating that it was a bearer of light. There is a rhythm intrinsic to art. But art is an act that carry mysterious potency. Even as it manifests, it absorbs and takes one on the fastest and easiest tastes of the experience of the divine. There was no literacy needed to experience this state through nāṭya, or drama. With this totality as opposed to modern-day compartmentalized minds, the Kashmiris contributed hugely to grammar, philosophy, literature, the nature of the self, and beyond. Kak summarizes all of the key contributions of the savants in these fields with great competence. This book is destined to be an expanded primer to *The Wonder that Was Kashmir*, Kak's earlier work, and should be read by every greater Indophile. It will also make for a treasured gift.'

Rakesh Kaul

Author and vice chairman, Indo American Arts Council

'*Whispers from the Past*, an encyclopaedic work by Subhash Kak, infuses life to the glories of Kashmir distilled during its classical period. With incisive focus, he highlights Kashmir's arts, music, medicine, grammar, metaphysics, and cosmology. Kak has skilfully assembled different domains of knowledge, including history and philosophy, with some of the finest illustrations to accompany the narrative. Just as Kak synthesizes narratives from *Pañcatantra*, *Yogavāsiṣṭha*, or *Kathā-sarit-sāgara*, he brings awareness to real history, exploring the contributions of Lalitāditya and Avantivarman. At the same time, Kak offers a synthesis of the philosophies of Patañjali, Kumārajīva, Vasugupta, and Abhinavagupta, making this book a must-read for grounding our knowledge about classical Kashmir.'

Sthaneshwar Timalsina
Professor of Asian and Asian American studies,
Stony Brook University, USA

'This book by Professor Subhash Kak, eminent scholar, philosopher, and scientist, is an intellectually stimulating and enlightening study of the history and culture of ancient Kashmir. "Dazzlingly erudite", the author offers in it, a refreshingly new perspective on the region's Sanskritic past, exploring, in his own words, "the extraordinary brilliance and creativity of Kashmir in various arts and sciences". The Kashmir that the book presents is not a mere geographical entity but a vibrant matrix of creative imagination from where emanated currents and cross-currents of intellectual thought and artistic activity that not only shaped the Indian mind over centuries but also had a transformative influence on cultural expressions in countries of Central Asia, North Asia, and East Asia, far beyond its geographical boundaries.

The book refers to the "great contributions" this small Valley situated in the lap of the mighty Himalayas made in the fields of art, aesthetics, sciences, literature, and philosophy and analyses conceptual foundations of its cultural symbols. The author considers the idea of universal consciousness and interconnectedness of all things, which is central to the philosophy of Kashmir Shaivism, as the common thread behind different forms of creative enterprises in Kashmir as it is "fundamental for self-understanding". He links his interpretation of the iconographies of the many faces of Kashmir's Shiva and Vishnu images to this idea. Based on the author's recent research, this study is uniquely original and engaging. While invaluable for historians of art and thought, it is also bound to be an immersive reading for others interested in knowing about Kashmir's intellectual and cultural traditions.'

Shashi Shekhar Toshkhani
Author and scholar

'Kashmir plays an important place in India's political imagination, yet there is little understanding of its contributions to Indian culture. For example, it is not widely known that sages such as Charaka and Patanjali, storybooks such as the *Panchtantra* and the *Katha-sarit-sagara*, and the *Chitrasutra*, India's oldest treatise on the art of painting, are from Kashmir. Subhash Kak's book *Whispers from the Past: Art and Wisdom of Kashmir* corrects this deficiency by presenting a broad survey of Kashmiri history that will be valuable to both scholars and the general reader. It's a must-read.'

Anand Ranganathan
Scientist and author

'In the last decade, there has been a resurgence of Indian identity deeply rooted in its indigenous art, philosophy, and science. But very few know, let alone acknowledge, that Kashmir has made a significant and substantial contribution to India's knowledge system. *Whispers from the Past: Art and Wisdom of Kashmir* by Subhash Kak beautifully and cogently demonstrates that connection of Kashmir with the rest of India's culture and philosophy on the basis of historical evidence and rigorous scholarship. The book navigates through ancient and medieval periods, covering the evolution of scientific streams, art, music, drama, and philosophy—Ayurveda, Yoga, grammar, cosmology, consciousness, and many other vital ideas that originated in Kashmir or were pioneered by the people of Kashmiri descent. What's remarkable in this book is Dr Kak's erudition and meticulous precision with which he has turned complex subjects into easily comprehensible ideas and lucid prose. This is a thoroughly researched guide that seamlessly synthesizes historical texts and epigraphic testaments, painting a vivid tableau of the socio-cultural and political dynamics that shaped not just ancient and medieval Kashmir but the rest of India as well. It will not be an overstatement to say that *Whispers from the Past* is easily the most important insight into the evolution of the Indian way of life which streamed out of Kashmir. Each chapter in the book unfolds like a historical detective story, weaving together disparate threads into a cohesive narrative of connecting India's rich past flowing out of Kashmir with its assertive present. This is an essential read for anyone interested in knowing Kashmir's place in the cultural landscape of India historically.'

Aarti Tikoo Singh
Editor-in-chief, *The New Indian*

'It isn't easy for us in the 21st century to grasp what Kashmir was a millennium ago, when Hindu India was the world's wealthiest and most advanced civilization and Kashmir was its nerve centre, its crest jewel. The efflorescence of Kashmir was the culmination of thousands of years of Vedanta and Tantra. It was founded upon the discovery that Ultimate Reality is Pure Consciousness, and this insight was married to an intense appreciation of this world in all its beauty. It birthed a stunning series of sadhakas, scientists, artists, and philosophers, whose impact on humanity is yet to be experienced in full. Ānandavardhana, Utpaladeva, Abhinavagupta, and Śārṅgadeva are not household names. This is not because they weren't special; rather, the majority of the world, to this day, remains simply incapable of even beginning to understand what they were working on.

Tragically, this extraordinary culture was almost annihilated nearly seven hundred years ago. Until the time comes when a critical mass of people in the world are able to appreciate the work of these giants, we can only hope to preserve and carry forward their legacy. In this stirring book, Professor Subhash Kak delivers a paean to the lives, stories, and ideas of Kashmir, not the fake squatter-occupied Kashmir from TV shows and newspapers but the real Kashmir, the eternal Kashmir, the Sanatan Kashmir. *Whispers from the Past* is a whirlwind tour through the masterpieces of Hindu history, art, philosophy, and science, and contains just enough material to whet your appetite. Beautifully illustrated and dense with insights, it is sure to appeal to a wide swathe of readers.'

Anand Venkatraman

Interventional neurologist and researcher of Hindu mind sciences

Whispers from the Past

Art and Wisdom of Kashmir

Subhash Kak

ink | OCCAM

ISBN: 978-81-967375-2-8

First published in India 2024
This edition published 2024

BluOne Ink Pvt. Ltd
A-76, 2nd Floor, Sector 136, Noida
Uttar Pradesh 201301
www.bluone.ink
publisher@bluone.ink

Printed and bound in India at Nutech Print Services - India

ink | OCCAM

Note

Standard IAST convention has been used to transcribe Sanskrit words except for words that have become a part of the English vocabulary. Thus, for example, we use Krishna, Vishnu, Charaka, and Ayurveda for Kṛṣṇa, Viṣṇu, Caraka, and Āyurveda, except where the words come in Sanskrit contexts. Where there may be confusion, the correct spellings are indicated within square brackets in the first occurrence of the word.

Contents

Preface xv

1. Introduction 1
2. Charaka and Ayurveda 26
3. Drama and the Arts 38
4. The *Panchatantra* 58
5. Patañjali, Sage of Grammar and Yoga 78
6. Kumārajīva and the Middle Way 88
7. Cosmology and Consciousness: The *Yoga Vāsiṣṭha* 99
8. Lalitāditya and His Campaigns 130
9. Vasugupta and the *Śiva Sutra* 141
10. The Age of Avantivarman 159
11. Abhinavagupta on the Bhagavad Gita 170
12. Somadeva and Stories from the *Kathā-sarit-sāgara* 182
13. Representations of Divinity 200
14. Art and Music 209
15. Epilogue 224

Notes 229
References 237
About the Author 243

Preface

This book provides an overview of the history and culture of classical Kashmir together with contributions to Yoga and consciousness science, in which it produced two great stars: Patañjali, the author of the *Yoga Sūtra*, and Abhinavagupta, the Śaivite sage and philosopher whose ideas remain central to contemporary research on the nature of reality.

For over a thousand years, Kashmir was one of the most creative places in the world. Its contributions to the arts, aesthetics, sciences, literature, and philosophy are of abiding interest. The common thread behind these works was the idea that universal consciousness binds humanity and this is fundamental for self-understanding and for achieving personal creativity.

Kashmir is steeped in fables and imaginative tales that instruct in wisdom, ethics, and morality for the real world. The enduring popularity of its fables of *Panchatantra* derives partly from their unlikely setting. In my own childhood, we were regaled by stories by people from my father's office who would drop in at home for tea and conversation to pass the many hours of wintry evenings.

This book covers currents of intellectual life, lives of prominent royals, writers, and sages, and abridged tales from the *Panchatantra*, the *Kathā-sarit-sāgara*, 'Ocean of the Stream of Stories', and the *Yoga Vāsiṣṭha*, arguable the greatest book of imagination that presents the conundrums of consciousness with a clarity that has never been equalled. The intuitions related to the *Yoga Vāsiṣṭha* were elaborated in subjects ranging from yoga to literary criticism.

There is a unity in the approach adopted in Kashmir to art and aesthetics. Great art was not mere cleverness, but rather the capacity to take the audience to the source of creativity in themselves. This view, where art's function to inspire and transform takes one to the heart of awareness, is valuable to all creativity. The Kashmiri tradition's emphasis on aesthetics and beauty for meaning in life resonates with modern sensibility.

Many scholarly reconstructions of ancient Kashmiri society are based on one-sided reliance on textual material that has led to wrong understanding. If I may extrapolate from my experience growing up in Kashmir and listening to and participating in debates with spiritual masters, abstract notions were always measured on the anvil of commonsensical realism.

It is hoped that this book will encourage the readers to further investigate the story of Kashmiri art and wisdom and be amazed by how its lessons are relevant for our times.

Stillwater
20 November 2023

1

Introduction

Kashmir's geographical location partly explains its cultural history. It may be that natural beauty and temperate climate were conducive toits traditions in the arts, sciences, literature, painting, drama, and dance. Sharada Peeth (Śāradā Pīṭha), the great centre of Kashmiri learning and a repository of manuscripts, was at the northwest corner of the valley, less than 200 miles north of the ancient Taxila University.

Its relative isolation, and the security provided by the ring of mountains, may have led its scholars to bold conceptions. Its climate and the long winters may explain its fascination for philosophical speculation and devotion to storytelling. The great sage Abhinavagupta says this of Kashmir of his times (c. 11th century):[1]

sarvo lokaḥ kavir atha budho yatra śūro 'pi vāgmī
candroddyotā masṛṇagatayaḥ pauranāryaś ca yatra

Where one sees poets or scholars, where even warriors are eloquent,
where the urbane ladies have gentle gait and a moon-like radiance.

He saw Shāradā's grace behind its Kashmir's creativity, and he viewed it as the best place both for worldly enjoyment and the attainment of wisdom.

Kashmir is at the centre of Puranic geography. In the Puranic conception, the earth's continents are arranged in the form of a lotus flower. Mount Meru stands at the centre of the world, as the pericarp or seed-vessel of the flower surrounded by circular ranges of mountains. Like lotus petals, four island-continents (*dvīpas*) are arranged around it, aligned to the four points of the compass: Uttarakuru to the north, Ketumāla to the west, Bhadrāśva to the east, and Bhārata or Jambudvīpa to the south.

Uttarakuru is Central Asia, Ketumāla is Iran and lands beyond, and Bhadrāśva is China and the Far East. Kashmir's centrality in this scheme was a recognition that it was a meeting ground of trade and ideas for the four main parts of the Old World. It was the land where an attempt was made to reconcile opposites by deeper analysis and intrepid imagination.

Its nearness to rich trade routes brought it considerable wealth and emboldened Kashmiris to take Sanskrit culture out of the country as missionaries. They became interpreters of Indian civilization, authoring many fundamental synthesizing and expository works. Some of these works are anonymous encyclopaedias, and for many other works the author's name is known but the details of the life and circumstances in Kashmir are barely remembered.

Kalhaṇa's *Rājataraṅginī*[2] (River of Kings), written in about 1150, provides a narrative of successive dynasties that ruled the land. Kalhaṇa claimed to have used eleven earlier works that are lost and the *Nīlamata Purāṇa*[3] (6th or 7th century) that has survived. The narrative in the *Rājataraṅginī* becomes more than mere names with the accession of the Kārkoṭa dynasty in the early 7th century.

The political boundaries of Kashmir have, on occasion, extended well beyond the valley and the adjoining regions.

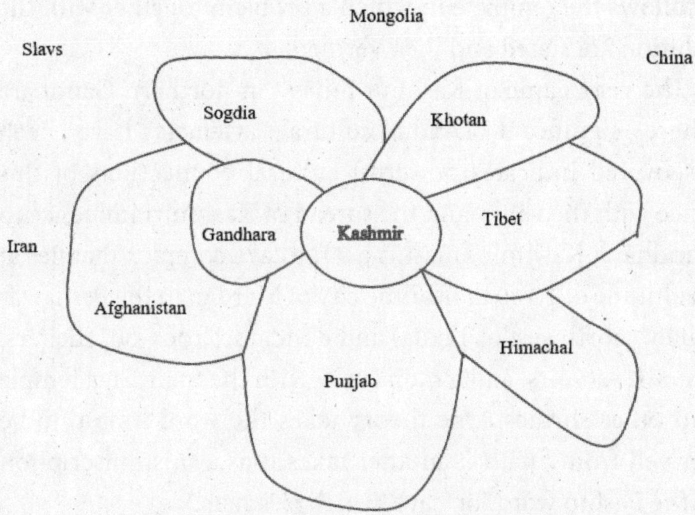

1.1. Kashmir and its neighbouring regions

According to the Chinese traveller Xuanzang (Hiuen Tsang), the adjacent territories to the west and south, down to the plains, were under the direct control of the king of Kashmir. With Durlabhavardhana of the Kārkoṭa dynasty, the power of Kashmir extended to parts of Punjab and Afghanistan.

It appears that during this early period the elite—if not the general population—of Gandhāra, Gilgit, Baltistan, and West Tibet spoke Kashmiri-related Dardic languages. Gāndhāri language was also in use in Khotan in Central Asia. It is not surprising that Dardic languages continue to be widely used in Gilgit, Baltistan, Chitral, and Eastern Afghanistan. The Gandhāra-jātaka (Jātaka 406) speaks of Kashmir and Gandhāra being ruled as a twinned kingdom.

The Sharada script was widely used in northwestern India between the 8th and 12th centuries. The Bakhshali manuscript found in Gandhāra and variously dated to the early or late first millennium is the oldest extant mathematics manuscript from India. A compendium of rules and illustrative examples, it follows the template in which a problem together with the solution are stated and then verified.

The very name of Kashmir Smast[4] in northern Gandhāra where significant Hindu cultural artefacts have been discovered indicates powerful cultural connections of this place with the valley and the spread of Kashmiri influence to Gandhāra. Kashmir Smast is a large cave complex that lies at an altitude of 1,100 m near the city of Mardan in the Peshawar Valley (northwest of Taxila) and it includes rock-cut shelters, water reservoirs, and a monastery with the main Śiva temple and other shrines. One theory takes the word 'smast' to be derived from 'maṭha'; another takes it as a mistranscription of the Pashto word for 'cave' which is 'smats'.

The main cave consists of two inner chambers up 33 m high with a total length of about 180 m. The numismatic finds show an uninterrupted sequence from the 2nd century BCE to the 11th century CE. It appears to have been an important Shaivite pilgrimage centre dedicated to Śiva Maheśvara and his consort, Bhīmā ('the fearful one'), venerated in her svayambhū manifestation, which the Chinese pilgrim Xuanzang noted in the 7th century.

In the 8th century, Lalitāditya (reigned 725–761), conquered parts of north India, Central Asia, and Tibet. His vision and exertions marked a new phase of Indian empire-building. Kashmir had become an important player in the rivalries amongst the various kingdoms of north India, Tibet, and China.

The jostling of the Kashmiri State within the circle of the north Indian powers led to an important political innovation. The *Viṣṇudharmottara Purāṇa*, believed to have been written in Kashmir at the time of the Kārkoṭa kings, recommends changes in the application of the rājasūya and the aśvamedha sacrifices. The latter, in its medieval interpretations, was

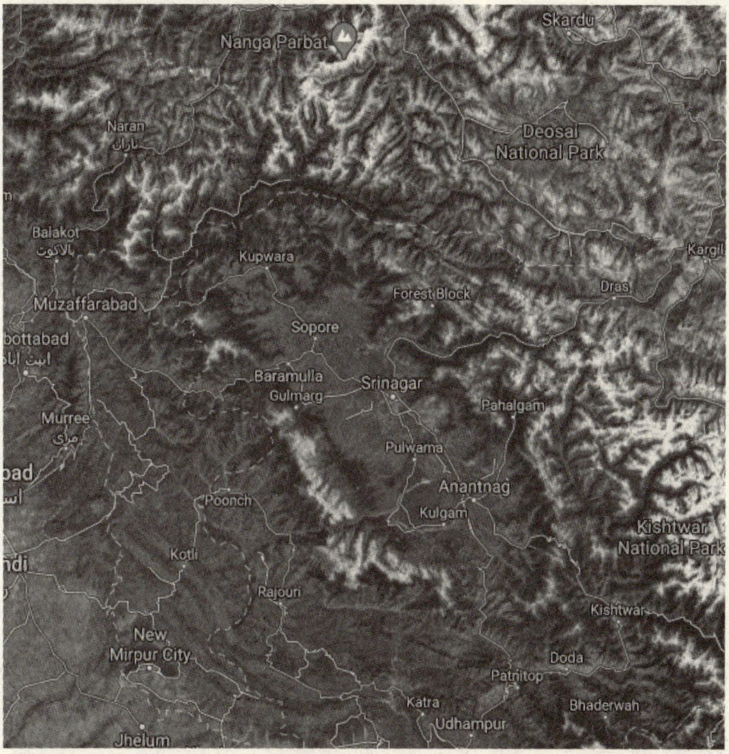

1.2. Vale of Kashmir, ringed by white mountains; Sharada Peeth is in the north of Kupwara on the Kishanganga (Neelum) river

responsible for much warfare amongst kings. In medieval times, the horse was left free to roam for a year and the king's soldiers tried to establish their rule in regions visited by the horse, which led to fighting. The *Viṣṇudharmottara Purāṇa* replaced these ancient rites with the rājyabhiṣeka (royal consecration) and surapratiṣṭhā (the fixing of the divine abode) rites.

Kashmir and Central Asia

The Tarim Basin in present-day Xinjiang has been in many ways Kashmir's cultural extension. The entire region was a part of the Sanskritic world for centuries. It was called Uttarakuru (perhaps the origin of the word Uyghur) in Indian texts and its languages included Indian Prakrits like Gandhāri that has some similarities with Kashmiri, Sanskrit, and Khotanese Saka, which itself has much Sanskritic vocabulary. We have attestation of the name Uttarakuru in local accounts. For example, a Tocharian B text from Kucha speaks of Uttarakuraṣṣe = Uttarakuruvāsī. Megasthenes, Strabo, and Ptolemy also use this name for the region.[5]

According to the Chinese pilgrim Xuanzang and Tibetan translations of Khotanese documents, Khotan was founded by immigrants from northwest India during the 3rd century BCE reign of Aśoka Maurya. These immigrants most likely included Kashmiris.

The region was part of the Kushan Empire of Kanishka in 2nd century CE. After the rule by the Kushans, the next centuries became the golden age of the Tarim Basin, and various Indic city-states thrived along the Silk Road such as Kashgar, Khotan, Turfan, Kucha, Niya, and Loulan.

The centrality of Kashmir to this area is clear from the fact that Kanishka chose it for the Fourth Buddhist Council. A stream of scholars and adventurers left Kashmir for the Tarim Basin to seek fame and fortune and to take Indic ideas to Central Asia.

The most prominent of the Tarim Basin states was the Kingdom of Khotan (Gaustana or Gosthāna in Sanskrit) that lasted until 1006 CE when it was conquered by the Karakhanid ruler Yusuf Kadir Khan of Kashgar.[6]

Jonarāja's *Rājataraṅginī*[7] takes Kashmir's story to the 15th century. According to Mongol accounts[8], Kashmir became a part of the expanding Mongol Empire during the reign of Ogedai, Chingiz Khan's son and successor, and two Kashmiri brothers Otochi and Namo joined Ogedai's court sometime after 1235. Namo rose to be the chief of all the Buddhist monks in the empire, and he played a key role in the adoption of Buddhism by the Mongols. Later, during Möngke's reign (1251–1259), there was a new invasion and Kashmir was plundered and the chief inhabitants of the capital were killed, and the rest, together with wives and children, were carried off into slavery.

Otochi was sent as administrative governor (darughchi) only to be killed in a local rebellion. By the time of Jonarāja, these events had been forgotten for he speaks of this period merely as unsettled conditions during the reigns of Rājadeva, Saṅgrāmadeva, and Rāmadeva. Rashīd al-Dīn's *Jāmiʿ al-Tawārīkh* (chronicles compiled around 1307–1316) is the source for these details, and he speaks of a further invasion of Kashmir in 1272–1273 by another Mongol force. These invasions weakened Kashmir in vital ways so that it ultimately fell in 1339, a total of 333 years after the similar fall of Khotan.

Here's the backstory to the events in Khotan. Satuq Bughra Khan was one of the first Turkic rulers to convert to Islam in 934. According to Tazkirah Bughra Khan, Satuq's conversion took place when he was twelve. His teacher in Islam was a Samanid merchant from Bukhara named Abu an-Nasr, who was befriended by the Khan of Kashgar, Satuq's stepfather and uncle Oghulchak Khan, and was granted permission to build a mosque in the town of Artux just outside Kashgar. Here Satuq would often come to watch the caravans arrive and this is how he met Nasr.

Oghulchak Arslan Khan was the last Karakhanid ruler professing native Turkic religion of Tengrism. Satuq kept his conversion secret from the king, but the king heard a rumour to this effect, and he demanded that Satuq build a new temple to Tengri to show his faith. Nasr advised Satuq to pretend to go along, and in the meanwhile issued a fatwa that permitted

Satuq to murder his stepfather, the Khan, after which he conquered Kashgar.

Khotan experienced waves of jihads unleashed by the Karakhanid leader Musa, the son of Satuq Bughra Khan, although the jihads were unsuccessful, and the Khotanese managed to briefly seize Kashgar. Khotan was finally conquered in 1006 CE when 140,000 mujahedeens under Karakhanid leader Yusuf Qadir Khan attacked them.

In the case of Kashmir, during the reign of Suhadeva (1301–1320), a Mongol chief by the name of Zulju (also called Dulcha in some records) with a large army of several thousand soldiers invaded Kashmir and ravaged it in an occupation that lasted nine months. According to the history called *Baharistan-Shahi*,[9] 'Zulju ordered a massacre of the natives. Men were killed; women and children were sold to the merchants and traders of China who had accompanied his troops. The buildings of the city and the villages were burnt. The invading army consumed as much of food grains as they needed and whatever remained was destroyed.'

The valley was effectively depopulated but Zulju continued to be harassed by fighters in the mountains. With the arrival of winter and looming food shortages, Zulju decided to leave. But rather than return the way he had entered, he took the advice of his Kashmiri prisoners and slaves who wanted to avenge the deaths of their people. They recommended a very dangerous mountain pass where Zulju, his army, and an estimated 5,000 prisoners perished in a terrible snowstorm.

During the Mongol invasion, Suhadeva had fled the country and his general Ramachandra had held on in the mountains. In these unsettled conditions, a Ladakhi aristocrat named Rinchan gained strength. After Zulju's exit, Ramachandra briefly occupied the throne, before being killed by Rinchan, who married Ramachandra's daughter,

Kota Rani, and appointed one Shah Mir as minister. Rinchan was killed by rebels after three years of rule (1320–1323) and the kingship passed to Udayanadeva (1323–1338) who made Kota Rani his queen. There was a new Turkish invasion during Udayanadeva's rule, but Kota Rani was able to repulse it by joining with Shah Mir and other nobles.

Upon Udayanadeva's death, Kota Rani ruled in her own right (1338–1339), but the Hindu rule ended when she was murdered by Shah Mir who began Islamic rule.[10]

Early Period

During the Vedic period, Kashmir was an important region because it was near the Mujavant Mountain, the region where Soma grew. Recent archaeological findings suggest that the mountain may have been in Kashmir Smast or the Kishtwar region. It is possible that in the Vedic era a large part of the valley was still under a lake as is stated in the Kashmiri tradition. Kalhaṇa's history begins with the Mahābhārata War, which he places in 2449 BCE in the chronology given by the 6th century astronomer Varāhamihira. But it is rather hazy with regard to the events prior to the Mauryan Emperor Aśoka. We know that the astronomer Āryabhaṭa (c. 500 CE) followed another tradition for the Mahābhārata War and placed it 35 years prior to the Kaliyuga calendar that has a starting point of 3102 BCE, and this was to become the dominant tradition.[11]

The grammarian Pāṇini (4th or 5th century BCE) held resident tenure at ancient Takshashila (present-day Taxila) University in Gandhāra, near Kashmir and close to the valley. At the time of Xuanzang (Hiuen Tsang), Takshashila was a tributary to Kashmir. It is generally accepted that Patañjali, the great author of the Mahābhāṣya commentary on Pāṇini's Aṣṭādhyāyī, was a Kashmiri.[12]

According to Bhartṛhari and other early scholars, Patañjali also contributed to Yoga (the *Yoga Sūtras*) and Ayurveda. He was educated at Takshashila and taught in Pāṭaliputra. From the textual references in his works, it can be safely said that he belonged to the 2nd century BCE.

The *Charaka Saṃhitā* of Ayurveda[13] had its final editing by Dṛdhabala of Kashmir, who added seventeen chapters to the sixth section and the whole of the eighth section; Patañjali may also have been involved in a prior editing of this book.

Takshashila and Sharada Peeth were centres of learning in the larger northwest Indian region. The early levels of buildings in Takshashila have been traced to 800 BCE. The first millennium BCE was a period of great intellectual activity in this region and attitudes that later came to be termed Kashmiri were an important element of this activity. Amongst these attitudes was a characteristic approach to classification in the arts and the interest in grammar.

Logical analysis was applied to various fields. The most extraordinary of these was Pāṇini's grammar that describes the Sanskrit language by a system of 4,000 algebraic rules, a feat that has not been equaled for any other language to this day. It set the tone for scientific studies in India with their emphasis on rational explanations. Patañjali's brilliant commentary on the Pāṇini grammar contributed to its prestige.

Pāṇini mentions images of deities in the Aṣṭādhyāyī. We have evidence of images of Krishna, Śiva, and the Goddess in regions just beyond Kashmir that go back to, at least, 3rd century BCE. The Indo-Greek king, Agathocles of Aï Khanum (180–170 BCE) in northern Afghanistan issued silver coins showing Balarāma-Saṅkarṣaṇa and Vāsudeva-Krishna. This appears to confirm the account in the

Nīlamata Purāṇa of a very old tradition of Vishnu worship in Kashmir where the Pāñcarātra emanations of Vishnu are described as the divinities of an ancient period. The earliest extant representation of Rāma is from the same general area in a bronze coin of Huvishka, who succeeded Kanishka.

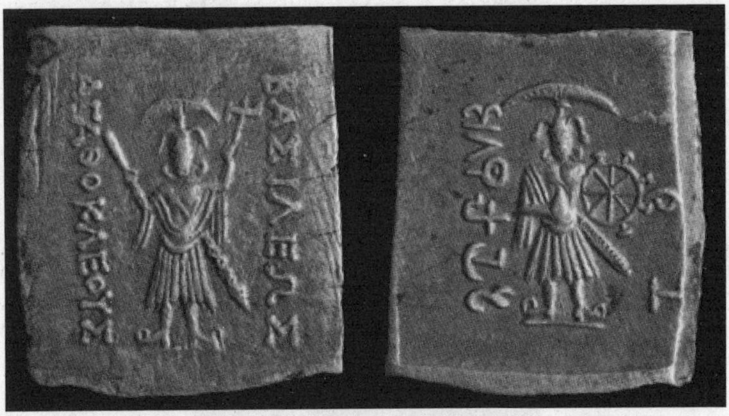

1.3 Agathocles 180–170 BCE. Saṅkarṣaṇa-Balarāma & Vāsudeva-Kṛṣṇa

Goddess Worship

Goddess worship is central to Kashmiri life. To see its antecedents, the Goddess proclaims in the Devī Sūkta, *Ṛgveda* 10.125: 'I am the sovereign queen of all existence … I bend the bow for Rudra; I pervade the heaven and earth.' Goddess Durgā is also called Ambikā, or Ambā (Mother), or Devi Ambā.

The Śrī Sūkta gives several other names of the Goddess, including Ārdrā ('of the waters'), and she is compared to the moon illumined by the sun; it is the light, the illuminating self behind the observation, that makes her auspicious. The image of the goddess with the lion represents both the free-will in Nature, which evolves by natural law (*ṛta*), as well as its control by a higher agency.

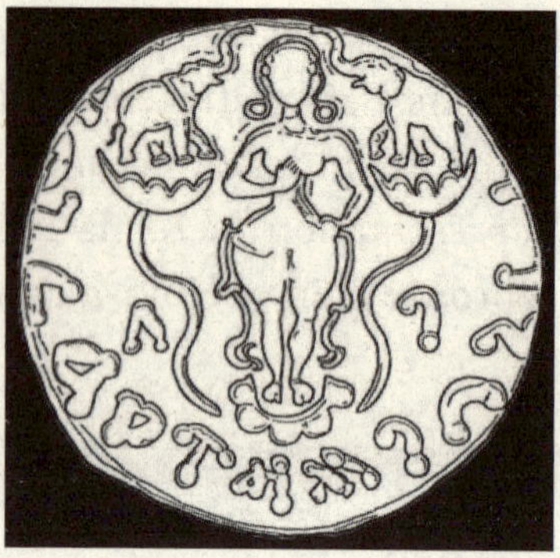

1.4 Lakshmi adored by elephants on a coin of Azilises (57–35 CE) in Gandhāra

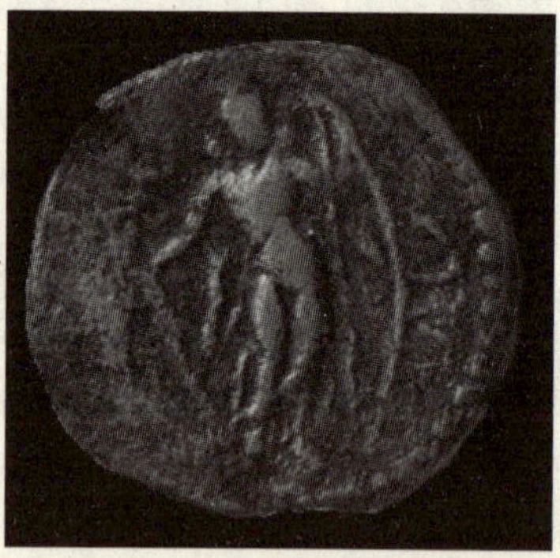

1.5 Huvishka (150–180 CE) bronze coin with earliest known representation of Rāma (British Museum)

Nanā is the name for mother and goddess (as in *Ṛgveda* 9.112.3 *kārurahaṃ tato bhiṣagupalaprakṣiṇī*), speech (Vāc), and daughter in Sanskrit. Nanā is attested by name on a coin of Sapadbizes, a first-century BCE king of Bactria, and she also appears on the coins and seals of the Kushans. The Rabatak inscription of Kanishka invokes her in claiming that the kingship was obtained from Nanā and the gods.

Devi Ambā has many names that emerge from the different facets of the mind. She is Sarasvatī, Lakṣmī, and Pārvatī seen through the lenses of learning and knowledge, fortune and prosperity, and strength and devotion. Durgā is the name of Pārvatī when she fights the demons of ignorance and materiality. Goddess Lalitā opens the doorway to the deepest understanding of the world and in Kashmir she is called Śārikā or Rāgnyā (Rājñī, the Queen).

According to the *Nīlamata Purāṇa*, the name Kashmir is derived from Kaśyapamar (the lake which covered much of the valley before it was drained), and this seems to be confirmed by Kasperia, the Greek name for the region. But it was eventually identified with the Goddess Kaśmīrā, a form of Umā.

In the Śāradā Māhātmya, Śāradā is the synonym of Sarasvatī, and she is visualized in three colours: white, red, and black, which represent the three guṇas of Sāṅkhya. She is Time (Śravaṇī) and Rudrāṇī (the energy of consciousness) as well.

The 18-armed Durgā from a temple in Tengpora in Pulwama in Kashmir is a masterpiece in stone that stresses her sovereignty in 18 different physical and psychological planes. This representation became the standard in Kashmir after the 8th century. The choice of 18 arms may be connected with the 36-tattva system of Kashmir Śaivism.

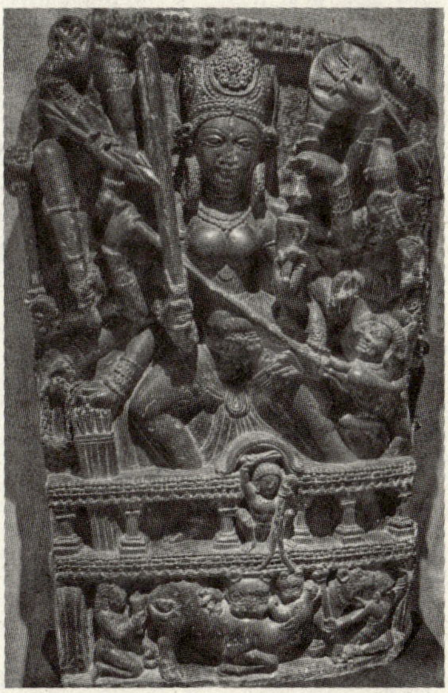

1.6 Tengpora Durgā with 18 arms (8th century) in stone, Sri Pratap Museum, Srinagar

A late ninth century image of four-armed Śāradāhas distinctive Kashmiri features. Her two lower hands rest on two diminutive male figures, each holding a manuscript, who embody the complementary elements of knowledge (vidyā) and wisdom (jñāna).

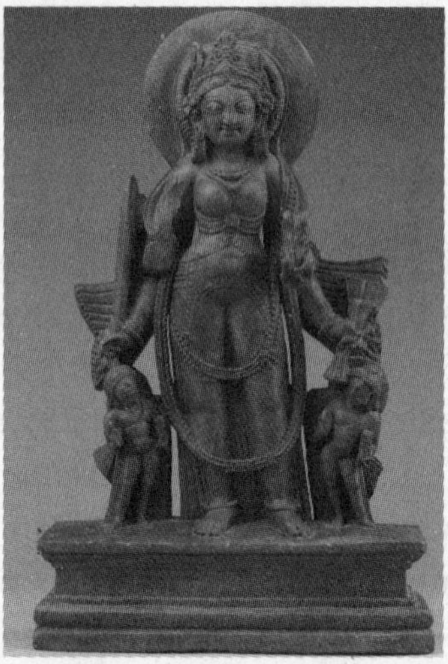

1.7 Goddess Shāradā, late 9th century (Metropolitan Museum, New York)

The *Nīlamata Purāṇa* informs us of the high status of women in Kashmiri life. They were trained in the fine arts, and they were encouraged to socialize freely, participate in sacred rituals, and in outer activities including watersports. For example, on the moon-lit night of Kaumudī Mahotsava we find the wife sitting at the sacred fire in the company of her husband, children, servants, and husband's friends.

Vishnu, Śiva, and Vishva

Kashmir's spiritual quest was centred on both Śiva and Vishnu, and common to these was representation with multiple faces. Vaikuṇṭha Caturmūrti, a representation of Vishnu with four faces, was the tutelary deity of Kashmir during the Kārkoṭa and Utpala dynasties (625–1003 CE), which is the period when the tradition of Kashmir Śaivism blossomed. The Utpala dynasty king Avantivarman (r. 855–883) built in Avantipur temples of Avantīśvara and Avantisvāmī dedicated to Śiva and Vishnu, respectively. The philosopher Abhinavagupta (c. 950–1020) wrote not only numerous texts on Śaivism and Tantra, but also a summary of the Bhagavad Gītā.

To understand the conception of the many faces of the image, one needs to go to the heart of knowing. Our experience of reality is within the frame of space, time, and consciousness. The universe interpenetrated by divinity is Vishnu (the one who pervades all), and space and time are intertwined because one can sense space only within the matrix of change. The finality that time represents is Death; it is the dual to life, but it is also experienced as vibration, as hearing or perception of change (Śravaṇa). As the foundation of life and reality, time is the Goddess (Devī), or more explicitly Kālī.

Consciousness transcends the material self, and it is Rudra-Śiva, Īśa or Īśvara. Another way to look at it is through the five faces of Śiva: Sadyojāta, Aghora, Tatpuruṣa, Vāmadeva, and Īśāna. Sadyojāta represents the beginning of the movement of consciousness; Aghora is another name for Rudra (another is Bhairava); Tatpuruṣa is the passive state where consciousness is hidden, Vāmadeva is the preserving side that is sometimes represented by Pārvatī; and Īśāna is the aspect that bestows grace. The five faces map the five senses through which we comprehend reality.

The one undivided reality is projected in space, time, and consciousness, and the three are often seen in pairs as Harihara (Vishnu and Śiva), Śiva-Vaiśravaṇa as dual, and Ardhanārīśvara (Śiva and Pārvatī).

Śravaṇa, as Time, became Zurvan in the Avesta. Both Śiva and Śravaṇa were represented as the axis of reality.

It is commonly known that Sarva—all—is the name for both Vishnu and Rudra-Śiva, but the fact that Viśva—the Universe—an epithet for Vishnu is also used for Śiva is less known.

This usage goes beyond the more commonly known Viśvanātha (lord of the universe), Mahādeva, Maheśa, Maheśvara, and Parameśvara. There is a deep philosophical insight behind this name for we apprehend reality in our consciousness. At the deepest level of experience, its aspect outsideus is identical to the consciousness of it, so we can proclaim with Skanda Purāṇa, 1.8.20–21: 'Viṣṇu is no one but Śiva, and he who is called Śiva is but identical with Viṣṇu.'

The naming of the projections of the transcendent is done recursively. If Vishnu, as preserver and Rudra as the destroyer are a pair in the perspective from outside-in, Aghora (Bhairava) and Vāmadeva, and Paśu and Paśupati are so from inside-out, this explains why Śiva's faces that capture phases of his continuous dance are shown in various combinations. Agni and Śiva, in the form of Bhairava, are shown with flaming hair.

As embodiment of change and movement, Śiva has contradictory aspects. He is both a yogi who lives outside of society and a king who rules the world. His function as a renunciate can be seen in the matted locks and the cobra that girdles his torso, and yet he wears a king's crown. He grants freedom from fear with the gesture of his upraised right hand.

The Upaniṣads speak of the three states of awareness: waking, dreaming, and deep sleep, together with the transcending fourth, or turīya. In the *Māṇḍūkya Upaniṣad*, the relationship between the object of experience and the experiencer appears in three-fold forms as Viśva (gross), Taijasa (subtle), and Prājña (blissful). Our sense of the identity or distinctness of Vishnu and Śiva depends on the state of our consciousness.

The Mahābhārata has mention of four-headed Vishnu and the iconography is described in later Pāñcarātra texts. According to *Viṣṇudharmottara Purāṇa* 3.85.1–42, the four vyūhas of Nārāyaṇa, that is Vāsudeva, Saṅkarṣaṇa, Pradyumna, and Aniruddha, may be depicted in human form. These are generally four different images fused together partially or fully. On the other hand, the image of Vishnu-Vaikuṇṭha is one body with eight (or four) arms, four heads, including a boar- and a lion-face.

Each face of Śiva represents a different state of awareness since our cognitions are a dance between veiling and unveiling of consciousness, between reflexive behaviour and freedom. On the other hand, the multiple faces of Vishnu are a representation of the descent (avataraṇa) in different world ages. Śiva's faces represent near simultaneity (as Śiva's dance occurs recursively at all scales and times), whereas Vishnu's are across time, excepting in Vishnu's Viśvarūpa in which the whole universe is contained within him.

Kashmiri Calendar: The New Saptarshi Era

According to Kalhaṇa, Kashmir followed the Saptarshi (*Saptarṣi*, Seven Rishis) Era that began in 3076 BCE and is still in use for horoscopes. The seven ṛiṣis, the stars of the Ursa Major, are mentioned in many stories of the *Ṛgveda.* The *Śatapatha Brahmana* speaks of a tradition where each 100 years was associated with a different nakṣatra, thus creating a cycle of 27 or 28 centuries (for there have existed competing tradition of 27 or 28 nakṣatras).

Research has shown that the original or Old Saptarshi Era commenced in 6676 BCE and used a total of 28 nakṣatras, and it was consistent with the start of the Kaliyuga in 3102 BCE. This appears to be the version mentioned by historians Pliny and Arrian, who wrote about Alexander's Indian campaign based on the accounts of the Seleucid Greek ambassador Megasthenes. Briefly, they mention the period from the beginning of Indian calendar to the time of Chandragupta to have had 153 or 154 kings in a duration of 6,451 years [Pliny, *Naturalis Historia*, 6.59–60].[14]

Later on, a new version of the Era arose in the South during the rule of the Sātavahānas that counted by 27 nakṣatras, requiring revision to the start of the Kaliyuga to 2414 BCE to ensure that the seven ṛṣis remain in Maghā, which was the accepted tradition. The idea of the reworking may have been the fact that the Vedāṅga Jyotiṣa accepts 27 nakṣatras. Varāhamihira tried to reconcile these two by keeping the Kaliyuga at 3102 BCE but moving down the Mahābhārata War to 2449 BCE, which created a gap of 653 years in the process. As mentioned earlier, Kalhaṇa in the *Rājataraṅginī* was following this new theory of Varāhamihira.

Given that the Old Saptarshi Calendar began in 6676 BCE, the Kashmiri Saptarshi Era took 3,600 years off it to make the beginning as close to the Kaliyuga of 3102 BCE as was possible. The choice of 3076 BCE for the beginning of what we may call the New Saptarshi Calendar attempted to harmonize the counting by 27 nakṣatras to the well-entrenched tradition of the start of the Kaliyuga. It is also possible that the New Saptarshi Calendar innovation did not take place in Kashmir and was originally current elsewhere also.

The *Nīlamata Purāṇa* presents the legend that Gonanda, the king of Kashmir, was allied with the Kauravas and was killed in a battle at Mathura. His young son, Dāmodara, lost his life in a subsequent battle in Gandhāra. Krishna arranged for the coronation of Dāmodara's pregnant queen, Yaśovatī, who in due course gave birth to a son, Bālagonanda. This child was too young to participate in the Mahābhārata War.

The Saptarshi Saṃvat is the Laukika Era of Kalhaṇa. In his account, Durlabhavardhana ascends the throne in 3677, Lalitāditya in 3776, Avantivarman in 3991, and Queen Diddā in 4056. Kalhana sometimes mixes up the Laukika and the Kaliyuga Era causing his chronology to be off by 25 years (as in the case of the Karkota dynasty). The traditional interest of the Kashmiris in celestial phenomena is clear from the comet sightings mentioned in the *Rājataraṅginī* of Jonarāja and Śrivara.

Rulers, Scholars, and Travellers

In addition to the *Nīlamata Purāṇa* and the *Rājataraṅginī* there are accounts of scholars such as Kumārajīva, and travellers like Faxian and Xuanzang, who went to Central Asia from Kashmir. At the time of Alexander's invasion, King Abhisāra ruled Kashmir, and it later became part of Mauryan and Kushan empires. For ready reference, the following pages provide a list of the more significant rulers with the names of scholars in italics.

Early Period: *Charaka, Pāṇini* (Gandhāra).

Maurya Dynasty (322–185 BCE): Aśoka (268–232 BCE)—*Vishnu Sharma.*

Śuṅga Dynasty (185–73 BCE): Puṣyamitra Śuṅga (185–149 BCE)—*Patañjali.*

Kushān Dynasty (113–247): Kanishka (127–151); Huvishka (151–190); Vāsudeva I (190–230)—*Kumārāyana, Kumārajīva, Bandhudatta, Buddhabhadra, Buddhayaśas, Dharmayaśas, Dharmagupta.*

Post-Kushān Period: The Kidāra Hūns conquered Gandhāra sometime between 390 and 410 BCE, around the end of the rule of Gupta emperor Chandragupta II or beginning of the rule of Kumāragupta I.

The earliest gold coins present the Kidarite king standing beside an altar on the obverse and an enthroned goddess on the reverse. Under the king's arm the legend Kidāra is written perpendicularly on the obverse while the reverse gives the names Śrī Shāhi Kidāra, Kritavīrya, Sarvayaśa, Bhavan, Śilāditya, and Prakāśa.

The Chinese Buddhist monk *Faxian* (337–422) arrived in the larger Kashmir region on his way to the pilgrimage places in India's Madhyadeśa. He saw the influence of India in Central Asia. In Loulan, people dressed like the Chinese but followed the customs of India. According to him, the local Buddhist clergy read Indian books and practised speaking in Indian languages. He describes the famous oasis city of Khotan on the southern rim of the Taklamakan as an important Buddhist centre in the region. 'Throughout the country,' he writes, 'the houses of the people stand apart like (separate) stars, and each family has a small tope (i.e., pagoda) reared in front of its door. The smallest of these may be twenty cubits high, or rather more. They make (in monasteries) rooms for monks from all quarters, the use of which is given to travelling monks who may arrive and are provided with whatever else they require.' He found the veneration of the relics of the Buddha at many places. In Peshawar, the rituals were associated with the worship of the Buddha's alms bowl.

Various kings such as Khingila (c. 405–465), Toramāṇa (c. 465–477), Mihirakula (c. 477–505), Toramāṇa II (c. 505–545), Pravarasena II (c. 505–565), Khinkhila Narendraditya (c. 572–600): *Vasubandhu*, *Asanga* (Gandhāra).

Kārkoṭa Dynasty (600–855): Durlabhavardhana (c. 600–636); Durlabhaka (662–712); Candrapīḍa (712–720); Lalitāditya Muktāpīḍa (c. 724–757 or 760)—*Vasugupta*, *Śivānanda*.

Xuanzang (c 600–664) arrived in India in 627 on a trip that lasted 16 years, of which he spent two years in Kashmir. His main reasons to undertake the arduous journey was to visit sacred Buddhist sites, procure original works, and learn the doctrines directly from Indian teachers. He took over 600 Buddhist texts with him, and made excellent translations himself. He noted the Indian influences on Central Asian kingdoms, reporting that the people of Yanqi (Agni), Kuchi (Kucha), and Khotan used Indic scripts.

Hyecho (704–787), Sanskrit: Prajñāvikrama, was a Buddhist monk from Gyeongju in Korea. On Kashmir, he wrote, 'The king, chiefs, and commoners are extremely reverent of the Three Jewels. When travelling, the king and the biggest chiefs ride elephants. Minor officials ride horses and the commoners walk.'

Utpala Dynasty (855–936): Avantivarman (855–883); Śaṅkaravarman (885–902)—*Ānandavardhana, Bhaṭṭa Kallaṭa, Somānanda, Eraka.*

Queen Diddā (958–1003): *Utpala, Rājānaka Rāma, Bhaṭṭa Rāmakaṇtha,* Śambhunātha, *Abhinavagupta.*

First Lohāra Dynasty (1012–1110): Saṅgrāmarāja (1003–1028)—*Bhāskara, Kṣemarāja, Nāga, Somadeva, Bilhaṇa, Kṣemendra, Varadarāja, Hrasvanātha, Maṅkha.*

Second Lohāra Dynasty (1101–1339): Uccala (1101–1111); Sussala (1112–1128); Jayasimha (1128–1154); Paramanuka (1154–1164); Vārttideva (1164–1171); Vopyadeva (1171–1181); Jassaka (1181–1199); Sri Jagadeva (1199–1213); Rājadeva (1213–1236); Saṅgrāmadeva (1236–1252); Rāmadeva (1252–1273)—*Kalhaṇa, Śārṅgadeva, Ramyadeva, Śrīvatsa, Śivānanda II, Jayaratha, Maheśvarānanda.*

Sultanate (1346–1580), Mughals and Durranis (1580–1819), Sikhs (1820–1846), Dogras (1846–1947).

Main Scholars

Charaka (Chapter 2)

Vishnu Sharma, 3rd century BCE, author of the *Panchatantra* (Chapter 4).

Patañjali (2nd century BCE; Chapter 5)

Nāgasena was a Sarvāstivādan Buddhist sage who lived around 150 BCE. His answers to questions about Buddhism posed by Menander I (Pali: Milinda), the Indo-Greek king of northwestern India, are recorded in the Milindapañhā and the Sanskrit Nāgasenabhiksusūtra.

Bhāmaha (Sanskrit poet believed to be contemporaneous with Daṇḍin). He is noted for writing a work called Kāvyālaṅkāra, 'The ornaments of poetry.'

Ānandavardhana (c. 820–890 CE) was the author of Dhvanyāloka, or A Light on Suggestion (*dhvani*), a work articulating the philosophy of 'aesthetic suggestion' (*dhvani, vyañjanā*). According to scholars, it occupies the same position in poetics as Pāṇini's Aṣṭādhyāyī in grammar and Śaṅkarācarya's commentary on Vedānta.

Vasugupta (c. 800–850 CE) was the author of the *Śiva Sutra*, an important text of the Advaita tradition of Kashmir Śaivism, also called Trika (Chapter 9).

Somānanda (875–925 CE) was a leading teacher of Kashmir Śaivism, in the lineage of Trayambaka, author of the first philosophical treatise of this school, Śivadṛṣṭi. A contemporary of Bhaṭṭa Kallaṭa, the two formed the first group of scholars to propose in a rigorous and logical way the concepts of non-dual Śaivism.

Jayanta Bhaṭṭa (c. 820–900 CE) was a poet, teacher, logician, and an advisor to King Sankaravarman. He was a philosopher of the Nyāya school of Hindu philosophy. He authored three works on Nyāya philosophy, an allegorical drama, and a commentary on Pāṇinian grammar.

Medhātithi, one of the earliest and most famous commentators on the Manusmṛti.

Vaṭeśvara (born 880) was a 10th century mathematician who presented several trigonometric identities. He was the author of Vaṭeśvara-siddhānta written in 904 CE, a treatise focusing on astronomy and applied mathematics. This work defended Āryabhaṭa.

Utpaladeva (c. 900–950 CE) was a philosopher who belonged to the Trika Shaiva tradition and is the most important thinker of the Pratyabhijñā School of monastic idealism. His Īśvarapratyabhijñā-Kārikā ('Verses on the Recognition of the Lord') is the most important and central work of the Pratyabhijñā school. Utpaladeva was a major influence on Abhinavagupta.

Abhinavagupta (c. 950–1020) was a sage and scholar. Autobiographical references scattered in his books are valuable in forming an idea of life in the valley (Chapter 11).

Utpala, also known as Bhaṭṭotpala (Bhaṭṭa-Utpala), was an astronomer, who lived in the 10th century (or according to one theory, in the 9th century). He wrote several Sanskrit-language texts on astrology and astronomy, the best-known being his commentaries on the works of the 6th century astrologer-astronomer Varāhamihira.

Kṣemendra (c.990–1070 CE) was an 11th century Sanskrit polymath, satirist, philosopher, historian, dramatist, and art-critic. Both his education and literary output were broad and varied. He studied literature under Abhinavagupta. His son, Somendra, provides details about his father in his introduction to the Avadāna Kalpalatā and other works. Kṣemendra refers to himself in his works as Vyāsadāsa, a title which was perhaps won or adopted after the completion of his Bhāratamañjari.

Kṣemarāja (late 10th to early 11th centuries) was a philosopher and disciple of Abhinavagupta, who was a master of tantra, yoga, poetics, and dramaturgy. Not much is known of his life. The Pratyabhijnahridayam, a work in which Kṣemarāja brings the main tenets of the Pratyabhijna system into a succinct set of sutras occupies a prominent place in Kashmir Shaivite literature.

Somadeva of the *Kathā-sarit-sāgara* (Chapter 12)

Bilhaṇa was an 11th century poet known for his love poem, the Caurapañcāśikā. He was born in a village called Khonmukh, about 24 km from Srinagar. He left his home sometime during the reign of King Kalaśa and set out on a journey which would take him to central India. The story goes that he had a secret love affair with Princess Yāmini-pūrṇa-tilaka, the daughter of King Madanabhirāma. On discovery, he was thrown into prison, where he wrote the poem while awaiting news of his execution or banishment. The poem was transmitted orally, and there are several variations. Bilhaṇa eventually left Kashmir in search of fame and fortune. Wandering through various cities, he finally found a generous patron in the western Chalukya king Vikramaditya VI (r. 1076–1126) who appointed him as Vidyāpati. Bilhaṇa reciprocated by composing the long panegyiric poem Vikramāṅkadevacarita, in the king's honour. Some accounts of his life suggest that Bilhana died in the year 1088, perhaps before reaching the age of 40.

Kalhaṇa (12th century) was the author of the *Rājataraṅginī*. Although a chronicle focused on kings, it does communicate something of the idea of life in the valley in the statement 'Learning, lofty houses, saffron, icy water, and grapes: things that even in heaven are difficult to find, are common there.'

Śārṅgadeva (1175–1247) was the 13th century musicologist who authored Saṅgīta Ratnākara, which is the most influential medieval Sanskrit text on music. Born in Kashmir, he migrated south and settled in the court of King Siṃhaṇa (r. 1210–1246) of the Yadava dynasty in the Deccan. His text systematically presents ideas on the nature of sound, register, the smallest distinct sounds that humans can hear and musical instruments can produce (*śruti*), musical scales and modes, 264 rāgas, beats and role of time (*tāla*), prosody (*chandas*), relation between performance arts and human emotions and sentiments, musical and vocal ornaments, the composition of drama and songs and the limitless opportunities available to the artist to express and affect his audience.

2

Charaka and Ayurveda

The medical compendium of Charaka (Sanskrit, *Caraka*) tells us a lot about social life in early India. Health and disease can be scientifically assessed only within an understanding of the complex of body and mind within an assumed nature of reality. It tells us not only about physiological processes, disease, and treatment, but also the use of logic and analysis for diagnosis, and causation in the discovery of drugs.

The Sanskrit word *caraka* is a term for the wandering religious student, and it is also used for the itinerant physician (*vaidya*) in a tradition that goes back to the *Atharvaveda*. The Caraṇavyuha, a pariśiṣṭa of the *Yajurveda*, states that the *Atharvaveda* had nine *shakhas*, or schools: Paippalāda, Stauda, Mauda, Śaunakīya, Jājala, Jalada, Brahmavada, Devadarśa, and Cāraṇavaidyā. Of these, the last, the Cāraṇavaidyā shakha, was the one associated with the wandering vaidya.

The *Atharvaveda* has material on medicine and surgery, and this was most likely compiled in the second millennium BCE. According to the Kāśikāvṛtti, a commentary on Pāṇini's grammar, Vyāsa's disciple Vaiśampāyana is Charaka, but this name is associated with several Vedic sages.

The sage Punarvasu Ātreya (c. 1000 BCE) is believed to have taught Ayurveda to his student Agniveśa, who composed the Agniveśa-samhita.[1] The Mahābhārata alludes to Kṛṣṇātreya (Krishna Ātreya) being the founder of medical science (*cikitsitam*). Later this text was organized by Charaka from Kashmir into what came to be known as the *Charaka Samhita*.[2] Punarvasu Ātreya had another five disciples—Bhela, Jātūkarṇa, Parāśara, Hārīta, and Kṣārapāṇi—who also composed medical samhitas.

The *Charaka Samhita* does not provide any clues on where and when Charaka lived. Most likely he preceded Buddhism (500 BCE) as there is no mention of the Buddha and the text style resembles that of the Brāhmaṇa books (c. 800 BCE or earlier). Some scholars believe that Charaka redacted his work as early as the 8th century BCE; others date him a few centuries later. Pāṇini's sutras mention Charaka (Aṣṭādhyāyī 4.3.107), and Agniveśa indirectly, in the appellation Gargādi. Clearly, these names must have been famous before Pāṇini's time.

One Charaka was the royal physician to Kanishka, who reigned during the 2nd century, 127–150 CE, with capital at Purushapura (present-day Peshawar) in Gandhāra. But he need not be the Charaka after whom the samhita is named. Kanishka had a fondness for Kashmir for he convened the fourth great Buddhist council here, which marks the beginnings of Mahāyāna Buddhism.

The current version of the *Charaka Samhita* is late, perhaps first century CE; it was completed by Dṛḍhabala who states that he had to write one-third of the book himself because that portion had been lost. He added seventeen chapters in the section on Therapeutics and two sections on Pharmaceutics and Success in Treatment.

Dṛḍhabala informs us that he is the son of Kapilabala and a native of Pañcanadapura ('five-streams town'); this place is now known as Panjnor, which is about seven miles north of Srinagar, not far from the confluence of five streams—

Trigama, Vitasta, Sindh (not Indus), Kshirabhavani, and Anchara. Early commentators Cakrapanidatta and Vijayaraksita also assert that the *Charaka Samhita* is from Kashmir.

The *Charaka Samhita* is considered the earliest of the three primary texts of Ayurveda, the other two being the *Sushruta* (*Suśruta*) *Samhita* and the *Aṣṭāṅgahṛdaya* of Vāgbhaṭa. The *Sushruta Samhita* is like the *Charaka Samhita* excepting that it includes surgery.

Charaka sees Ayurveda as a distinct Veda, for good health is the basis of all other enjoyments. Vāgbhaṭa, the elder, speaks of Ayurveda as an upaveda of the *Atharvaveda*, and the Mahābhārata tells us that there are four upavedas: Ayurveda, *Dhanurveda*, *Gandharva-veda*, and *Arthaśāstra*. Charaka's approach to health and medicine is based on the Vedic schools of Nyāya and Vaiśeṣika that deal with logic and the material world. Ayurveda uses the Vedic doctrine that a human being is a microcosmic replica of the universe.

Charaka divided the treatise into eight parts, or *aṣṭāṅga sthāna*: *sūtra* (general principles), *nidāna* (pathology), *vimāna* (specific determination), *śarīra* (anatomy), *indriya* (sensory organ-based prognosis), *cikitsā* (therapeutics), *kalpa* (pharmaceutics and toxicology), and *siddha* (success in treatment). The *Aṣṭāṅga Āyurveda* is mentioned in the Mahābhārata along with the three constituents (*dhātu*): *vāyu* (wind), *pitta* (bile) and *śleṣman* (mucus). There is mention that by these three the body is sustained and that by their decay the body decays.

Suśruta has a division of Ayurveda into eight subjects ranging from surgery to treatment of various diseases such as those of the head (*śālākya*), ordinary diseases (*kāya-cikitsā*), diseases of the mind (*bhūta-vidyā*), child diseases (*kaumāra-bhṛtya*), antidotes to poisons (*agada-tantra*), the science of rejuvenating the body (*rasāyana*), and the science of sexual function (*vājīkaraṇa*). The *Aṣṭāṅgahṛdaya Samhita* also has an eight-fold division that is a variation on that of Charaka.[3]

At the beginning of the 8th century, *Charaka Samhita* was translated into Arabic. Charaka's name appears as 'Sharaka Indiansus' in the Latin translations of Avicena, Razes, and Serapion. Al-Biruni's chief source of medicine was the Arabic edition of Charaka.

The body consists of innumerable cells which, in turn, are composed of five mahābhūtas, namely, pṛthivī, āpas, tejas, vāyu, and ākāśa, but since ākāśa is all-pervasive, the body shows only four of them. The three doshas, namely, vāta, pitta, and kapha play a vital role in normal as well as abnormal functions of the body, and in the treatment of diseases. Their balance gives positive health, and any disturbance in the equilibrium results in disease. They also regulate the functions of the mind.

The vāta dosha is a combination of ākāśa and air with the qualities of cold, dry, light, and mobile; the pitta dosha is a combination of fire and water with the qualities of hot, wet, light, and mobile; and the kapha doṣa is a combination of water and earth with the qualities of cold, wet, heavy, and stable.

Charaka knew that blood circulates, and the heart is the controlling organ that provides life to other organs. Many descriptions of human physiology recorded in Ayurveda literature are quite accurate. The samhita describes 149 significant diseases; 341 plants and plant products, 177 animal products, and 64 minerals are mentioned along with the properties of most of them for the treatment of diseases.

Charaka understood the germ theory of the causation of diseases, but he rejected the idea that germs are the only causative factor. His theory is that the imbalance of doshas and vitiation of dhatus are the primary causes of disease, and germs will grow in the body only when they get a congenial environment. Both for metabolic diseases and infective ones, the correction of the imbalance of doshas and dhātus constitutes the basic principle of therapeutics.

Charaka is modern in his emphasis on the prevention of diseases. Similarly, his theories of immunity, digestion, and metabolism are logical. Charaka's emphasis on experimental scientific methodology, repudiation of dogmatism, heredity, and many advanced concepts of pathogenesis and management of diseases are consistent with modern ideas. He takes a rational approach to the causation and cure of disease and prescribes objective methods of clinical examination.

The Aim of Life

Life is of four kinds: sukha (happy), duhkha (unhappy), hita (good), and ahita (bad).

Sukham-āyuḥ is a life unaffected by bodily or psychic diseases, endowed with vigour, capabilities, energy, vitality, activity, knowledge, successes, and enjoyments. The lack of these attributes characterizes the asukham-āyuḥ.

Hitam-āyuḥ is the life of a person who is willing to do good to all living beings, is truthful, non-stealing, calm, self-restrained, virtuous, achieving fulfilment in life without conflict with others, devoted to knowledge-understanding-serenity of mind, and to charity and peace. The opposite of these attributes constitutes the ahitam-āyuḥ.

Charaka asserts that there are four important parts to the treatment: the patient, the physician, the nurse, and the medicines, and all four are essential to recovery and return to health. The physician provides knowledge and coordinates the treatment, for he is the one who must explore the dark interior of the body with the lamp of knowledge.

Since there is no end to the knowledge of medical science, the physician must constantly learn and devote himself to it, as well as discuss his findings and questions with other physicians.

Food is more than a source of energy; its purpose is to provide proper stimulation of the cognitive centres. The transformations of food are called vipāka, and prabhāva is the corresponding subtle effect on the body. Food is converted into rasa by the digestive action of jāṭharāgni, or the fire in the stomach.

Taste is one of the five primary senses. The six basic tastes are sweet, sour, salty, pungent, bitter, and astringent (hatuc, āmla, lavaṇa, tikta, kaṭu, and kaśāya). Each rasa that is recognized by taste is a result of the predominance of two elements. Madhura, āmla, and lavaṇa are believed to work well against vāta; hatuc, tikta, and kaśāya against pitta; and kaṭu and kaśāya against kapha.

Food has additional properties (guṇas) that are arranged in 10 pairs of opposites, namely, heavy/light, cold/hot, unctuous/dry, dull/sharp, stable/mobile, soft/hard, non-slimy/slimy, smooth/coarse, minute/gross, viscous/liquid.

The vāta is cold, dry, light, and mobile, so foods that are sweet (heavy and wet), sour (warm, moist, and heavy) and salty (warm, moist, and heavy) are good for it. The pitta is hot, wet, light, and mobile, so foods that are sweet (cool and heavy), bitter (cool and dry) and astringent (cool and dry) are appropriate. Since the kapha is cold, wet, heavy, and stable, foods that work to counter these qualities are pungent (hot, dry, light), bitter (dry, light) and astringent (dry, light).

The purpose of taste is going beyond the processes that convert food into energy to engage with the cognitive elements of the self. Foods are also classified according to whether they are sāttvic, rājasic, and tāmasic, which lead to clear-headedness, energy, and dullness, respectively.

The five elements, in various proportions, are said to form seven kinds of tissues (*hatu*). These are: rasa (plasma), rakta (blood), māṃsa (flesh), medas (fat), asthi (bone), majjā (marrow), and śukra (semen). The activity of the hatu is represented by ojas (vitality) or bala (strength). Ojas is mediated through an oily, white fluid that permeates the whole body. The functions of the vital organs like the heart, brain, spleen, and liver are explained based on the flow and exchange of tissues. The heart is the chief receptacle of the three chief fluids of the body: rasa, rakta, and ojas.

Charaka documents three different kinds of blood vessels: sirāḥ (vessels that carry the contents without pulsating), dhamanyaḥ (vessels that pulsate), and srotāṃsi (vessels from which fluids move out).[4] This points to the presence of three distinct segments in the vascular tree: the pulsating (arteries) segment, the exchange (capillaries) segment, and the transporting (veins) segment. He asserts that all parts of the body are nourished in a circular fashion, like that of a rotating wheel.[5]

The heart and the different vessels attached to it are described to transport four vital entities: i) rasa, the nutrient fluid that nourishes the tissues; ii) rakta, the red fraction that is essential for life; iii) ojas, a white fraction, the functions of which are closely associated with immunity; and iv) prāṇa, life-force derived through the act of respiration. Therefore, what is known as 'blood' should include all these components.

Prāṇa, along with rakta, is transformed into māṃsa (flesh) and other bodily tissues. The text further says that the heart and the 10 prominent blood vessels attached to it forming the system (rasavāha srotas) are responsible for the distribution of nutrients to all parts of the body.[6]

Assessment of Disequilibrium of the Dhātus

The original source of disequilibrium of the dhātus can be inferred only after the emergence of disorder. The action (*kārya*) of the physician is to help in the restoration of the equilibrium of the dhātus. The physician may sometimes arrive at the wrong inference by focusing on the overtly manifested symptoms in the patient. A small and lean body could be strong, like the small ants that carry a big load, therefore, the essence (*sāratā*) of the dhātus needs to be examined before understanding the strength (*bala*) of the patient.

The significance of the *Charaka Samhita* for our modern times is in its holistic (or ecological) view of the body and the consistent use of logic and analysis in diagnosis as well as treatment. It takes the various processes being in harmony as a sign of good health, and in disharmony, a sign of disease. This is an objective of contemporary personalized medicine as well. More significantly, it uses a ternary logic (three doshas and three guṇas), which mathematics has shown is superior to the binary logic used in Western medicine.[7]

The Physician and Society

The *Charaka Samhita* has extensive material that throws light on society and the role of a physician in it. Since Dṛḍhabala was the final editor of the samhita, we can be certain that it presents a picture consistent with Kashmiri manners and customs.

The physician should be diligent, dexterous, virtuous, with a skilled hand, and free from ego, envy, or anger. He should seek the highest good for all beings. After finding a worthy teacher, he should work hard and continually attempt to improve his knowledge, understand (hidden) meanings, with the comprehension of ideas and power of speech. The means for enhancing the depth of knowledge are study, teaching, and discussion with knowledgeable people.

When the student first arrives for his course of study, the preceptor should make a rectangular platform measuring four cubits and sloping eastward or northward, in an even and pure place. This should be covered with sacred grass and bound on borders with paridhi. At the fire ceremony, he should go round the fire keeping it to the right. The teacher should begin his teachings at the end of this ritual.

The text dedicates numerous verses to discussing the code of the physician. It mandates that the physician must speak the truth, dress modestly, seek consent before entering a patient's quarters, must be accompanied by a male member of the family if attending a woman or minor, must inform and gain consent from patient or the guardians if the patient is a minor, must never resort to extortion for his service, never involve himself in any business activities with the patient or patient's family, speak gently with appropriate consideration for the feelings of the patient. The physician must do that which serves the greatest good of the patient and maintain their privacy.

Charaka exhorts the physician to be on good terms with everyone, without pointing the defects in others. He says: for the wise, the whole world is the teacher, while for the unwise it is the enemy; the wise follow sensible advice even if it comes from the enemy.

The physician's role is also to guide the patient to take charge of the connection between their mind and body. This is aided by the faith the patient has in the doctor, which requires the highest ethical behaviour from the latter. This was ensured by the oath that the doctor had to take at the initiation. The initiation ceremony of the Charaka physician was called upanayana, and it involved the teacher leading the student three times around the sacred fire. This ceremony made the student thrice born (trija).

The Āyurvedic oath:[8] At the closing of the initiation, the guru gave a solemn address to the students, directing them to a life of chastity, honesty, and vegetarianism. The student was to strive with all his being for the health of the sick. He was not allowed to betray patients for his own advantage. He was to dress modestly and avoid strong drinks. He was to be collected and self-controlled, and always measured in speech. He was to constantly improve his knowledge and technical skill. In the home of the patient, he was to be courteous and modest, directing all attention to the patient's welfare. He was not to divulge any knowledge about the patient and his family. If the patient was incurable, he was to keep this to himself if it was likely to harm the patient or others.

Logic and Reasoning

Continuous learning was to be obtained through study, experiments, and discussion with other physicians, removing doubts, increasing confidence in one's knowledge, and bringing forth new ideas hitherto unknown. This learning was based on rational arguments and logical reasoning.

An open discussion with another person is called a vāda. This is of two types: jalpa and vitanḍa. In jalpa, the speaker makes his case and contradicts the opponent's view. In vitanḍa, the speaker has no position of his own and only finds faults in the opponent's position.

The statement to be proved is called pratijñā (proposition); sthāpana is establishing the same proposition on firm ground with the help of hetu (reason), dṛṣṭānta (instance), upanaya (correlation) and nigamana (conclusion).

For example, if the proposition is: 'purusha is eternal', the reason (hetu) is: 'because of not being created'; the instance (dṛṣṭānta) is: 'as sky'; the correlation (upanaya) is: 'as the sky is uncreated and is eternal so is purusha'; conclusion (nigamana) is: 'therefore, purusha is eternal'.

Giving a statement contrary to the one before the assembly is called pratiṣṭhāpanā. For instance, 'the self is non-eternal' is the proposition (pratijñā); 'because of being perceived by the senses' is the reason (hetu); 'as a pitcher' is the instance (dṛṣṭānta); 'as a pitcher is perceived by the senses and is non-eternal so is the self' is the correlation (upanaya); and, therefore, 'the self is non-eternal' is the conclusion (nigamana).

Knowledge flows out of reasoning (hetu) and evidence related to direct perception (pratyakṣa), anumāna (inference), traditional instruction (aitihya) (authoritative testimony) and analogy (aupamya). That which is revealed by such reasoning is tattva (truth). The conclusion established after doing experiments and tests and developing a theory is called a siddhānta.

The application of treatment, as in other matters of life, comes with saṃśayaḥ, or doubt and uncertainty. For instance, of two critically ill patients, one may respond to treatment better than the other. If one dies, the doubt may arise whether it was a case of untimely death. If it were indeed untimely death, there is need to use life-promoting measures in future situations.

Charaka speaks of 10 entities in relation to therapeutics, which the physician must keep in mind. The physician is part of a larger system where the disease is the cause (kāraṇa) that may be of different origins, drugs act like instrument (karaṇa), and what needs to be determined is the imbalance of the dhātus (kāryayoni), for action by the physician to restore the balance of the dhātus (kārya), for attainment of health and happiness (kāryaphala), to increase the life-span (anubandha), at a specific place (deśa), considering the time and phase of the disease (kāla), with the initiation of therapy (pravṛtti), by use of excellence in treatment (upāya).

3

Drama and the Arts

One of the central ideas of Bharata Muni's *Nāṭya Śāstra* is that of rasa, the fulfilment aesthetic flavour of any visual, literary or musical work that evokes an emotion or feeling in the reader or audience. Kashmir has a long tradition of scholars over centuries continuing to work on aesthetic theory and rasa. It has also been proposed that the count of 36 chapters of the *Nāṭya* Śāstra was deliberately chosen to conform to the theory of 36 tattvas or elements of reality (25 tattvas as described in the Saṅkhya system together with the 11 Rudras that represent states of consciousness), which count was later formalized in Kashmir Śaivism. Also note that the bhāṇa, a one-actor play described by Bharata, is still performed in Kashmir by actors called bhāṇḍ pather (bhāṇa pātra, in Sanskrit).

Manomohan Ghosh,[1] the modern translator of the *Nāṭya Śāstra*, believes that it belongs to the 5th century BCE. He bases his assessment on the archaic pre-Pāṇinian features of the language and the fact that Bharata mentions the *Arthaśāstra* of Bṛhaspati and not that of the 4th century BCE Kauṭilya.

It Is also noteworthy that there are close connections between Kashmir and South India in the dramatic tradition and the worship of Śiva, Pāñcarāṭra, Tantra, and the arts. A few years ago, when I pointed this out to Vasundharā Filliozat, the art historian who has worked on Karnataka, she said that the inscriptional evidence indicates a continuous movement of teachers from Kashmir to the South and that Kashmir was likely the original source of many of the early Shaivite, Tantric, and Sthāpatya Āgamas. While this is true of the period when scholars were compelled to leave Kashmir due to its unsettled conditions, a migration of teachers from the South to Kashmir in the earlier periods is a distinct possibility.

The *Nāṭya Śāstra* not only presents the language of creative expression, but is also the world's first book on stagecraft. It is so comprehensive that it lists 108 different postures that can be combined to give the various movements of dance. Bharat's ideas are the key to proper understanding of Indian arts, music, and sculpture. They provide an insight into how different Indian arts are expressions of a celebratory attitude to the universe.

The term nāṭya is synonymous with drama. According to Bharata, the nāṭya was created by taking elements from each of the four Vedas: recitation (pāṭhya) from the *Ṛgveda*, song, or melody (gīta) from the *Sāmaveda*, acting (abhinaya) from the *Yajurveda*, and sentiments (rasa) from the *Atharvaveda*. By this synthesis, the Nāṭya Śāstra became the fifth Veda, meant to take the spirit of the Vedic vision to the common man.

The *Nāṭya Śāstra* classified the diverse arts that are embodied in the classical Indian concept of the drama, including dance, music, poetics, and general aesthetics. Later, the *Viṣṇudharmottara Purāṇa* of the 4th century CE (compiled during the Karkotas) describes canonical conventions of architecture, iconography, and painting.

Five of the thirty-six chapters of the *Nāṭya Śāstra* are devoted to music. Bharata speaks of the 22 śrutis of the octave, the seven notes and the number of śrutis in each of them.

He explains how the vīṇā is to be tuned and describes the dhruvapada songs that were part of musical performances.

The concept of rasa, enduring sentiment, lies behind the aesthetics of the *Nāṭya Śāstra*. The artist, through movement, voice, music, or any other creative act, attempts to evoke them in the listener and the spectator. This evocation helps to plumb the depths of one's experience, thereby facilitating self-knowledge. Love poems are suffused with śṛṅgāra rasa in one of two modes: union (sambhoga) and separation (vipralambha) and, of course, they can be joined with other rasas. If love is about the impending sense of loss, it is bound with the deepest emotions related to being.

The ideas of the *Nāṭya Śāstra* provide an overarching framework to the Indian theory on sculpture, temple architecture, performance, dance, and storytelling. But unlike other technical śāstras that were written for the scholar, Bharat's work influenced millions directly. For these reasons alone, the *Nāṭya Śāstra* is one of the most important books ever written.

Bharata stresses the transformative power of creative art. He says,

> It teaches duty to those who have no sense of duty, love to those who are eager for its fulfilment, and it chastises those who are ill-bred or unruly, promotes self-restraint in those who are disciplined, gives courage to cowards, energy to heroic persons, enlightens men of poor intellect and gives wisdom to the learned.

Our life is spent learning one language or another. Words in themselves are not enough, we must learn the languages of relationships, ideas, music, games, business, power, and nature. There are some languages that one wishes did not exist, like those of brute power and domination. But evil, resulting from ignorance that makes humans act like animals, is part of nature and confronting it starts by acknowledging its presence and influence.

Rules and Creativity

Even though Pāṇini, perhaps the greatest grammarian of all time, and Bharata Muni, with his theories of art, drama, and music, worked in different domains, their motivation was similar. Speaking of grammar in the same breath as art is not as incongruous as one thinks when considering that both language and creations of art are governed by rules and conventions. The challenge in each is to express meaning and feeling in novel ways, and both Pāṇini and Bharata indicate that at the basis of their productions lie the universal, which is, therefore, a means to the knowledge of the self.

Pāṇini's grammar, the *Aṣṭādhyāyī*, gave the rules to generate all Sanskrit sentences and it collected roots in the dhātupāṭha and primitive nominal stems in the gaṇapāṭha.[2] The *Aṣṭādhyāyī* is a wonderful resource for the culture and history of his times, and it mentions the *Naṭasūtra* of Śilālin, the canonical text on drama in his times.

Behind the rules of grammar was the idea clearly expressed in the *Muṇḍaka Upaniṣad* that all linguistic thought or representation can only hope to approximate reality, which, at its deepest level, is transcendent (parā). The success of the poet and the artist owes not only to the canonical rules and conventions of the medium (surface structure), but also to the inexpressible intuition behind the conception (deep structure).

The artist strives to represent the intuition in a manner that facilitates the aesthete receiving a similar deep experience. The roots of this approach trace back to the Vedic ritual with representation of the cosmos in the fire altar which, later, became the model for the temple, fine arts, and music.

In the *Viṣṇudharmottara Purāṇa*, the sage Mārkaṇḍeya says that although divinity is formless, worship and meditation are possible only when it is endowed with form. Therefore, the artist observes nature carefully and moulds that inspiration, using the conventions that he has internalized in the realm of his imagination.

The model for the creative sciences in India is the churning of the ocean (*samudra-manthana*) that occurs within the heart of the artist. This is a dance between mechanicity and freedom, represented respectively by the demons who symbolize materiality, and the gods who symbolize the senses. Out of this arises new vision and insight.

The creative process depends on rules and precepts, but the artist must reach for an understanding that is authentic and meaningful. This is similar to how the poet cannot depend on the rules of grammar alone to find words that communicate felt experience. The driving force must thus be the transcendent self which informs the reflective mind.

Pāṇini's grammar, along with its word-lists, presents invaluable incidental information about life and society in the 5th century BCE. It provides us names of cities, towns, villages, and cultural and political entities called Janapadas, details regarding social life, economic conditions, education and learning, religion, and political conditions.[3]

The Janapada states had different kinds of government. Some Janapadas were republics, others were monarchies. We learn that the king did not have absolute power and he shared authority with his ministers. This balancing of the powers created an environment that was conducive for inquiry, out of which emerged the many sciences that have been passed down to us.

Pāṇini's references shed light on the way religion was practised. We find that images were used to represent deities in temples and open shrines. There were images in the possession of the custodians of shrines. The *Mahābhāṣya*, the 2nd century BCE commentary on Pāṇini's grammar describes temples of Dhanapati, Rāma, Krishna, Śiva, and Vishnu.

Emotion and Drama

After the *Nāṭya Śāstra*, additional contributions to the structure of Indian classical music and dance were made by Mataṅga Muni's *Bṛhaddeśi* (about 600 CE), Abhinavagupta's *Abhinavabhāratī,* and Śārṅgadeva's *Saṅgīta Ratnākara* (13th century).[4]

Bharata explains the relationship between the bhāvas, the emotions evoked in the spectators, and the rasa, which is the essence of the performance or the work of art. He says that the artist should be conscious of the bhāva and the rasa that are being established. The word rasa means 'essence' which emerges from the interplay of vibhāva (stimulus that may be a word or a gesture), anubhāva (reaction) and vyabhicārī bhāva (fleeting or transitory emotion). A performance that displays perfect technique but has no emotion would be wanting in rasa. According to Abhinavagupta, rasa is a universal mental state, and the highest purpose of all creative arts is to help the connoisseur reach such a state, for the arts are the aesthetic means to knowing the self.

Bharata explains rasa by the analogy of the combination of various condiments. Each has its own taste, which when combined creates a unique lingering taste. The corresponding combination in drama leads to a feeling (sthāyībhāva) that is the nāṭyarasa. In both these cases, the subject, whose mind reflects cultural and personal experience, is central to the appreciation of the creation.

The eight sthāyibhāvas are rati (love), hāsa (mirth), krodha (anger), śoka (grief), utsāha (heroism), bhaya (fear), jugupsā (disgust), and vismaya (wonder). Corresponding to these are the eight rasas of the *Nāṭya Śāstra* that form four pairs:

śṛngāra, love, devotion (dark hue), and *hāsya*, laughter, mirth (white)
raudra, fury, anger (red), and *kāruṇya*, compassion, sadness (dove coloured)
vīra, heroism, courage (yellowish), and *bhayānaka*, fear, terror (dark)
bībhatsa, repulsion, aversion (blue), *adbhuta*, wonder, astonishment (yellow)

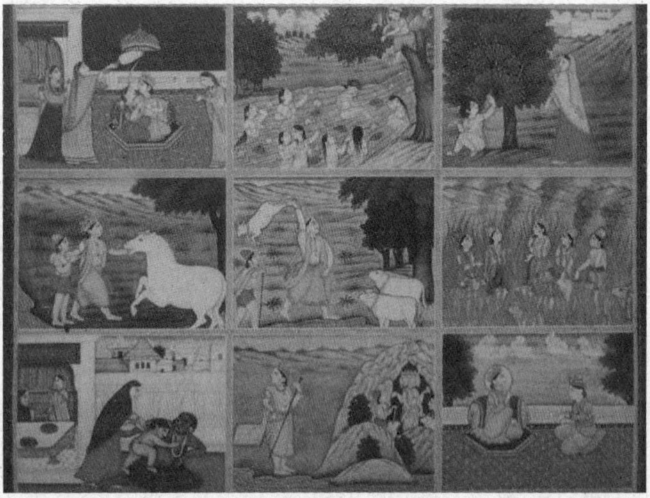

3.1 The nine rasas in Krishna's leela, Pahari, by a painter from the Kashmiri Nainsukh Raina family, ca. 1815

The deities associated with these are Vishnu, Pramatha, Rudra, Yama, Indra, Kāla, Mahākala, and Brahmā, respectively. Later, a ninth rasa śānta, peace or tranquility, with the colour of white and Vishnu as deity, and the expression navarasa (the nine rasas) became popular. Nāṭya is a sharpened representation of life wherein the various emotions are dramatically enhanced so that the spectator gains the flavour of the portrayed pleasure and pain, connecting him to the source of the same within himself.

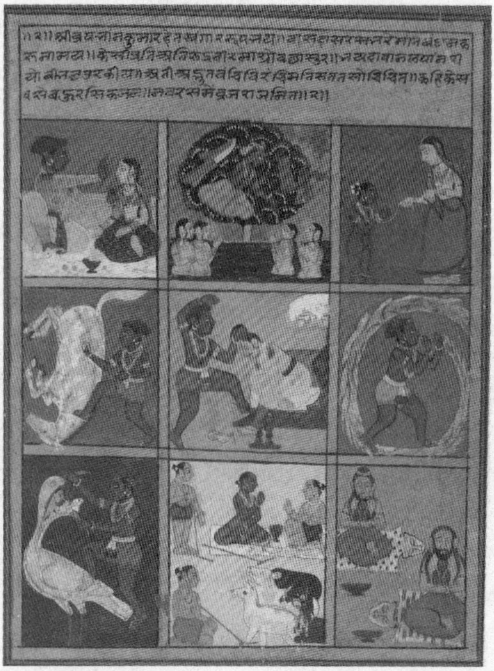

3.2 The nine rasas in Krishna's leela, ca. 1700

There are three types of bhāva, namely sthāyī (eight types), vyabhicārī (thirty-three), and sattvika (eight), for a total of forty-nine. The eight sthāyī bhavas are the bases of the eight rasas.

nirveda (depression)	dhṛti (fortitude)	supta (overcome by sleep)
glāni (languor, emptiness)	vrīḍā (shame)	vibodha (awakening)
śaṅkā (suspicion)	capalatā (nervousness)	amarṣa (intolerance)
asūyā (jealousy)	harṣa (joy)	avahittham (dissimulation)
mada (intoxication)	āvega (excitement)	ugratā (fierceness)
śrama (fatigue)	jaḍatā (slothfulness)	mati (understanding)

ālasya (laziness)	garva (pride)	vyādhai (illness)
dainya (misery)	viṣāda (sorrow)	unmāda (insanity)
cintā (anxiety)	autsukya (unease)	maraṇam (death)
moha (fainting, calamity)	nidrā (sleepiness)	trāsa (dread)
smṛti (memory)	apasmāra (forgetfulness)	vitarka (argumentation)

The sāttvika bhāvas are the physical manifestation of genuine emotion. They are: stambha (stupefaction), sveda (perspiration), romāñca (thrill), svarabheda (voice change), vepathu (trembling), vaivarṇya (facial colour change), aśru (tears), and pralaya (swoon, fainting).

Vibhāva as the cause has two fundamental components: the ālambana vibhāva which is the basic stimulant and the uddīpana vibhāva which is the enhancing stimulant related to the environment and the context. If the heroine is the ālambana vibhāva, the location, like a garden, is the uddīpana vibhāva.

Much after Bharata Muni, Abhinavagupta asks the question whether nāṭya is representation of reality (tattva) or its likeness (sadṛṣya) as in the case of a twin, or mere error (bhrānti) as in the case of silver being taken as a piece of mother-of-pearl, or superimposition (āropa), or as replica (pratikṛti) as in the case of a painting of a model, and so on. He asserts that nāṭya is neither of these for each of these lacks transcendence (asādhāraṇatā) without which there cannot be rasa.

The aesthetic experience is a doorway to the innate dispositions of the self for in that moment the connoisseur has become more than his own self. In the contemplation of characters depicted in the work of art, or in the absorption in an abstract composition, the mind feels the breath of the universal spirit.

These ideas have inspired scholars to look at the sciences of human behaviour. Language, drama, music, and social relations in a society have their own underlying rules and grammar. Eventually these ideas were applied to disciplines beyond linguistics, such as anthropology and literary theory. Modern linguistics seeks not only to determine the type of language, but also its specific characteristics and linguistic universals as the study of the general features of languages in the world.

The works of Pāṇini and Bharata Muni also presage the modern field of semiotics, or the study of signs and symbols as a significant part of communications. The *Nāṭya Śāstra* has rich material on acting, signs, gestures, and postures, each communicating its own specific meaning to the spectator.

The search for universal laws of grammar underlying the diversity of languages is ultimately an exploration of the very nature of the human mind. The other side to this grammar is the idea that a formal system cannot describe reality completely since it leaves out the self. As human society evolves, signs and symbols in use lose their original meaning, manners change, and fashions come and go.

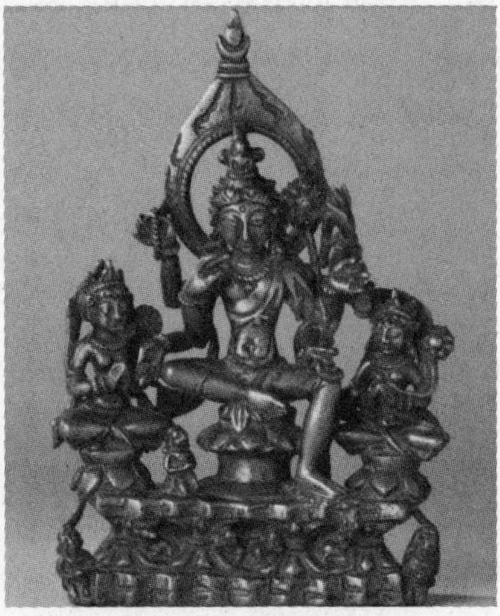

3.3 Six-armed Avalokiteśvara flanked by goddesses, ca. 1000, Rubin Museum of Art

The Art of Painting

The *Citrasūtra* is the part of the *Viṣṇudharmottara* that deals with the art of painting.[5] It considers measurements and proportions of the different parts of the body and the distinguishing features of the five male and female types and hair and eye types. It also has details on auspicious marks that divine images, both sculpture and painting, and different postures (sthānas) for figures, and explains how to mix paints, prepare the surface, and apply the paints. It defines four types of paintings, and prescribes the manner in which a large number of beings, such as royalty, priests, nature and heavenly sprites, demons, wives, courtesans, attendants of Vaiṣṇava deities, warriors, merchants, and others should be depicted; it also speaks of the nine rasas in painting.

The *Citrasūtra* says that of all arts, the best is chitra (reprentation of form and movment). Art is the greatest treasure of mankind, far more valuable than gold or jewels, and the purpose of art is to show one the grace that underlies all of creation, to help one on the path towards reintegration with that which pervades the universe.

The *Citrasūtra* employs the structure of a conversation between the sage Mārkaṇḍeya and King Vajra to inform about the task of the artist. King Vajra asks, 'How can one make a representation, in painting or image, of a Supreme Being who is devoid of form, smell and emotion, and destitute of sound and touch?'

The sage Mārkaṇḍeya responds, 'The entire universe should be understood as the modification (vikṛti) of the formless (prakṛti). The worship and meditation of the Supreme is possible for an ordinary person only when the formless is endowed with a form, and when that form is full of significance. The best worship of the Supreme is, of course, contemplation of the formless with eyes closed and all senses subdued in meditation.'

In another passage, the *Citrasūtra* says that the natural environment and society of the artist is the source of his inspiration. The text says that in dance and painting, as in other arts, the world must be reflected in as charming a manner as possible. To ensure this, the understanding of drama is essential for the artist.

Mārkaṇḍeya says that without the knowledge of music, one cannot understand Nāṭya. And, without the knowledge of Nāṭya, one can scarcely understand the technique of painting. Furthermore, who does not know the art of painting cannot understand the art of image-making (śilpa), and it is difficult to know painting without any knowledge of dancing and, in turn, it rests on the knowledge of instrumental music (vādya) that, in turn, must be grouded on a knowledge of vocal music (gāna). Thus, music was seen at the base of all fine arts.

While the term *citra* is generally translated as 'painting', the texts use the term in a more abstract sense as a 'mental image' that can be differently interpreted in both painting and sculpture.

Nāṭya and Chitra

The intimate connection between drama and representation implies that the rhythm, fluidity and grace of the Nāṭya must be transferred to painting. The abstract dance form, *nṛtta* is meant to beautify a dramatic performance.

Some specific gestures are called *rahasyamudras*, which are meant to communicate mystical experience. There is discussion of the origin of dancing and since the work is devoted to the worship of Vishnu, the author views Vishnu as the originator of the art of dancing.

The Citrasūtra recognized the value and the significance of the spatial perspective. It adds:

> He who paints rolling waves, darting flames, smokey streaks, fluttering banners and Apsaras floating in the sky, indicating the direction and movement of the wind, should be considered a great painter.
>
> He who knows how to show the difference between a sleeping, an unconscious and a dead man, or who can portray the visual gradations of a highland and a low land is a great artist.

Sculpture and painting are closely related to Nāṭya (dance) for additional reasons. Not only are the rules of iconography (pratimā lakṣaṇa) derived from the *Nāṭya-śāstra*, but the sculptures are also often the frozen versions or representations of the gestures and poses of dance. The sculpture and the painting use a system of medians (sūtras), measures (mānas), postures of symmetry (bhaṅgas) and asymmetry (abhaṅga, dvibhaṅga and tribhaṅga) together with positions of standing, sitting, and reclining.

The Nāṭya and Śilpa śāstras developed a remarkable approach to the structure of the human body and delineated the relation between its central point (*nābhi*, the navel), the verticals and horizontals. It then coordinated them, first with the positions and movements of the principal joints of neck, pelvis, knees and ankles, and, then with the emotive states, and the expressions. Based on these principles, *Nāṭya-*śāstra enumerated many standing and sitting positions that demonstrate the principles of stasis, balance, repose, and perfect symmetry. But it is true that painting, as a two-dimensional form, can communicate and articulate space, distance, time, and the more complex ideas in ways that are easier than in sculpture.

The education of an urbane man (nāgarika) of the town included knowledge and skill of several arts in addition to erudition in literature, rhetoric, grammar, philosophy and allied subjects. The art of painting was a pleasant diversion from other concerns but essential in the upbringing of children of 'good families'.

With regard to the depiction of deities, it is explained that it is a *bimba*, the reflection, or *pratimā*, the image but not the god itself. The *Citrasūtra* says, those qualities that we admire in a divine being are within us, and, when we respond to those images brought to us in art, we awaken those finer aspects latent in us. When we are filled by that grace, it lifts us above base desires and pain, and we become that deity.

When we view a great work of art, we experience the joy brought to us by its sublime beauty (ānanda, āhlāda), as we allow it to dissolve our identities and attachments and become one with the object of beauty. It is a moment that bestows on us the grace that underlies the whole creation. Art provides a path to liberation and takes one from the superficial or the outer to the deeper and the paradoxical.

Even though the *Citrasūtra* was written in Kashmir, examples of Kashmiri paintings have not survived the destruction to art that occurred in the Islamic period. However, recently a painted panel in wood, dated to about 900 CE, has come to light that can be clearly traced to Kashmir itself. This panel apparently served as a book cover.

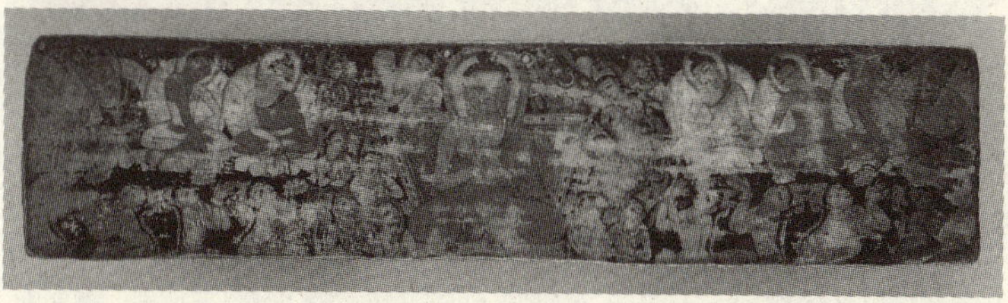

3.4 The oldest surviving painting from Kashmir as a book cover (Pal, 2008)

The analysis of this painitng tells us a lot about the complex symbolism described in the *Citrasūtra*. This cover shows a Central Buddha in a cosmic scene preaching to a congregation of other Buddhas, Bodhisattvas, serpent kings, and mortals, where the serpent kings (nāgarājas) may be identified by their snake-like tails. The eight nāgarājas, which represent the eight directions (four look inwards and other four look away), are in the gesture of offering (añjalimudrā) with expression of intense devotion. The four nearer the central Buddha are oriented towards him while four others at the two ends turn the other way. The Central Buddha is garbed in the red robes of a monk. Here's how Pratapaditya Pal analyzes the painting:[6]

> With his hands the Buddha expresses the gesture of preaching the Law (dharmachakrapravartanamudrā). Distinctive are the extremely narrow eyes emphasizing his trance-like gaze. The oval nimbus is bordered by a band of flames rendered in mauve.

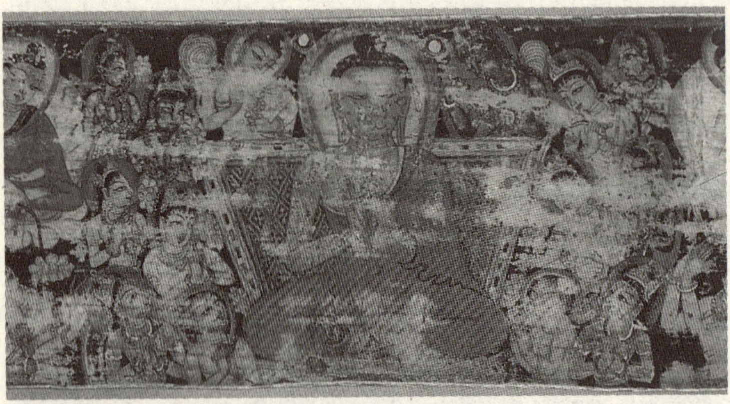

3.5 Details of the Central Buddha preaching

> The halo is flanked by a Buddha standing behind the throne back holding a flywhisk with his right hand and a lotus flower with the left. On the other side is a crowned bodhisattva of a dark green complexion, also with a flywhisk but in his left hand. Surrounding

the Buddha are eight other figures, six of whom are crowned and bejeweled, while the two near the Buddha's knees are monks. Beyond this group of adorers on the upper tier are seven larger seated Buddhas. Four on the left of the central Buddha can be clearly recognized. There may have been an eighth Buddha at the other end but the form is unclear.

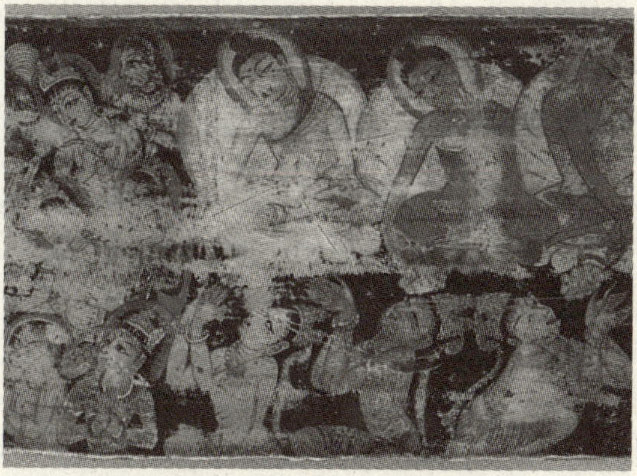

3.6 Details of the adoration of the Buddhas

Pal has argued[7] that the figures are in a style that is close to those at Tabo, indicating that it belongs to the Kashmiri pictorial tradition. He adds,

> To date no painted book cover has been found in Western Tibet, where the practice seems to have been to illuminate only the pages, whereas among the Gilgit manuscripts only the covers were painted. Thus, the painted panel or cover with the scene of the Buddha preaching before a celestial audience must have been painted in Kashmir rather than in Western Tibet by Kashmiri artists or their Tibetan pupils.

Sculpture and Bronze Images

Amongst the early sculptures from Bijbehara in South Kashmir is a large six-armed Skanda (Kārtikeya) standing with his ahana, the peacock that is dated to about 450 CE.[8]

Although Skanda is primarily worshipped in South India today, there was a time when he was an extremely popular deity in Kashmir.

The figure stands in a strictly frontal pose with a massive frame, broad shoulders, and thick, powerful limbs. Although it is badly damaged, one can identify a bow framing the body held at shoulder height in the upper left hand, the shaft of a long lance held at the top on the opposite side, and an upright arrow that passes before the peacock's breast is held in the lower right hand. The upper left arm is lowered, probably holding a rooster, and the right raised, probably holding an akṣamālā.

The hair is drawn up in a large topknot with the bunched hair bulging outwards at the sides, while a long wavy lock of hair falls onto each shoulder. Two distinguishing features of the early period are the short single-stranded sacred thread and the garland that clings tightly to the thighs and reaches the knees.

Around the middle of the 5th century, Gupta features begin to appear in the form of regalia and jewellry. Sculptures of this phase are carved from both gray chlorite and limestone, of which there are many examples from Bijbihara and Baramula.[9]

Images of Śiva retain the double-looped topknot, whereas the Vishnu crown is now of a turreted form. In the mature Kashmir style, there is frequent portrayal of the deity with three lateral heads, and the use of personified weapons in the form of diminutive side attendants.

Many of the new features can be linked to post-Gupta developments elsewhere in North India, predominantly in the workshops of Sarnath and Nalanda, from where there was selective borrowing, especially of the window effect and the form of the dhoti. A North Indian influence is most notably lacking in the upper garment of the female figure, since during this period elsewhere in North India the female deity is usually bare-breasted.

The fully developed Buddha type, and thus the entire Classical style, emerged in the 7th century. The evidence for this is an inscription in metrical Sanskrit on the pedestal of a standing Buddha in the Potala Palace in Lhasa, which records its dedication during the reign of King Durlabha, who could have been either Durlabhavardhana (r. 626–662) or Durlabhaka (r. 662–712). Below is a masterpiece of Buddha Shakyamuni and adorants on the cosmic Mount Meru shown as a transcendental figure.

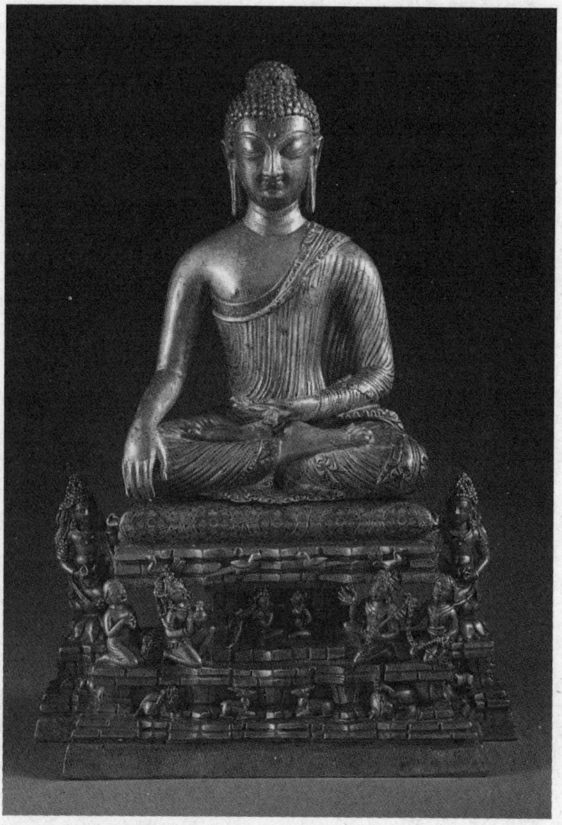

3.7 Buddha Shakyamuni, 700 CE, Norton Simon Museum

In this masterpiece of Indian metal sculpture, Buddha Shakyamuni sits in the meditation posture on a thick cushion. Beneath him is a rocky formation divided into three realms—animal, human and celestial—from bottom to top. The face is oval with arched eyebrows, an urna, large almond-shaped eyes, long nose, compact smiling lips, and small round chin. In profile, the nose and the brow form a continuous line, while the lower half of the face recedes.

Several stone sculptures in Classical style have survived in the valley, of which many are three-headed, a feature peculiar to Kashmir. These were placed in shrines or set in the niches of the peristyle that enclosed the courtyard of most temples. The most outstanding sculpture in the style is undoubtedly the majestic, richly ornamented three-headed Vishnu, holding his attributes, the lotus and the conch, which must date from the 7th century.

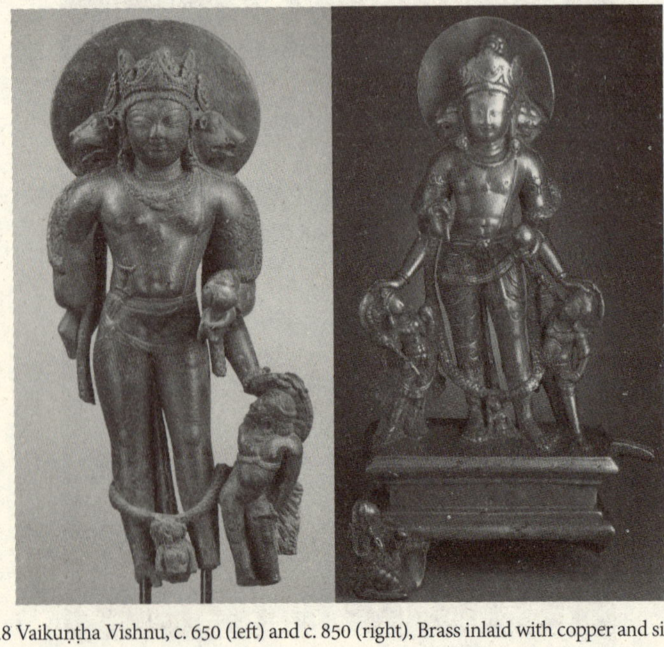

3.8 Vaikuṇṭha Vishnu, c. 650 (left) and c. 850 (right), Brass inlaid with copper and silver

This complex form of Vishnu, first referred to by the name Vaikuṇṭha in the *Viṣṇudharmottara Purāṇa*,[10] is four-faced (caturmūrti), with the heads of a lion (right) and a boar (left) flanking a human head. He is also identifiable in this form by the epithet Parā-Vāsudeva, 'the highest god'. The lion and boar represent Vishnu's Varāha and Narasiṃha avatars. Carved in low relief on the back of the halo is the fourth face, a demonic, grimacing representation with fangs and a vertical third eye on the forehead. The small attendant on Vishnu's left is Cakrapuruṣa, the personification of his war discus, originally balanced on his right by Gadādevi, the female personification of his battle mace. The earth goddess Prithvī stands between Vishnu's legs. From the 8th through the 10th century, this four-faced Vishnu was the paramount icon in the kingdom of Kashmir. The philosophical basis behind it is that just as Śiva has aspects that are simultaneously present, so does Vishnu, in both the auspicious and fierce forms.

The style underwent a brief revival in the mid-9th century during the reign of Avantivarman (r. 855–883), as can be seen in the sculptures of the Vishnu and Śiva temples at Avantipura, which are carved from a highly polished black marble. However, though they show new vigour, much stylization has crept in, and the facial features are hardened. The earlier complex patterning of the open edge of the lower garment and the foliate design of the crown is crudely interpreted, and the headdress is out of proportion to the head. Two iconographical changes are evident: the sacred thread is now triple-stranded, and a reverse Kapila (angry) head is added to three-headed images of Vishnu.

4

The *Panchatantra*

The *Panchatantra* of Vishnu Sharma is one of the world's most widely translated and popular books. It is a storehouse of practical wisdom and is a model for the genre of tales embedded in frame stories, of which we will see other examples later in this book.[1] The German scholar Johannes Hertel who researched the many recensions of the text believed that the original was composed in Kashmir around 200 BCE, although the individual stories are more ancient.[2]

The background story to the creation of the *Panchatantra* is fascinating as well. King Amara Śakti of Mahilāropa was unhappy that his three sons were hostile towards education and, therefore, lacked in proper judgement. He approached his ministers for counsel and was told that learning grammar required 12 years of study, and the sciences, politics, and diplomacy were disciplines that took a lifetime to master. Instead of instruction in scriptures and texts, the princes should be taught the wisdom inherent in them, and the aged scholar Vishnu Sharma was the man to do it.

Vishnu Sharma was invited to the court, and the king asked him if he could turn the princes into 'incomparable masters of the art of practical life, and if he did, he will be given one-hundred land grants'.

Vishnu Sharma said, 'King, listen, here's the plain truth. I'm not the man to sell learning for a 100 land-grants. But if

I do not aquaint the boys with the art of intelligent learning, in six months, I will give up my own name. Let's cut the matter short. My boasting is not from a need for money. I am 80 years old, and objects of sensual desires have lost their charm. But to fulfil your request, I will show the play of knowledge (*Sarasvatī-vinoda*). Mark this date. If I fail to make your sons extraordinary masters of wisdom in six months, let God bar my way to heaven.'

The king was astonished and happy to hear this promise. The princes were sent off with Vishnu Sharma. The time was short and clearly a conventional curriculum would be useless, so Vishnu Sharma hit upon instruction by interwoven animal fables. Adapting stories that were undoubtedly in currency, the *Panchatantra* was created as an entertaining text to communicate the essence of diplomacy, relationships, politics and administration to the princes. Stories with anthropomorphic animals are found in ancient Sanskrit texts of the 1st millennium BCE, such as the *Chāndogya Upaniṣad*. So this was a familiar form.

The earliest known translation of the *Panchatantra* into a non-Indian language is into Middle Persian (Pahlavi, 550 CE) by Burzoe. This became the basis for a Syriac translation as *Kalīlāh* and *Damnag* and a translation into Arabic in 750 CE by Persian scholar Abdullah Ibn al-Muqaffa as *Kalīlah wa Dimnah*.[3]

The *Panchatantra* collection is divided into five (Skt. *Panca*) central teachings (*tantras*) with each part having a core story and other stories woven into it. These five parts are:

1. Loss of friend (mitra bheda)
2. Winning of friends (mitra lābha)
3. On crows and owls (kākolūkīyam)
4. Loss of gains (labdhapraṇāśam)
5. Ill-considered actions (aparīkṣitakārakaṃ)

The first book features a jackal named Damanaka as the unemployed minister in a kingdom ruled by a lion. He and his moralizing sidekick Karataka conspire to break up alliances of the lion king. A series of fables describe the conspiracies and causes that lead to the break-up of close and inseparable friends.

The overall focus of the second book is the reverse of the first book by the emphasis on friendship, teamwork, and alliances. It teaches that weak animals with very different skills working together can accomplish what they cannot when they work alone.

The third book discusses war and peace, showing how strategic means can be employed to neutralize the army of a vastly superior opponent. The fourth book is a compilation of ancient morality fables and examples of what should be avoided. The fifth book has fables about hasty actions or jumping to conclusions without establishing facts and due diligence.

One of the fables in the last book is the story of a woman who has a pet mongoose. She has to step out of her home, and she leaves the child in the care of the mongoose. Returning, she sees blood on the mongoose's mouth, and fearing that her child was hurt, kills the mongoose. Soon she discovers that her child is alive, and the blood on the mongoose' mouth came from killing a snake that was trying to harm the child. She now regrets having killed a friend due to hasty action.

The following stories have been adapted from the first book on the loss of friends.[4]

The Story of the Ox Abandoned in the Forest

Once upon a time a rich merchant's son was going to the city of Mathurā to trade a bull named Sañjīvaka. But in a forest, on the way, the bull slipped, fell into a ravine, and lay there paralyzed. The merchant's son was unable to raise the bull from the ravine, and at last in despair abandoned it and went off. As fate would have it, the bull slowly revived, and eating grass that was in rich supply in the forest recovered his former condition. Soon, fat, and strong with a full hump, he was roaming free like the bull of Śiva, tearing up anthills with his horns, and bellowing loudly.

At the time there lived in a neighbouring wood a lion named Piṅgalaka, who had subdued the forest by his might. This king of beasts had two jackals for ministers named Damanaka and Karaṭaka. One day, on his way to the bank of the Yamunā to drink water, Piṅgalaka heard the resounding roar of Sañjīvaka. This roar, the likes of which he had never heard before, made him think, 'Surely this is a creature greater than me who dwells nearby; I will depart, for if it saw me, it might slay me, or expel me from the forest.' Thereupon the lion quickly returned to the forest without drinking water, and continued to hide his fears from his followers.

The wise jackal Damanaka said secretly to Karaṭaka, the second minister, 'Our master went to drink water; so how come he has returned so quickly without drinking? We must ask him the reason.' But Karaṭaka said, 'What business is this of ours? Have you not heard the story of the ape that pulled out the wedge?'

The Story of the Monkey That Pulled Out the Wedge

In a certain town, a merchant who wished to build a temple to a divinity, gathered much timber. The workmen, having sawed through the upper half of a plank, placed a wedge in it, and went away on a food-break. In the meanwhile, a monkey came there and bounding up sat on the plank, the parts of which were separated by the wedge. As he sat in the gap, in purposeless mischief, he pulled out the wedge and was crushed and killed.

'Thus, a person is ruined by meddling in what is not one's own business. So, what is the use of probing into the mind of the king of beasts?' When the grave Damanaka heard Karaṭaka say this, he answered: 'Certainly wise ministers must observe the peculiarities of their master's character.' But Karaṭaka said, 'Prying for one's own gratification is not the duty of a servant.' Damanaka replied, 'Do not speak thus. Everyone desires action suited to his character; the dog is satisfied with a bone.'

Karaṭaka said, 'And supposing under these circumstances the master gets angry, instead of being pleased? Lords, like mountains, are exceedingly rough, firm, uneven, difficult to access, and surrounded by nasty creatures.' Then Damanaka said, 'This is true, but he who is wise, gradually gets influence over his master by penetrating his character.'

Karaṭaka agreed with this, and Damanaka went into the presence of his master. After being received kindly by the lion, he bowed and said, 'King, I am a hereditary useful servant of yours. One who is useful is to be cherished, even if he were a stranger, and a disagreeable one is to be condemned. A cat, being useful, is bought with money, and held dear; but a mouse, being harmful, is destroyed, even if it was born in one's own house. A king, who desires prosperity, must listen to good servants, who must give their lord at the right time useful counsel, even without being asked. So, King, if you feel confidence in me, if you are not angry, and do not wish to conceal your feelings from me, nor disturbed by my boldness, I will ask you a certain question.' When Damanaka said this, the lion Piṅgalaka answered, 'You are trustworthy, you are attached to me, so speak without fear.'

Damanaka said: 'King, being thirsty, you went to drink water; so why did you return without drinking, like one despondent?'

The lion thought, 'I have been found out, so why should I try to hide the truth from this devoted servant?' He said, 'Listen, when I went to drink water, I heard a noise that I had never heard before, and I think it is the terrible roar of an animal superior to myself in strength. As a rule, the might of a creature is proportionate to its roar, and it is well known that God has made animals in infinitely varying regular gradations. Now that this powerful animal has entered this forest, I cannot call my body nor my forest my own. So, I must depart to some other place.'

To the lion's plight, Damanaka replied, 'You are brave, O King, why do you wish to leave the wood for so slight a reason? Water breaks a bridge, secret whisperings break friendship, counsel is ruined by garrulity, but only cowards are routed by mere noise. There are many noises, such as those of machines, which are terrible till one knows the real cause. Your Highness must not be afraid. Hear, by way of illustration, the story of the jackal and the drum.'

The Story of the Jackal and the Drum

Long ago there lived a jackal in a certain forest. He was roaming about in search of food and came upon a field where a battle had taken place, and hearing from a certain quarter a booming sound, he looked in that direction.

There, he saw a drum lying on the ground, a thing he had never seen before. He thought, 'What kind of animal is this that makes such sound?' He noticed that it was motionless. He approached it for a better view and decided that it was not an animal. He suspected that the noise was produced by the parchment being struck by the shaft of an arrow, moved by the wind. So the jackal laid aside his fear, tore open the drum, and peeped inside to see if there was any food in it.

'King, why do you fear a mere sound? If you approve, I will go to investigate the matter.' The lion answered, 'Go there, by all means, if you dare.' So Damanaka went to the bank of the Yamunā. While he was roaming slowly, guided by an unfamiliar sound, he discovered the bull eating grass. He approached him and made his acquaintance, then returned to tell the lion what he had discovered.

The lion Piṅgalaka was delighted and said, 'If you have really seen that great ox, and made friends with him, bring him here by some artifice, that I may see what he is like.' Damanaka went to the bull and said, 'Come. Our master, the king of beasts, is pleased to summon you.' But the bull would not consent, for he was afraid.

The jackal returned to the forest and induced his master to grant the bull protection. Once he had the King's word, he brought Sañjīvaka over. When the lion saw him come and bow before him, he treated him with kindness, and said, 'Remain here now about my person, and entertain no fear.' The bull was happy and gradually gained the confidence of the king of the jungle. Slowly, the lion turned his back on his other ministers, and was entirely governed by the bull.

Damanaka was annoyed by the turn of events and said to Karaṭaka in secret: 'See, our master has been possessed by Sañjīvaka, and he pays us no attention. He eats alone, and never gives us a share, and the fool is now taught his duty by the bull. I am responsible for this mischief, and I will now take steps to have the bull killed and save our master from his unbecoming infatuation.'

When Karaṭaka heard this from Damanaka, he said, 'Friend, even you won't be able to do this now.' Then Damanaka said, 'I shall certainly be able to accomplish it by judiciousness.

Anything can be achieved if wisdom does not fail in calamity. As proof, hear the story of the makara that killed the crane.'

The Story of the Crane and the Makara

In olden times there dwelt a crane in a certain tank rich in fish, who in terror would flee out of his sight. Not being able to catch the fish, the crane lied to them. 'There has come to this place a fisherman who will soon catch you all and kill you. If you have any faith in me, please act on my advice. There is in far-off place a translucent lake, which is unknown to the fishermen of these parts. I will take you there one by one, and drop you into it, so that you may happily live there.'

When the foolish fish heard this, they said in fear, 'Do so, we have faith in you.' The treacherous crane took the fish away one by one, and, putting them down on a rock, devoured them.

A certain makara dwelling in that lake, noticed these activities of the crane and asked, 'Where are you taking the fish?' The crane said to him exactly what he had told the fish. The makara was also terrified and said, 'Take me there too.'

The crane, whose reason was clouded by thoughts of so much flesh, carried the makara, soaring aloft, towards the slab of the rock. When the makara neared the rock, he saw the bone fragments of the fish that the crane had eaten and understood what had happened. No sooner was he put down on the rock that the sagacious makara cut off the crane's head. And he returned and told the fish what had happened.They were delighted, and hailed him as their deliverer from death.

'Prudence indeed is power, so what has a man, devoid of prudence, to do with power? Hear this other story of the lion and the hare.'

The Story of the Lion and the Hare

There was in a certain forest a lion, who was invincible and the sole master of it. Whatever creature he came across, he killed. The animals met and deliberated upon their predicament. They made the following petition to that king of the beasts: 'Why do you by killing us indiscriminately ruin your own interests? We will send you one animal every day for dinner.'

The lion consented to their proposal, for he was in the habit of eating only one animal of the many he would kill everyday.

It so happened that one day it was the turn of the hare to present himself for the meal. On the way the wise hare thought, 'He is truly brave who does not become bewildered even in time of calamity. Now that Death stares me in the face, I will devise a way to get out of my situation.'

Thinking thus, the hare presented himself before the lion, but only after the appointed hour. The lion was furious and said, 'Why didn't you arrive at the dinner hour? What penalty worse than death can I inflict on you, scoundrel?'

The hare bowed and said: 'It is not my fault, your Highness, I have not been my own master today, for another lion detained me on the road, and only let me go after much entreating.'

When the lion heard that, he lashed his tail, his eyes became red with fury, and he bellowed, 'Who is that second lion? Show him to me.'

The hare said, 'Let your majesty come and see for yourself.' The hare took him away to a distant well. 'Here he lives, behold him,' said the hare, and the lion looked into the well, roaring with anger.

Seeing his own reflection in the clear water, and hearing the echo of his own roar, the lion thought there was a rival who was roaring louder than him. In anger, he threw himself into the well to kill the second lion, and there, the fool was drowned. The hare, having escaped death by his wisdom, went to the assembly of animals who were delighted when they heard his story.

'So, you see that wisdom is the supreme power, and not strength.' When Damanaka said this, Karaṭaka remained silent.

Damanaka went before the king Piṅgalaka, assuming a visage of depression. When Piṅgalaka asked him the reason, he said in a whisper, 'I will tell you, king, for if one knows anything, one ought not to conceal it. And one should speak even without being commanded to do so if one desires the welfare of one's master. Here is what I know.

'This bull Sañjīvaka intends to kill you and gain possession of the kingdom. In his position of minister, he has concluded that you are timid. Longing to slay you, he is going about flashing his horns, his natural weapons, and he talks over the animals in the forest, encouraging them with speeches of this kind: "We will kill this meat-eating king of beasts, and then you can live in security under me, who am an eater of grass. Think, my master. As long as this bull is alive, there is no security for you."'

Piṅgalaka answered, 'What can that miserable herb-eating bull do to me? But how can I kill a creature that has sought my protection, and to whom I have promised immunity from injury?' Damanaka said, 'When a king makes another equal to himself, luck does not proceed as favourably as before. If the fickle Goddess of Fortune places her foot at the same time upon two exalted persons, she will certainly abandon one of the two. And a king, who hates a good servant and honours a bad servant, is to be avoided by the wise, as a wicked patient by the physician.'

Damanaka added, 'Where there is a speaker and a hearer of advice that seems disagreeable at first, but in the end is useful, there Goddess of Fortune sets her foot. He, who does not accept good advice and follows the bad, falls into calamity in a short time. What is the meaning of this love of yours for the bull, O king? And what does it matter that you gave him protection, or that he came as a suppliant, if he plots against your life?

'Moreover, if this bull remains about your person, you will have worms produced in you by his excretions. And they will infect your body, which is covered with the scars of wounds by the tusks of infuriated elephants. If a wicked person is wise enough not to harm directly, the injury will happen indirectly. Hear is a story in proof of it.'

The Story of the Louse and the Flea

In the bed of a certain king lived a louse, which had crept in from somewhere or other, by name Mandavisarpiṇī, who was undiscovered for a long time and so lived a happy life. And suddenly a flea, named Ṭiṭṭibha, entered that bed, wafted there by the wind.

When Mandavisarpiṇī saw him, she said, 'Why have you invaded my home? Go elsewhere.' Ṭiṭṭibha answered, 'I wish to drink the blood of a king, something I have never tasted before, so permit me to dwell here.'

Then, to please him, the louse said to him, 'If this is the case, remain. But, my friend, you must not bite the king at unreasonable times; you must bite him gently when he is asleep.' Ṭiṭṭibha heard that and agreed to the condition. But at night he bit the king hard when he was in bed and not quite asleep. Then the king rose up, exclaiming, 'I am bitten,' but the wicked flea fled quickly, and when the king's servants made a search in the bed, they discovered the louse and killed it.

'So Mandavisarpiṇī perished by associating with Ṭiṭṭibha. Accordingly, your association with Sañjīvaka will not be to your advantage. If you do not believe what I say, imagine seeing him approach you, flashing his horns, which are sharp as lances.'

These words changed Piṅgalaka's feelings towards the bull, and Damanaka induced him to form in his heart the resolve to kill his rival. Having ascertained the state of the lion's feelings, Damanaka immediately went off on his own accord to Sañjīvaka, and sat in his presence with a despondent air. The bull said to him, 'Friend, why are you in this state? Are you in good health?'

The jackal answered, 'What can be good with a servant's situation? Who is permanently dear to a king? What petitioner is not despised? Who is not subject to time?' The bull probed further, 'Why are you so despondent today, my friend, tell me?'

Damanaka said, 'Listen, I speak out of friendship. The lion Piṅgalaka has become hostile to you. So unstable is his affection that, without regard to friendship, he wishes to kill you and eat you, and I see that his evilly disposed courtiers have instigated him to this resolve.'

The simple-minded bull, on account of the confidence he had previously reposed in the jackal, said to him: 'Alas, a mean master, with mean retainers, though he be won over by faithful service, becomes estranged; in proof of it hear this story.'

The Story of the Lion, the Panther, the Crow, and the Jackal

There lived once in a certain forest a lion, named Madotkaṭa, and he had three followers, a panther, a crow, and a jackal. That lion once saw a camel, which had escaped from a caravan, enter his forest; this was a creature of ridiculous appearance that he was unfamiliar with.

That king of the beasts said in astonishment, 'What is this creature?' And the crow, who knew when it behooved him to speak, said, 'It is a camel.' Out of curiosity, the lion had the camel summoned, and giving him promise of protection, made him a courtier.

One day the lion was wounded in a fight with an elephant, and his injury forced him to stop hunting, even though he was surrounded by attendants who were in good health. The exhausted lion roamed about in search of food, but not finding any, secretly asked all his courtiers, except the camel, what was to be done. They said to him, 'Your Highness, we must give advice which is appropriate for the present situation. What friendship can you have with a camel, and why do you not eat him?'

'He is a grass-eating animal, and therefore meant to be devoured by us flesh-eaters. And why should not one be sacrificed to supply food to many? If your Highness should object on the ground that you cannot slay one to whom you have granted protection, we will contrive a plot by which we shall induce the camel himself to offer his body.'

The lion heard this and agreed to the scheme. The crow went and said to the camel, 'This master of ours is overpowered with hunger, although he says nothing about it, so we intend to make him well-disposed to us by offering him our bodies, and you had better do the same, in order that he may be well-disposed towards you.'

When the crow said this to the camel, the simple-minded camel agreed, and came to the lion with the crow. Then the crow said, 'King, eat me, for I am my own master.' The lion said, 'What is the use of eating such a small creature as you?' Thereupon the jackal said, 'Eat me,' and the lion rejected him in the same way. Then the panther said, 'Eat me,' and yet the lion would not eat him; and at last, the camel said 'Eat me.'

So the lion, and the crow, and others, taking him at his word, killed him, divided him into portions, and ate him.

'In the same way some treacherous person has instigated Piṅgalaka against me without cause. Now fate will decide. It is better to be the servant of a vulture-king with swans for courtiers, than to serve a swan as king, if his courtiers be vultures.'

When the dishonest Damanaka heard Sanjívaka say that, he replied, 'Everything is accomplished by resolution and people must follow good advice, otherwise they will be ruined.'

The Story of the Tortoise and the Two Swans

Once upon a time, there was in a certain lake a tortoise named Kambugrīva, who had two swans, Vikaṭa and Sankaṭa, for friends. Soon the lake dried up due to drought, and they wanted to go to another lake. The tortoise said to them, 'Take me also to the lake you are planning to go to.' When the swans heard this, they said to him, 'The lake, to which we wish to go, is a tremendous distance off; but, if you wish to go there too, you must do what we tell you. You must take in your teeth a stick held by us, and while travelling through the air, you must remain perfectly silent, otherwise you will fall and be killed.'

The tortoise agreed and took the stick in his teeth, and the two swans flew up into the air, holding the two ends of it. Gradually, they drew near that lake and were seen by men living in a town below. The thoughtless tortoise heard the people say, 'What a strange thing could the swans be carrying?' The tortoise asked the swans about the chattering below, and in so doing let go of the stick from its mouth. He fell down to the earth and was killed by the men.

Thus, you see that a person who loses common sense will be ruined, like the tortoise that let go of the stick. 'This is true, my dear, but hear this story also.'

The Story of the Three Fishes

In old times there were three fishes in a lake near a river. One was called Anāgatavidhātṛi, a second Pratyutpannamati and the third Yadbhaviṣya, and they were companions. One day they heard some fishermen, who passed that way, saying to one another, 'It looks like there are plenty of fish in this lake.' Thereupon the prudent Anāgatavidhātṛi, fearing to be killed by the fishermen, entered the current of the river, and went to another place.

But Pratyutpannamati remained where he was, without fear, saying to himself, 'I will take the expedient course if any danger should arise.' And Yadbhaviṣya remained there, saying to himself, 'What must be, must be.'

Then the fishermen came and threw a net into the lake. But the cunning Pratyutpannamati made himself rigid and pretended to be dead the moment he felt himself hauled up in the net. The fishermen, who were killing the fish, did not kill him, thinking that he was already dead, so he jumped into the current of the river, and went off somewhere else as fast as he could. But Yadbhaviṣya, like a foolish fish, jumped around and wriggled in the net, so the fishermen laid hold of him and killed him.

'So I too will adopt an expedient when the time arrives. You must be wise in calamity and not let go of your resolve. Now a battle with Piṅgalaka is at hand. When his tail gets erect, and he rises with his feet together, then you will know that he is about to strike you. You must have your head ready, and gore him in the stomach, and tear out his entrails.'

After Damanaka had said this to the bull Sañjīvaka, he went to Karaṭaka, and told him that he had succeeded in setting the two up against each other.

Then Sañjīvaka slowly approached Piṅgalaka, being desirous of reading the mind of the king of beasts by his face and gestures. He saw that the lion was evenly balanced on all four legs, his tail was erect, and he was prepared to fight. The lion saw that the bull had tossed up his head in fear, and he sprang on the bull and struck him with his claws. The bull countered with his horns, and so their fight went on. Seeing this, the virtuous Karaṭaka said to Damanaka, 'Why have you brought calamity on our master to gain your own ends? Wealth obtained by oppression of subjects, friendship obtained by deceit, and a lady-love gained by violence, will not last long. But enough! A person who despises good advice, incurs misfortune, as did Sūcīmukha, the bird.'

The Story of the Monkeys, the Firefly, and the Bird

Once upon a time, there was a troop of monkeys wandering in some wood. In the cold weather they saw a firefly and thought it was real fire. They placed grass and leaves upon it, and tried to warm themselves, and one monkey fanned the firefly with his breath.

A bird named Sūcīmukha saw this and said to him, 'This is not fire, this is a firefly, do not fatigue yourself.' Though the monkey heard it, he did not stop, and thereupon the bird came down from the tree, and earnestly dissuaded him. The ape was annoyed by this and throwing a stone at Sūcīmukha, crushed him.

'Therefore, one ought not to stop one who will not act on good advice. Why then should I speak? You well know that you brought about this quarrel with a mischievous objective, and that which is done with evil intentions cannot turn out well.'

The Story of Dharmabuddhi and Duṣṭabuddhi

Long ago, there lived in a certain village two brothers, Dharmabuddhi and Duṣṭabuddhi, the sons of a merchant. They left their father's house and went to another country in search of wealth. With much effort they acquired two thousand gold dīnārs. With these they returned to their own city, and for future business expenses they buried those dīnārs at the foot of a tree, except for one hundred that they divided equally.

One day Duṣṭabuddhi went by himself and dug up the dinars that were buried at the foot of the tree. And after one month had passed, he said to Dharmabuddhi, 'Come, my elder brother, let us divide those dinars; I have expenses.' Dharmabuddhi agreed, and they went to the place and did the digging at the burial spot but did not find any dinars.

The treacherous Duṣṭabuddhi said to Dharmabuddhi: 'You have taken away the dinars, so give me my half.' But Dharmabuddhi answered: 'I have not taken them; you must have taken them.'

A quarrel arose, and Duṣṭabuddhi hit Dharmabuddhi on the head and dragged him into the king's court. There they both stated their case, and as the king's officers could not judge, they were proceeding to detain them both for a trial by ordeal. Then Duṣṭabuddhi said to the king's officers, 'The tree, at the foot of which these dinars were hidden will depose as a witness that they were taken away by this Dharmabuddhi.' The officers were astonished, and said, 'We will question it tomorrow.' Then they let both Dharmabuddhi and Duṣṭabuddhi go on bail.

Duṣṭabuddhi, who was his father's favourite, told the whole matter to his father, and secretly giving him money, said, 'Hide in the trunk of the tree and be my witness.'

His father consented, and at night he hid in the capacious trunk of the tree. In the morning the two brothers, together with the king's officers, went to question the tree. The father, who was hidden in the trunk of the tree, replied in a loud clear voice: 'Dharmabuddhi took away the dinars.' When the king's officers heard this surprising utterance, they said, 'Surely Duṣṭabuddhi has hidden someone in the trunk of the tree.'

They made a fire and fumigated the trunk of the tree. The father fell out of the trunk on to the ground and died. When the king's officers saw this, they understood the whole matter, and they ordered Duṣṭabuddhi to return the dinars to his elder brother, and he was banished from the city. Dharmabuddhi was honoured as a man who deserved his name.

You see that a deed done with an unrighteous mind is sure to bring calamity, therefore one should act righteously as in the story of the crane and the snake.

The Story of the Crane, the Snake, and the Mungoose

Once upon a time a snake came and ate the nestlings of a certain crane as soon as they were born. This grieved the crane. On the advice of a crab, he went and strewed pieces of fish starting from the dwelling of a certain stratagem to the hole of the snake, and when the stratagem came out, it followed up the pieces of fish until it was led to the hole of the snake. It entered the hole and killed the snake and his offspring.

So, by stratagem one can succeed.

The Story of the Mice That Ate an Iron Balance

Once upon a time there was a young man who had spent all his father's wealth and had only an iron balance left. He decided to deposit the balance in the care of a merchant and go to another land to seek fortune. On his return, he came to ask for his balance, but the merchant said, 'It has been eaten by mice,' adding, 'It is quite true, for this iron was particularly sweet, and the mice could not resist it.' This he said with an outward show of sorrow, although he was laughing in his heart.

Then the young man asked for some food, and the merchant, being in a good mood, gave him some. The young man went to bathe, taking with him the young son of the merchant, whom he persuaded to accompany him by giving him sweets. And after he had bathed, the young man left the boy in the care of a friend and returned alone to the house of the merchant. The merchant asked, 'Where is my son?' He replied, 'A kite swooped down from the air and carried him off.'

The merchant raged, 'You have abducted my son,' and he took him to the court; and there the young man made the same statement. The officers of the court said, 'This is impossible. How could a kite carry off a boy?' But the young man answered, 'In a country where a large balance of iron was eaten by mice, a kite might carry off an elephant, not to mention a boy.'

When the officers heard this, they made the merchant restore the balance to the young man, who then brought back the merchant's child.

'Thus, you see, persons of eminent ability attain their ends by stratagem. But you, by your reckless impetuosness, have put our master in danger.'

When Damanaka heard Karaṭaka, he laughed and said, 'Don't talk like this. What chance is there of a bull being victorious over a lion? There is great difference between a lion, whose body is adorned with scars of wounds from the tusks of infuriated elephants, and a tame ox, whose body was pricked by the goad.'

While the jackals were carrying on this discussion, the lion killed the bull Sañjīvaka. When he was slain, Damanaka recovered his position of minister without a rival, and remained for a long time about the person of the king of the beasts in perfect happiness.

5

Patañjali, Sage of Grammar and Yoga

The *Yoga Sūtra* of Patañjali is one of the two central texts of classical yoga, the other being the Bhagavad Gītā. Many Yoga practices begin with an invocation to Patañjali. Given the worldwide popularity of Yoga, almost everyone has heard of him, but books say very little about his life, and most don't know why his images show a serpent tail.

There is an Indian tradition going back at least to King Bhoja Paramāra of the 11th century in his commentary on the *Yoga Sūtras* called the *Bhojavṛtti* that Patañjali authored not only the book on Yoga but also the Mahābhāṣya ('Great Commentary' on grammar and language) and a treatise on Āyurveda. An earlier remark by the poet and linguist Bhartṛhari (c. 500 CE) also speaks of a sage who did all three, namely Yoga, grammar, and Āyurveda and since his time is not that far removed from the time of the *Mahābhāṣya*, it seems reasonable to assume that he was referring to Patañjali.

The medical text attributed to Patañjali is the now-lost *Pātañjalatantra*, which is considered a medical authority in several Sanskrit texts such as *Yogaratnākara*, *Yogaratnasamuccaya*, and *Padārthavijñāna*.

The Indian tradition accepts that many great early grammarians of Sanskrit hailed from the region of Takshashila (Taxila) that some see as part of Greater Kashmir. As the Maurya Empire became the predominant power in north

India in 4th century BCE, a stream of scholars left Takshashila to seek fortune in Pāṭaliputra.

Thus, Rājaśekhara in his Kāvya-Mīmaṃsā (9th century) says that grammarians like Upavarṣa, Varṣa, Pāṇini, Piṅgala, Vyāḍi, Vararuci, and Patañjali obtained fame in Pāṭaliputra.[1] It is likely that Patañjali lived for some years there, which later led to the belief that he was from the east (Gauḍa), and as his fame multiplied this location was transferred to south India, and even Thailand.

The *Mahābhāṣya* has been the authority on classical Sanskrit for more than 2,000 years. Its ideas on structure, grammar, and philosophy of language have been extremely influential in the Sanskrit tradition.

Understanding Patañjali as a person is important to those who do Yoga; it is also relevant to those who are interested in mapping of cognitive content of text to derived meaning in artificial intelligence, and to the search for a new paradigm for medicine as a holistic discipline, where Ayurveda appears to offer solutions. There is a mathematical theorem that proves three-way logic is more efficient than binary logic. Recasting medicine in three-classes may make it more patient-centred. For context remember that Ayurveda has three doshas and three guṇas, whereas allopathy uses only two states of wellness and illness.

In his grammar, Patañjali speaks of the idea of sphoṭa, which is the utterance that remains unaffected by individual speaker differences. Later, Bhartṛhari (6th century CE) made sphoṭa central to his theory that the sentence (rather than just the stringing together of words) is indivisible (akhaṇḍa), conveying meaning that owes to the cognitive content (saṃvit) of the entire utterance. The idea that the sentence is more than a mere concatenation of words is of great significance to the ongoing debates in artificial intelligence (AI).

The overall aim of Sanskrit grammar was not to list out the rules and to standardize the language, but to clearly bring out the apt and the intended meaning of the structure of words. As Yāska says in the *Nirukta* (the oldest available Indian treatise on etymology, philology, and semantics), the aim is to understand the real significance of the word.

The *Nirukta* became necessary to help understand archaic, uncommon words used mainly in the *Ṛgveda* since almost a quarter of the words in the Vedic texts composed in the 2nd-millennium BCE appear once; and their meaning and intent have gradually become unclear.

A Grammatical Background

There were several Niruktas prior to the time of Yāska (c. 7th or 6th century BCE), who refers to about 12 such texts prior to his time, but these works are lost. Yaska's *Nirukta* is a commentary on the *Nighaṇṭu*, which is a glossary of words occurring in the *Ṛgveda*, and functions as a complement to vyākaraṇa (grammar).

The grammars of the three Great Sages (Munitraya), Pāṇini, Kātyāyana, and Patañjali, raised the question of the intended meaning of the spoken word. Debates were carried out on the question: 'What is the basic unit of the language that gives forth a meaning? Is it the word or the sentence?'

The words come together to form a sentence, and just as a word has no separate entity without its constituent letters, a sentence has no separate entity without words that give it structure. Also, though the words are parts of a sentence, the meaning of the sentence does not independently arise out of them.

Meaning is the function of the sentence so that the meaning of a word is context dependent. Yet the process by which the context is fixed in the mind of the listener is dependent on several factors, including the mood of the reader. This is the reason why a good poem yields different meanings on new readings, since the reader's context is partly established by their state of mind.

The next question was whether the words have an independent existence of their own or whether they are merely segments of a sentence which, in truth, is an indivisible entity producing a definite meaning.

There was a line of argument which asserted that a word, though a part (khaṇḍa) of a sentence is, in fact, an independent unit of thought and meaning, which came to be known as khaṇḍa-pakṣa.

The other school posited that the sentence is the fundamental, indivisible (akhaṇḍa) linguistic unit; words are just the components of a sentence, and the school which advocated this argument was known as the akhaṇḍa-pakṣa.

According to Yāska, every word is derived from a root; and by analyzing the root, its disposition and the suffix, it is possible to establish the relation between word and meaning.

Like Pāṇini, Patañjali also focuses on words. According to him, the basic linguistic unit is the word. His commentary, the *Mahābhāṣya*, commences with the statement *atha śabdānuśāsanam*, 'here begins the science of words'. He deals with the formation of words, determination of meaning, and the relation between a word and its meaning.

The *Aṣṭādhyāyī* of Pāṇini shows how to produce words and sentences based on verbal roots (dhātu), noun-base (prātipadika), and suffixes (pratyaya). These constituent elements are invested with meaning, and derived from them, words and sentences are formed to express collection of meanings as held by these elements.

The *Mahābhāṣya* enlarges the focus. The purpose of a grammar is to account for the words by writing a set of general (sāmānya) rules (lakṣaṇa) and by pointing out exceptions (viśeṣa). These general rules must be derived from the usage of the learned. In this he follows Kātyāyana.

Bhartṛhari explained that, initially, the thought exists in a unified way in the mind of the speaker. When uttered, the sequence of sounds (dhvani) that follow one after the other produces certain specific sound-patterns (nāda). Although the articulated word-sounds are separated in time and space, as they reach the listener in a sequence, the listener grasps the completed sentence as a single unit, as its meaning bursts forth (sphoṭa) in a flash of understanding or insight (pratibhā). Understanding of the meaning must be the immediate and intuitive grasp of the sentence as a whole. The articulated sound's (dhvani, nāda) sphoṭa is the inner unity conveying the meaning.

Patañjali and His Times

The date of the Patañjali is known to be mid-2nd century BCE from the fact that the Mahābhāṣya mentions Puṣyamitra of the Śuṅga dynasty (ruled from 185–149 BCE) as a contemporary. Patañjali's authorship of seminal books in three different fields is declared in the following popular invocation:

> *yōgena cittasya padena vācāṃ malaṃ śarīrasya ca vaidyakena.*
> *yō'pākarōttaṃ pravaraṃ munīnāṃ patañjaliṃ prāñjalirāṇatō 'smi.*

> He who removed the impurities of the mind through yoga, of speech through grammar, and of the body through medicine, to that illustrious sage, Patañjali, I bow with folded hands.

Recently a series of papers by Ashok Aklujkar has provided the definitive judgment that Patañjali's provenance was

Kashmir. The main points of evidence considered by Aklujkar are:[2]

1. Patañjali's familiarity with the geography of Kashmir. He is also familiar with the eastern regions, but that may be due to his having spent part of his life in Pāṭaliputra, which was the great royal capital of his times.

As another example, Jinendra-buddhi, author of the Pañcikā commentary on the Kāśikā was a Kashmiri, a resident of Varāhamūla (modern Baramulla) but his work was most known in eastern India, particularly Bengal. Patanjali shows no familiarity with the geography of South India, and his association with the Tamil lands is explained by conveyance of his fame along the eastern coast of India, and in a similar way further beyond to Thailand.

2. Gonanda is the name of a mythical figure in the history of Kashmir, and one of the names of Patañjali is Gonandīya. The name 'Gonanda', written incorrectly as 'Gonarda', led some scholars astray and assigned him to the Gauḍa lands.

3. The scholar Yudhiṣṭhira Mīmāṃsaka has pointed out that Kashmiri rulers such as Jayāpīḍa (c. 775 CE) revived the teaching of the Mahābhāṣya, indicating that Patañjali had a special relationship with the place.

4. An astronomical argument on the duration of morning mentioned by Patañjali is true only for the northern regions of Kashmir and Gandhāra.

5. Patañjali's closeness to the *Atharvaveda*, which was popular in Kashmir in ancient times.

The Snake Tail

The Kashmiri tradition considers Nāgas (literally, snakes, but really a totem for the residents of the valley) as connected with its geography. Existing customs include propitiation of Nāga deities, of which as a Kashmiri, I have personal knowledge. Patañjali was seen as an incarnation of Ananta Nāga (or

Śeṣanāga, the snake on whom Vishnu sleeps between cycles of creation) who, under the guidance of sage Kaśyapa and Vishnu, created the outlet that drained the lake that covered the valley in prehistoric times. The worship of Nāgas is prescribed in the *Nīlamata Purāṇa.*[3]

Nāga as a totem is also seen in the name Kārkoṭa, the dynasty to which Kashmiri Emperor Lalitāditya belonged. Karkoṭa is the Nāga who presides over the month of Pauṣa (in winter), and he and other Nāgas are assumed to reside in Pātāla (the nether world). Their characteristics mirror those of the Gandharvas, musicians, and singers to the gods, who have been associated with the historical Gandhāra region.

Karkoṭa is also the name of a serpent (nāga) associated with Karaṅkaka, the western cremation ground (śmaśāna) that indicates spiritual practice within Śaivism.

The totem of Nāga may have something to do with esoteric Yoga practices that involve the kuṇḍalinī, literally 'coiled snake', a form of divine feminine energy located at the base of the spine; these practices have been popular in Kashmir, and further support for this comes from the worship of Goddess Kubjikā, whose girdle is called Karkoṭa.

The Nāga-kings, variously known as Nāgarāja, are traditionally depicted as wearing white ornaments; they have human torsos above their coiled snaketails and raised hoods above their heads. This is precisely how Patañjali is shown.

Yoga is most associated with Śiva, the Great Yogi, who internalizes the oppositions of our lived experience: life and death are a pair, as are love and aversion, or ambition and directionlessness. Śiva lives in the cremation grounds, although he is the ideal husband to Pārvatī; his is another name for the Light that illuminates the mind, but he is also Mahākāla, the Great End personified. He wears the coiled snake, Vāsuki, around his neck.

Nāgas are also associated with Vishnu who, between cyclic creations, reclines on the Śeṣa, the first king of the snakes, Vāsuki's elder brother, whose uncoiling represents the movement of time. In the incarnation of Krishna, he narrates the Bhagavad Gītā, the greatest teachings of Yoga and is, therefore, called Yogeśvara.

The *Yoga Sūtra*

Patañjali's *Yoga Sūtra* speaks of eight elements (*aṣṭāṅga*) of practice with culmination in samādhi. The eight elements are *yama* (abstinences), *niyama* (observances), āsana (yoga posture), *prāṇāyāma* (breath control), *pratyāhāra* (withdrawal of the senses), *dhāraṇā* (concentration of the mind), *dhyāna* (contemplation), and *samādhi* (absorption). The main aim of practice is *kaivalya*, the discernment of purusha, the witness-consciousness, as distinct from prakriti, the cognitive apparatus.[4]

The first part is the *Samādhi Pāda*, which deals with methods of contemplation. It begins with the definitional verse (YS 1.2): *yogaś-citta-vṛtti-nirodhaḥ*, Yoga is the restriction of the fluctuations of the mind. When the mind is stilled, the seer or real Self is revealed, and the seer abides in his own nature. Otherwise, he assumes the form of the fluctuations. YS 1.33–39 mentions seven practices to still the mind, the seventh being meditative absorption.

On starting the journey of self-understanding, one must get a sense of how the mind works, and how thoughts and emotions colour one's experience. Our knowledge is erroneous if it is based on wrong perceptions. We may believe in something that simply is not true, and our recollections are selective.

To be grounded in truth, one must not be influenced by fleeting external stimuli that cloud the mind, nor swayed by a perceived connection or feelings of attachment.

We can strive to practice non-attachment in order to steady the mind. This can become easier by balancing the gunas. The practice of non-attachment may lead to samādhi by total devotion and dedication to Īśvara (Lord). Chanting the sacred sound of 'Om' in meditation can be an aid to blocking out all else to reach the Self.

In the second part, the *Sādhana Pāda*, Patañjali speaks of the yoga of action (Kriyā Yoga) and the Aṣṭāṅga Yoga (eightlimbed yoga). The *yama*, restraints or ethical behaviour, consists of: *ahiṃsā* (non-violence), *satya* (truthfulness), *asteya* (non-stealing), *brahmacarya* (path of Brahman), *aparigraha* (*non-possession*).

The *niyama*, observances, consists of: śauca (cleanliness), *santoṣa* (contentment), *tapas* (austerity), *svādhyāya* (self-study), and īśvara praṇidhāna (devotion to the lord).

Kriya yoga is preparation with stress on *tapas*, austerity, *svādhyāya*, self-study, and īśvara praṇidhāna, devotion to the lord.

The karmas are our experience, present and future, determined by our actions. A constant fluctuation of the gunas results from discrimination between this and that and what we may like at one moment and have an aversion to the next. Suffering can be avoided with steady practice of non-attachment balanced in the gunas. We can also detach from our perceptions to try to be free from ignorance to live our truth.

Practising the eight limbs of yoga can ready the mind, body, and spirit for samādhi or the superconscious state. We can practice *pratipakṣa bhāvanā*, which is to cultivate a positive thought every time a negative thought enters the mind.

The third part, the *Vibhūti Pāda*, outlines the many accomplishments that can be achieved through the practice of yoga. These accomplishments are the *siddhis* (extraordinary powers, abilities, attainments) which can be cultivated by practising the final three limbs of Rāja Yoga: dhāraṇā (concentration), dhyāna (meditation), and samādhi (complete integration).

Combining all three in the practice of *saṃyama* can guide us towards the light of knowledge by steadying the continuous input of new information to the mind. Observing or being a witness to one's self through saṃyama can lead to knowledge, insight, and a powerful sense of the self. With more practice, the need to focus on external or mind object becomes unnecessary.

The final state of samādhi is reached where nothing is needed. One has to observe the self to know the self and then see the true light of the self after the veil of external influence is lifted. Kaivalya (detachment), the goal of yoga, is achieved when the seed of attachment is gone. Of course, in life there are many necessary distractions and attachments and so we just visit the practice to come inward to manage our connection with our Self.

The fourth part, the *Kaivalya Pāda*, brings the threads together, explaining how the yogi's state of being leads to absoluteness. The state of kaivalya is the state of freedom. This is because the non-yogi's actions are a part of the karmic chain with the past and the environment determining the future.

The path of yoga is the path of freedom. As one stills the mind, the power of the past emotions or attachments that normally lead to reflexive behaviour fades. Abiding in pure consciousness, the yogi has true freedom of choice in behaviour.

Patañjali explains the karmic fate of those who do not take into consideration their life's journey and actions in affecting their future. They will unintentionally repeat behaviour that will take away their true agency.

6

Kumārajīva and the Middle Way

Most people are surprised when told that Indian Gāndhārī, Khotan Saka, and Kuchean were the main languages of Tarim Basin, Xinjiang until about 1000 CE. Both Khotan Saka and Kuchean were also strongly connected to Sanskrit.[1]

It was in this region that the Kashmiri scholar Kumārajīva (344-413) was to make extraordinary contributions to the translation of Sanskrit texts into Chinese. Many scholars believe that his skills as a translator and his passion for the Middle Way helped define the direction that China's culture took in the succeeding centuries.

The role of the Vedic tradition in the culture of Central Asia becomes clear from the many representations of Śiva, Maheśvara, Umā, Kṛṣṇa, Gaṇeśa, and other deities that have been found in the ruins of temples and monasteries. Vedic hermeneutics also played a fundamental role in the development of the Madhyamaka sect in Central Asia and China. In the success of this, Kumārajīva played a prominent role.

When the Chinese pilgrim Xuanzang visited Kucha in 630 CE, he received the favours of Suvarṇa-deva, the son and successor of Suvarṇa-puṣpa, and Hīnayāna king of Kucha. Of the religion of the people of Kucha, he says that they were followers of Sarvāstivāda, an influential Hīnayāna school:[2]

> There are about one hundred convents (saṅghārāmas) in this country, with five thousand and more disciples. These belong to the Little Vehicle of the school of the Sarvāstivādas (Shwo-yih-tsai-yu-po). Their doctrine (teaching of Sūtras) and their rules of discipline (principles of the Vinaya) are like those of India, and those who read them use the same (originals).

We will now speak of the beliefs of the Sarvāstivādins in the background of other currents of thought that will give us an idea of the intellectual life in the centuries before Xuanzang and provide a fair assessment of Kumārajīva's contribution in influencing then prevailing thought.

Bharat 2,000 Years Ago

Two thousand years ago in India, there were powerful intellectual currents not unlike what is happening in the world now. The Buddha's doctrine of anatta (anātmā), 'no-self', or the teaching that the sense of a permanent, autonomous self is an illusion, led to questions such as: What is it that gives the individual a sense of continuity? Is there free will? Somewhat similarly, modern science, which is based on reductionism and materialism, is grappling with the question of the origins of human agency, which is driving increasing scientific interest in the phenomenon of consciousness.

The theory of anatta arose within the context of the Vedic tradition, which does not suffer from the problem of free will for it postulates ātman, or self or consciousness as the ground-stuff of reality, further speaking of two kinds of knowledge, higher relating to the experiencing self, and lower relating to objects of observation. The Vedic tradition enjoins the use of different lenses (darśanas) that provide complementary cognitions to the further understanding of reality. To be sure, it leads to different kinds of questions and paradoxes, such as how individuals forget their true nature and the tradition provides answers to this. The Vedic tradition requires postulation of a category that goes beyond ordinary rationality. Buddha was trying to avoid this.

The school of Sarvāstivāda arose to provide a logical basis to Buddha's idea of anatta. The name of the school is from Sanskrit *sarvām asti*, that is 'everything exists/all is'. It assumed that dharmas, universal entities that combine momentarily to form a person's life flux, were eternal. Despite its limitations, this view became the most favoured in the famous council in Kashmir, during the reign of the Kushan Emperor Kanishka (2nd century CE) and remained highly influential for centuries, not only in India, but also in Central Asia.[3]

The doctrine of Sarvāstivāda had to compete with Nāgārjuna's Madhyamaka, the Middle Way, according to which reality, at the deepest level, is śūnyatā, or emptiness. Since the self is predicated on emptiness, phenomena take existence only as they relate to other phenomena, and it is pointless to postulate whether something exists or does not. The middle way stands between affirmation and negation.

According to the Sarvāstivāda school, living beings are formed by a temporary union of five elements and there is no real or permanent self, but that the dharmas, or elements of existence that constitute the living being, are real and have their own existence throughout the past, present, and future. This doctrine has been described as an eternalist theory of time.

Kashmiri Sarvāstivādins

The orthodox Kashmiri branch of the Sarvāstivāda School composed the large and encyclopaedic *Abhidharma Mahāvibhāṣa Śāstra* around the time of Kanishka. Because of this, orthodox Sarvāstivādins who upheld the doctrines in the Mahāvibhāṣa were called Vaibhāṣikas. The Sarvāstivādin School is sometimes seen as a transitional stage between the Hīnayāna and the Mahāyāna.

Vasubandhu's Abhidharmakośa-bhāṣya states, 'He who affirms the existence of the dharmas of the three time-periods (past, present, and future) is held to be a Sarvāstivādin.' The Sarvāstivāda was also known by other names, particularly hetuvāda and yuktivāda, stressing their use of logic and reasoning to turn the idea of momentariness on its head and claim eternalism.

The most important Sarvāstivāda Abhidharma text was rewritten and revised in Sanskrit and known as *Jñānaprasthāna* (Course of Understanding), which came to have its own commentary called the Mahāvibhaṣa, which was compiled by the Kashmir Sarvāstivāda council under the supervision of Vasumitra. The *Jñānaprasthāna* and its Mahāvibhaṣa were then declared to be the new orthodoxy by the Vaibhāṣikas.

The teaching of the Sarvāstivāda is a radical pluralism based on denial of the reality of a self as a substance (anātman) and the affirmation of the existence of momentary entities, the so-called dharmas.

The Sarvāstivādins postulate 75 different dharmas, which (like the ancient notion of atoms) represent final, indivisible units that are viewed as real. These dharmas include elements as well as form or matter (rūpa), consciousness (vijñāna), mental factors (caitasika saṃskāras), and various psychological processes. These conditioned dharmas do not come into being but rather exist from beginningless time and only change from a latent to a manifest state.

To explain how a dharma remains the same, yet undergoes change as it moves through the three times, the Vaibhāṣika held that dharmas have a unchanging essence (svabhāva) which persists through the three times. The term was also identified as a unique mark or own characteristic (svalakṣaṇa) that remains unchangeable throughout its existence. Svabhāvas are those things that exist substantially as opposed to other things that are made up of aggregations of dharmas which only have a nominal existence.

The Sautrāntikas (those who uphold the sūtras), also known as Dārṣṭāntikas, did not uphold the Mahāvibhāṣa Śāstra, but rather emphasized the Buddhist sūtras as being authoritative. These groups were called 'the western masters' (pāścātya), the foreign masters (bahirdeśaka; also called 'the masters outside Kaśmīra', and the 'Gāndhārian masters'). They studied the same Abhidharma texts as other Sarvāstivādins, but in a more critical way.

The most important Sautrāntika was Vasubandhu (ca. 350–430), a native of Gandhāra who wrote the Abhidharmakośa (Kośa), which became an influential abhidharma work. He famously converted to the Yogācāra school of Mahāyāna, a tradition that itself developed out of the Sarvāstivāda Abhidharma.

The Kośa was so influential that it became the Abhidharma text par excellence in both East Asian Buddhism and Indo-Tibetan Buddhism, and remains so even today.

The Mahāvibhāṣā illustrates the accommodations reached between the Hīnayāna and Mahāyāna traditions, which paved the way for the acceptance of Mahāyāna doctrines.

The Mahāyāna also came up with the idea of Buddha Nature, which is taken to be the fundamental nature of all beings. To its critics, the Mahāyāna brought in 'ātman' through the back door, but it did so only in a half-hearted way, for it does not admit the possibility of self by itself.

We know that Mahāyāna eventually triumphed in China. Perhaps, the individual most behind this triumph was Kumārajīva whose role in interpretation is as important as his translations. Much of the material on his life comes from the Lives of Eminent Monks, *Gaoseng Zhuan*, which was compiled in c. 530.

Kumārāyana

Kumārajīva's father, Kumārāyana, who was from a prominent Kashmiri family that had produced a long line of ministers, renounced his home to become a monk to seek fortune in far lands. His path took him to Kucha, on the northern rim of the Tarim Basin of Xinjiang, where the king, aware of his stature, persuaded him to stay and appointed him the state preceptor.[4]

While in Kucha, Kumārāyana fell in love with the King's sister, Princess Jīva, who was a scholar in her own right. They married and in due course (344) they had a son, whom they named Kumārajīva. The boy showed signs of exceptional promise, and he had much interest in subtle argumentation.

But Jīva's marriage didn't go as well as she had hoped, and she became a nun and joined a monastery together with her seven-year-old son. He spent the next two years studying the Āgamas and Abhidharma texts. When he was nine, mother and son travelled to Kashmir to study under the famed Buddhist teacher, Bandhudatta. In addition to the texts of the Sarvāstivāda School, the boy also learnt the Vedas, the darśanas, Ayurveda, astronomy, and other sciences.

After three years of study, they began their return journey, but as they passed through Kashgar (Kāśīgiri, the Mountain of Light, also known as Kashi), the local king, who had heard of the precocious boy, asked the mother and son to stay on for some time. While in Kashgar, Kumārajīva's Sarvāstivāda position was challenged by a teacher named Sūryasoma, a prince of Yarkand, who began to instruct him in Mahāyāna texts.

Kumārajīva, having studied the Veda and aware of the basic problem of the self in his earlier position, accepted the Mahāyāna position and was to become its most articulate votary. In the Mahāyāna view, all dharmas are themselves unreal; ontologically, dharmas are like empty space and assume distinct existence only in their ephemeral combinations.

Kumārajīva was so impressed by his new understanding that he invited Bandhudatta, his first teacher in India, to come to Kashgar and soon converted him to his new position. He became so adept in debates on Madhyamaka, that scholars and monks came from all over to learn from him.

Knowing that her son had established himself as a teacher and convinced that he was going to do great things, Jīva reportedly told her son, 'You should propagate the profound teachings of the Vaipulya-sūtras (the most important of the Mahayana sutras) in China. Its dissemination in the eastern countries depend on you. It should not matter that there will be no personal advantage for you in this.' To which he famously replied, 'The teachings of the great master are there to serve (others) and to forget oneself (in the process). If one is able to spread the great conversion and awaken the blind masses, then, even if one's body were burning in a red-hot oven, one will suffer but feel no regret.'

Jīva was pleased and decided it was best for her to return to Kashmir to continue her own studies. Mother and son never saw each other again.

General's Prisoner

Buddhism had already made much headway in China, but given its many competing sects, its exact trajectory wasn't clear. To the east of Kucha, Qin Emperor Fu-Chien (Fu- Jiān,

337–385) of Ch'ang-an (then the capital of China, present-day Xi'an) had a deepening interest in Buddhism and had assembled a team of Indian and Chinese scholars to translate Buddhist texts. Alhough it was not the first translation team in China, Fu-Chien's academy was the first to receive direct royal patronage.

Emperor Fu-Chien was convinced by regional kings and princes to subjugate the western lands by force. In 383, he asked General Lu Kuang (Lu Guang, 337–400) to lead 70,000 men to take Kucha and nearby lands. One of the motivations for the emperor was to bring Kumārajīva to his translation project. He told his general, 'I have heard that Kumārajīva in the western country has a deep understanding of the Dharma, is knowledgeable in all temporal and divine matters, and a role model and teacher for younger disciples. I yearn for him. A virtuous and wise man is the great treasure of a country. When you have defeated Kuchi, then send Kumārajīva post haste.'

Kucha resisted, was put under siege, and eventually submitted in 384. Meanwhile, in 385, Fu Jiān was decisively defeated and killed by the numerically inferior army of Later Qin.

When Lu Guang heard of the defeat of his emperor, he declared himself independent, and set up a state now known as Later Liang at Guzang. Lu Guang had no interest in Buddhism and held Kumārajīva captive in his own court, possibly as an advisor. For more than 16 years, Kumārajīva remained in Lu Guang's territory and had to keep his knowledge of the Buddha's teachings to himself.

Eventually Yao Xing, second ruler of the new dynasty at Chang'an, sent his army and conquered Guzang. Kumārajīva was rescued unharmed, and in 402 he was welcomed into Chang'an. He was invited to reside in the Great Monastery and was treated with immense respect and honour.

Translation Centre in Chang'an

When Kumārajīva arrived in Chang'an, Emperor Yao Xing bestowed upon him the title 'Teacher of the Nation'. The emperor gathered the best scholar-monk translators from India and China to form a translation academy that was even more ambitious than the one that Emperor Fu Jiān had formed some 20 years earlier.

He also constructed a special building for Kumārajīva and his team in the city centre. The beginning of the translation of a new text was a widely celebrated public event attended by up to 3,000 monks and lay people. During these gatherings, Kumārajīva lectured on the subject matter of the texts; these commentaries were recorded and distributed throughout the empire. As evidenced by the extant fragments of letters with Kumārajīva, Emperor Yao Xing was personally invested in the elucidation of the obscure doctrinal philosophies contained in the texts.

Now began the most productive phase of his life, which resulted in works that were to profoundly influence Chinese Buddhist tradition to the present day. In a short period that was to last barely a decade, he translated almost 50 works including the Prajñāpāramitā literature such as the *Vajracchedikā Prajñāpāramitā Sūtra* (Diamond Sutra), the *Vimalakīrti Sūtra,* the *Lotus Sūtra,* and the *Śūraṅgama Sūtra,* that add up to nearly 300 volumes. Chang'an had at this time many international scholars who enlivened its intellectual atmosphere, and these included people such as Buddhabhadra, Buddhayaśas, Dharmayaśas, and Dharmagupta. He and his disciples established the Chinese branch of the Madhyamaka, known as the San-lun, or 'Three Treatises School'.

An early 6th century source attributes 35 works in 294 fascicles to Kumārajīva. The central corpus of these works is well attested by contemporary prefaces, and dates of translation are known for 23 titles. The core of works translated by Kumārajīva shows that his main interest was in the *Śūnyavādin Sutras*, particularly those of the Prajñāpāramitā class, and the Mādhyamika treatises. His interests were broad, however, and he also translated pietist, Vinaya, and *sutras sutras*, as well as other texts.

Kumārajīva, his chief assistants, and the translation bureau devised new transcriptions of names and Buddhist technical terms and utilized interpolated glosses when specific words could not be translated adequately.

Kumārajīva's main contribution to the translation enterprise was to abandon the old style of literal translation that had proven ineffective in previous centuries. He chose to be guided by the intuition of an independent ontological position for consciousness, which made him give greater importance to the communication of deeper meaning. He and his colleagues produced texts which were readable and inspiring, and after a millennium and a half his translations are still read and admired.

Kumārajīva's most famous and enduring work is the rendition of the *Lotus Sūtra*, known in Sanskrit as the *Saddharma Puṇḍarīka Sūtra*, 'Sūtra on the White Lotus of the Sublime Dharma'. In part, due to the excellent quality of the translation, devout Buddhists in East Asia believe that the *Lotus Sūtra* contains the final teaching of the Buddha, and that it is complete and sufficient for salvation. The world's oldest datable printed book is the *Diamond Sutra* of 868 CE that was found in the Dunhuang Caves.

His translation of the *Pañcaviṃśatisāhasrikā-prajñāpāramitā Sūtra* shows that he advanced an interpretation that appears to be consistent with Vedanta. Thus, speaking of śūnyatā, emptiness, he says:

> What is seen does not differ from what is empty, what is empty does not differ from what is seen. Form is emptiness, emptiness is form. It is the same for feeling, perception, intention, and consciousness.

Scholars normally take śūnyatā to be the central theme of *Prajñāpāramitā Sūtras*. Kumārajīva gave it a twist so that one could take fullness of form to be equivalent to it, quite like how the Upaniṣads speak of reality in its two conceptions. This explains why lived Buddhism in the East is different from what is taught in the academy.

Around 412, Kumārajīva felt unwell and knew that his death was near. Deeply distraught during his final years because he had not managed, for personal and cultural reasons, to fully inculcate China with Buddha's Mahayana teachings, he said, 'It is unspeakably sad that I am now leaving the world behind. May what I have made known and translated spread further among future generations and be fathomed fully!'

7

Cosmology and Consciousness: The *Yoga Vāsiṣṭha*

The *Yoga Vāsiṣṭha* (YV) is a Kashmiri book that has had enduring influence over Indian thought.[1] As a book of instruction on the nature of consciousness, it has many fascinating and subtle passages on time, space, matter, and cognition that are relevant for our age.

As background, note that whereas reality is unitary, we experience it through the dichotomy of mind and matter. We must assume that we can comprehend it only because we are already equipped to do so. Innate ideas give rational organization to our sensations.

The YV is over 29,000 verses, and it is traditionally attributed to Vālmīki, the author of the epic Rāmāyaṇa, but scholars believe it was composed in the early centuries in Kashmir. The historian of philosophy, Dasgupta, dated it to about the 6th century CE on the basis that one of its verses appears to be copied from one of Kālidāsa's plays, where he considered Kālidāsa to have lived around the 5th century. But some scholars support the traditional date of Kālidāsa, that is 50 BCE, and so it is possible that this text is older than generally believed. And then of course this may be an irrelevant argument if this verse is a later interpolation.

The YV argues that whereas physical nature is taken to be analyzable it is defined only in relation to observers. It takes consciousness to be the fundamental category. Consistent with the Vedic emphasis on ṛta, YV accepts the idea that laws are intrinsic to the universe. Some have argued that the parallels between YV and recent ideas of physics are a result of the abstraction that is common to both; or it may be assumed that the parallels reflect the inherent structure of the mind.

The frame story in the YV is about Rishi Vālmīki compiling this teaching given by Sage Vasiṣṭha to Rāma. It deals with the subject of effecting union of the the jīvātman (the individual's atman) with the paramātman (the cosmic atman). It is considered the crest-jewel of all works on Vedanta.

The YV was abridged some centuries ago by Abhinanda Pandita, a Kashmiri scholar, into 6,000 couplets, which go by the name of Laghu *Yoga Vāsiṣṭha*.[2] A philosophical summary of this work was made long ago, by an unknown author, into about 230 verses divided into 10 chapters, as the *Yoga Vāsiṣṭha Sāra*,[3] of which a translation was made by Swami Sureshananda, a devotee of Sri Ramana Maharshi.

This chapter will present brief excerpts from the *Yoga Vāsiṣṭha*, including an abridged Story of Līlā, which is one of the most subtle parts of the book. At the end, I will present a further abridgement of the *Yoga Vāsiṣṭha Sāra*.[4]

Rāma on the Human Condition

Rāma's summary of the human predicament as is given in this section. He begins by saying that this world is a creation of the mind, even as the blueness of the sky is an optical illusion. Neither freedom from sorrow nor realization of one's real nature is possible if the conviction does not arise in one that the world appearance is unreal.

Moksha or liberation is the total abandonment of all vāsanā or mental conditioning. Mental conditioning is of two types—the pure and the impure. The impure is the cause of beginnings, and the pure leads to freedom. The impure is of the nature of egosense, and it takes one from one beginning to its unfoldment, and end and then the next beginning. The mental conditioning that merely sustains the body, is of a pure nature, and it exists even in those who have been liberated while living.

What do people call happiness, and can it be had in the everchanging objects of this world? All beings in this world take birth but to die, and they die to be born. Unrelated beings come together, and the mind conjures up a relationship between them. Everything in this world is dependent upon the mind, that is, upon one's mental attitude. Upon examination, the mind itself appears to be unreal.

Equally useless is wealth which deludes the ignorant. Unsteady and fleeting, wealth gives birth to numerous worries and generates an insatiable craving for more. It is no respecter of persons: both the good and the wicked can become wealthy. People may be good, compassionate, and friendly but their hearts are hardened by the pursuit of wealth, and this happens even to the wise scholar, hero, a man of gratitude and softspoken person. Wealth and happiness do not dwell together. Rare is that wealthy man who does not have rivals and enemies who scandalize him.

The short duration of life is also a source of sorrow. Its duration is like that of a water droplet on a leaf. The life is meaningful only to those who have self-knowledge. We may encompass the wind, we may break up space, we may string waves into a garland, but we can never know how long we will live. Man vainly seeks to extend his lifespan, and thereby he earns more sorrow and extends the period of suffering. Only he lives who strives to gain self-knowledge, which alone is worth gaining in this world. To the unwise, knowledge of texts is a burden; to one who is full of desires, wisdom is a burden; to one who is restless, the mind is a burden; and to one who has no self-knowledge, the body is a burden.

Egotism is another dreadful enemy of wisdom. It comes into being in the darkness of ignorance, and flourishes in ignorance. Spreading the net of worldly objects of pleasure, it traps living beings. Terrible calamities in this world are born of egotism; it eclipses self-control, destroys virtue, and dissipates equanimity.

Bereft of the grace earned through the service of the holy ones, the impure mind is like the lion in a cage, restless as the wind. It is dissatisfied with whatever it gets and grows more and more restless by the day. The sieve can never be filled with water, nor can the mind ever reach the state of fulfilment however much of worldly objects one acquires. The mind flits in all directions all the time but is unable to find happiness anywhere.

Even as the rushing waters of a river uproot the trees on its bank, the restless mind uproots one's whole being. It is the mind alone which is the cause of all objects in the world, and the three worlds exist because of the mindstuff. When the mind vanishes, the worlds vanish too.

When the mind is enveloped by craving, it dries up sweetness and gentleness of disposition, and makes one hard and cruel. It drives one in one direction now and the very next moment it takes one away in another direction like a mad horse. This craving is responsible for bondage and misfortune, and it creates delusion. Caught by this goblin, one is unable to enjoy even the pleasures that are within reach. Though it appears as if the craving is for happiness, it leads neither to happiness nor to fruitfulness in this life. On the stage of life, this craving is like an aged actress who is incapable of performing anything good and noble and suffers defeat and discomfiture at every turn yet does not give up dancing.

Craving now ascends to the skies, now dives into the depths of the netherworld, it is ever restless, for it is based on the emptiness of the mind. In the mind the light of wisdom momentarily shines, but there is delusion the next moment.

This pitiable body composed of veins, arteries, and nerves is also a source of pain. One may compare the body to a tree, with branches for arms, trunk for the torso, holes for eyes, fruits for head, and leaves for numerous illnesses. This tree is born in the forest known as Saṃsāra (repetitive existence), the restless monkey (mind) plays on it, it is the abode of crickets (worries), it is constantly eaten by insects (of endless suffering), it shelters the venomous serpent (of craving), and the wild crow (of anger). On it there may be flowers (of laughter), its fruits are good and evil, it is animated by the wind (of lifeforce), it supports the birds (of senses), it is resorted to by the traveller (lust or desire) for it provides the shade of pleasure, the formidable vulture (egotism) is seated on it, and it is hollow and empty. It is certainly not meant to promote happiness.

This body is the home of illness, the field for mental distress and changing emotions and mental states. Wealth, kingdom, and the body are mercilessly cut down by time.

Even childhood, the part of life which people ignorantly regard as enjoyable and happy, is full of sorrow. Helplessness, mishaps, cravings, inability to express oneself, utter foolishness, playfulness, instability, weakness—all these characterize childhood. The child is easily offended, easily roused to anger, easily bursts into tears. In childhood one's state is comparable truly to that of an animal living at the mercy of others.

The child is exposed to the countless happenings around it; they puzzle the child, confuse the child, and arouse in it various phantasies and fears. The child is impressionable and is easily influenced by the wicked: in consequence, the child is subjected to control and punishment by its parents.

Though the child may appear to be innocent, the truth is that all sorts of defects, sinful tendencies, and neurotic behaviour lie hidden and dormant in it, even as an owl lies hidden in a dark hole during the daytime. What can be worse suffering than a restless mind? And the child's mind is extremely restless. Unless the child gets something new every day, it is unhappy. Crying and weeping seem to be the child's foremost activity. When the child does not get what it wants, it looks as if its heart is broken.

When the child goes to school, it receives punishment in the hands of its teachers; and all this adds to its unhappiness. When the child cries, its parents, in order to pacify it, promise to give it the world; and from then on, the child begins to value the world, to desire the worldly objects. The parents say, 'I shall give you the moon for a toy,' and the child, believing their words, thinks that it can hold the moon in its hands. Thus, the seeds of delusion are sown in the little heart.

Leaving this period of childhood behind, the human goes on to the stage of youth, but is unable to leave the unhappiness behind. The shortlived pleasures of youth are quickly followed by longlasting suffering. What is worse still, it is during youth that one indulges in actions that bring unhappiness to many others.

Though youthfulness appears to be very desirable to the body, it is destructive to the mind. In youth, the man is tempted by the mirage of happiness, and in its pursuit, he falls into the well of sorrow.

In youth, the man is a slave of sexual attraction. In the body which is no more than the aggregate of flesh, blood, bone, hair and skin, he perceives beauty and charm. If this beauty were permanent, there would be some justification to the imagination, but, alas, it does not last long. On the contrary, very soon the very flesh that contributed to the attractiveness, the charm and the beauty of the beloved is transformed first into the shrivelled ugliness of old age, and later consumed by fire, or by worms, or by vultures. Yet, while it lasts this sexual attraction consumes the heart and the wisdom of the man.

When the child is dissatisfied with its childhood, youth takes over, and when youth is plagued by dissatisfaction and frustration, old age overpowers it. Even as wind tosses a dew-drop from a leaf, old age destroys the body. Even as a drop of poison when it enters the system soon pervades it, senility pervades the entire body and breaks it down and makes it the laughingstock of other people.

Though the old man is unable to satisfy his desires physically, the desires themselves flourish and grow. He begins to ask himself, 'Who am I? What should I do?' etc., when it is too late for him to change his life's course to make his life more meaningful. With the onset of senility, dyspepsia, and emaciation manifest themselves.

All the hopes of man in this world are consistently destroyed by Time. Time wears everything out: there is nothing in creation which is beyond its reach. Time creates innumerable universes, and in a very short time it destroys everything.

Time allows a glimpse of itself through its partial manifestation as the year, the age, and the epoch; but its essential nature is hidden. Time is merciless, inexorable, cruel, greedy, and insatiable. Time is the greatest magician, full of deceptive tricks.

To the lotus of youthfulness, Time is the nightfall; to the elephant of lifespan, Time is the lion. In this world there is nothing, high or low, that Time does not destroy.

The mind vainly seeks to find such happiness in the objects of this world. In ignorance, man binds himself to wife, son, and friends. He knows not that this world is like a large pilgrim centre where countless people come together fortuitously and they whom he calls his wife, son, and friends are among them.

This world is like a potter's wheel: the wheel looks as if it stands still though it revolves at a terrific speed—even so to the deluded person this world appears to be stable even though it is constantly changing.

Many aeons have come and gone; they are but moments in time— for there is essentially no difference between an epoch and a moment, both being measures. Whatever appears to be permanent or transient in this world—it is all like a dream. What is a crater today was a mountain before; what is a mountain today becomes a hole in the earth in a short while; what is a dense forest today is soon transformed into a big city; what is fertile soil now becomes arid desert. Similar is the change in one's body and in one's fortune.

This life-and-death cycle appears to be a skillful dancer whose skirt is made up of living souls, and her dancing gestures consist of lifting the souls up to heaven, hurling them down into hell, or bringing them back to this earth. All the mighty deeds, even the great religious rites that people perform here, are soon consigned to memory. In this world sense-objects appear to be pleasant to one only till one remembers their inevitable destruction. Just as a child playing with earth makes different designs with a clod, the ordainer of the universe keeps creating new things and destroying them.

What is that condition or state in which one does not experience any grief? What is that attitude that enables one not to be influenced by various kinds of activities and experiences? This world is full of pain and death. How does it become a source of joy, without befuddling one's heart? The mind is full of impurities; how can it be cleansed and with what cleanser? How should one live here so as not to fall a victim to the twin currents of love and hate?

Summary of the Book

With Rāma's summary of the human condition as background, let us speak of the book, which consists of six sections, namely: *vairāgya* (dispassion), *mumukṣu* (longing for liberation), *utpatti* (creation or origins), *sthiti* (existence), *upaśānti* (dissolution), and *nirvāṇa* (on liberation).

The book takes the world of experience is a creation of the mind, which is the doctrine of *dṛṣṭi-sṛṣṭivāda*. Just as objects are created by the mind in a dream, so also everything is created by the mind in the waking state also, although clearly the waking state creations must conform to certain constraints that are not required of dream states. The expansion of the mind is called *saṅkalpa*, which through its power of differentiation, generates this universe. Time and space are only mental creations. The play of the mind is with objects, and therefore distances in time and space are quite flexible.

Through the force of the mind, an age (kalpa) is experienced as a moment and a moment can stretch out. The mind is endowed with creative power, and it is the cause of bondage and the means to liberation.

Moksha (mokṣa) is the attainment of freedom through knowledge of the self. It has neither space nor time in itself; nor is there in it any external or internal state. If the illusory idea of 'I' perishes, one experiences the end of thoughts, which leads to freedom. This is identical to the assertion in the very first sūtra of the *Yoga Sūtra*.

Moksha is not a thing to be achieved for it is already there. If one were really bound, one could never become free. The Absolute is non-dual, partless, infinite, self-luminous, changeless, and eternal. It is the unity behind the subject and the object of experience. It is one homogeneous essence, and it is all pervading, and beyond description.

He whose mind is calm, who is endowed with the 'four means' of salvation, who is free from defects and impurities can realize the self intuitively. The scriptures and the spiritual preceptor cannot show Brahman; they can only guide and provide hints by way of analogies and illustrations.

Śānti (quiescence of mind), santoṣa (contentment), satsaṅga (association with sages), and vicāra (inquiry) are the four sentinels who guard the gates of moksha. If one makes friendship with them, one will easily enter the kingdom of moksha. Keeping company with any one of them opens the doorway to the other three. The student should have an unshakable conviction that consciousnesss is the only reality. Then one will realize this truth through direct cognition and intuition.

There is little difference between the waking and dream experiences. The waking state is a long dream. The dream experiences become unreal as soon as man comes back to his waking state. Similarly, the waking state becomes unreal for a sage who has attained self-realization. For the man who dreams, the waking state is unreal.

If one attains knowledge of the self, all doubts vanish, and all karmas perish. The sankalpas that are the drivers of the mind are given life by the vāsanās, which are the past impressions that influence behaviour. The universe is nothing but the mind manifesting through the power of consciousness. The mind contemplating on the body becomes the body itself and then, enmeshed in it, is afflicted by it.

The mind subjectively is consciousness; objectively, it is this universe. Without self-enquiry, one will see the physical world as the only reality. The jīvanmukta has no attachments; he is free from desires, egoism, and greed. He is in solitude though he works in the busiest part of the city.

The feeling that one is bound psychologically and the resolve to get out of this prison are necessary qualifications of one who wishes to learn from the text. Why do despair and fear arise in life? Why does one get attached and how does one hate? All these arise from hope or desire for happiness, and for peace of mind, but this hope inevitably leads one to unhappiness. Vasiṣṭha says, 'Give up all these ideas of running away from this world. Don't even try to examine what despair is, don't even try to investigate whatever is a passing phenomenon. Don't even let your mind dwell on what has been considered unreal.'

Consciousness, being omnipresent and infinite, manifests itself in infinite ways everywhere. It is not possible for this diversity to disappear, but what can and should disappear is seeing it as diverse objects opposed to one another. Vasiṣṭha says that this objective creation is like uncut figures in a marble slab; the sculptor can carve wonderful images from it. One can say that these figures already existed in the marble slab, although only as potential.

The world exists not as a reality that is independent of our mind. Our experiences form impressions on the mind, strengthening attachment or rather strengthening the idea we have of attachment.

The external world and external circumstances arise in the cosmic consciousness, and within the individual they become subjective experiences, which change. Realizing this, one is freed from the delusion of considering these appearances as the reality.

Your life is not your life. It is part of this cosmic being and whatever that cosmic being decides will happen. The direct understanding of this is surrender. To see this, one must have passed through despair. One realizes that the mind, freed from its attachments is pure consciousness. This leads to a life that is totally free and divine.

The Story of Līlā

The story of Līlā in the *Yoga Vāsiṣṭha* goes to the very heart of our predicament in life and shows how changing perspective alters our experience of reality.

Once upon a time, the virtuous King Padma ruled his kingdom in an ideal way. He was learned and just and he subdued his enemies and destroyed evil in society. His queen Līlā was beautiful and accomplished and the two were intensely devoted to each other. Their love for each other was pure without hypocrisy and artificiality.

One day, Līlā thought: 'My handsome husband is dearer to me than my own life. What should I do so that he and I may live for ever enjoying the pleasures of life?' She sought counsel and was told it was not possible to attain immortality in this world.

She thought if she were to die before her husband, she will attain self-knowledge and be free of sorrow. But what if her husband were to leave before her? She resolved to propitiate goddess Sarasvatī to have the boon that even if her husband were to die before her, his jīvātman will not leave the palace and she and her husband will always be together.

Without discussing this with her husband, she began to intensely worship Sarasvatī, eating only once every three nights. After hundred such sessions, Sarasvatī appeared before her and granted her the boons of her choice. Līlā said,

'Divine mother, grant me two boons. First, when my husband departs from his body, let his jīvātman remain in the palace and, second, whenever I pray to you, let me see you. Sarasvatī granted these boons and disappeared.'

Time passed and King Padma was mortally wounded on the battlefield. Līlā was inconsolate with grief. An ākāshic voice spoke to her, 'Child, cover the king's body. It will not decay, and he will not leave the palace.' She arranged for the body to be thus preserved.

But Līlā was not satisfied, and she invoked the goddess, who appeared before her. The Goddess said, 'My child, why do you grieve? Sorrow is an illusion, like water in a mirage.'

Līlā said, 'Where is my husband now?'

Sarasvatī explains that there are three types of space: psychological, physical, and the infinite space of consciousness which is the most subtle of the three. She explained, 'By intense meditation on the infinite space of consciousness, you can see and experience the presence of one like your husband, whose body is that infinite space, even though you do not see him here. This infinite space exists when there are no thoughts, or between those moments when the finite intelligence is not attached to one thing or another. Normally, only one who is truly absorbed in the non-permanence of this universe can experience it, but I shall, with my grace, make it possible for you to be there.'

Līlā saw the king again on a throne surrounded by kings and sages who were chanting Vedic hymns. Some people in the court were from the court of King Padma that she knew. She wondered if they were dead also.

She returned to her palace and thinking about all this she wondered, 'These people seem to exist in two places at the same time. Just as a mountain is seen both inside the mirror, and outside it, this creation is seen both within consciousness and outside it.'

She asked Sarasvatī which of these two was real, and which was the reflection. Līlā said, 'I'm here and you are in front of me, that's real. The region where I see my husband now, is unreal.'

Sarasvatī said, 'How can the unreal be the effect of the real? The effect is the cause, there is no essential difference. Material effects are produced by material causes. When you find no immediate cause of an effect, surely then that existed in the past. Memory is like space, empty. Even the birth of your husband is an illusory product of memory.'

To teach Līlā the method of seeing and visiting the various worlds that interpenetrate our world and to take her to the world of her husband's experience, Sarasvatī tells her the story of a holy man named Vasiṣṭha and his wife Arundhatī. One day, after witnessing the pompous royal procession and wishing to be born a king, the poor man died. His wife, Arundhatī, asked for and received the boon to keep the jīvātman of her husband confined in her house after his death.

Due to the power of his wish, the man was born into a royal family and became a mighty king who ruled over a great empire. Arundhatī was also reunited with him as queen. The holy man died eight days ago, and now the same holy man is your husband, and you are the same Arundhatī who was his wife.

Līlā did not believe this story. She said, 'It is like saying that a huge elephant is bound in the centre of a mustard seed, or that in an atom a mosquito fought with a lion, or that there is a mountain in a lotus pod.'

Sarasvatī replied, 'Your house, you, I and all this is pure consciousness. Your house was itself in the house of the holy man. Even after the creation in the house of the holy man, everthing remained as before. In every atom, there are worlds within worlds.'

Līlā said that it all happened only 8 days ago, yet my husband and I have lived together for many years. So how to explain this discrepancy.

Sarasvatī explained that just as space does not have a fixed span, neither does time, and it can unfold at different rates for different embodiments. Just as the world and its creations are mere appearances, a moment and an epoch are also imaginary. There is no essential difference between the experience of this world and that of another, for they are thought forms in the infinite consciousness.

Sarasvatī now took Līlā to different worlds, and eventually to the holy man's home where the family was in mourning. Līlā laid his hand on the head of the son of the dead man and he and the other members of the family seemed relieved of their sorrow.

Līlā and Sarasvatī then returned to the present world of the king, who was now named Vidūratha, and 70 years old. His present wife was also named Līlā. They manifested themselves before the king in his private apartment and reminded him of his previous existence as Padma.

He expressed a desire to be Padma again. His present wife propitiated Sarasvatī to confer a boon upon her to be the wife of her husband even in his future world.

Meanwhile, there arose a conflict with another king Sindhu that led to war in which King Vidūratha was killed. His jīvātman, which was present throughout in the palace where the body of Padma was lying, now re-entered the dead body and he rose again as King Padma, and standing before him were his two wives, Līlā I and Līlā II, who are reflections of each other, with whom he lived happily for a long time in this world.

Abridged *Yoga Vāsiṣṭha Sāra*

Many centuries ago, an abridgement of the YV was made by Abhinanda Paṇḍita, a Kashmiri scholar, into 6,000 couplets, which go by the name of *Laghu Yoga Vāsiṣṭha*. Later, a summary of the essence of the book in 230 verses, and named the *Yoga Vāsiṣṭha Sāra*, was made by an unknown author. Here we present an abridgement of the summary.

1. **Dispassion**

- Just as one learns how to steady a boat from a boatman, so also the method of crossing the ocean of Saṃsāra is learnt by association with great people.
- The great remedy for the long-lasting disease of Saṃsāra is the inquiry, 'Who am I? To whom does this Saṃsāra belong?' The sages are to be approached even if they do not teach, for even their conversation in a light vein contain wisdom. Real wisdom imparted to a worthy disciple makes him dispassionate.
- The customary method of teaching is only for preserving the tradition. Pure awareness results solely from the clarity of the disciple's understanding.
- The self cannot be seen with the help of the sacred texts or the Guru. The self is seen by the self alone.
- Whereas the arts acquired by humans are lost by lack of practice, the art of wisdom grows steadily.
- Just as an ornament worn round the neck is considered lost through forgetfulness and gained when the mistake is realized, so also the self is attained when the delusion is removed.
- That man who, even after knowing that worldly objects are deceptive, still thinks of them as the only truth, is an ass. Even the slightest thought immerses a man in sorrow, whereas when devoid of thoughts one is serene.

- Just as we experience the delusion of hundreds of years in a dream lasting an hour, so also we experience the sport of maya in our waking state.
- He is a happy man whose mind is inwardly cool and free from attachment and aversion and who looks upon this world as a spectator.
- The wise person has understood how to abandon ideas of acceptance and rejection and be one with the consciousness which is within the innermost heart.
- On the dissolution of the body the self-consciousness limited by the heart alone ceases to exist.
- When pots are broken the space within them becomes unlimited. Likewise, when a body dies, the self remains eternal and unattached.
- Nothing whatsoever is born or dies anywhere at any time. It is Brahman alone who appears illusorily as form in the world.
- The self is more extensive than space; it is pure, subtle, undecaying, and auspicious. It is tranquil, one without beginning, middle or end, which cannot be said to be existent or non-existent. Know this and be happy.

2. Unreality of the world

- The illusion of saṃsāra comes to an end when the mind is stilled. Saṃsāra rises when the mind becomes active and ceases when it is made still by controlling the breath and latent desires (vāsanās).
- This saṃsāra is born of one's imagination and vanishes in the absence of imagination. The appearance of a snake ceases to be fearful when it is realized it is only in a picture. Similarly, saṃsāra ceases to exist when the Truth is realized.

- Maya is amazing in that it brings delight through its own destruction. Its nature is inscrutable, and it fades away when it is observed.
- This maya which deludes the world is full of wonder. It is on account of it that the self is not perceived even though it pervades all the limbs of the body. Whatever is seen does not truly exist, and the world is like the mythical city of Gandharvas, or a mirage.
- That which is not seen, though within us, is called the eternal and indestructible self. Just as the trees on the bank of a lake are reflected in the water, so also all varied objects are reflected in the vast mirror of our consciousness.
- This creation, which is a play of consciousness, arises like the delusion of the snake in a rope (when there is ignorance) and comes to an end when there is right knowledge.
- Even though bondage does not really exist, it becomes strong through desire for worldly enjoyments; when this desire subsides, bondage becomes weak.
- Like waves rising from the ocean, the unstable mind rises out of the vast and stable expanse of the supreme self. It is from this expanse that the magical show (of the world) is projected in the waking state.
- This world, though unreal, appears to exist and is the cause of life-long suffering to an ignorant person, just as a (non-existent) ghost (is the cause of fear) to a boy.
- One who has no idea of gold sees only the bracelet. Similarly, towns, houses, mountains, serpents, and so on are in the eyes of the ignorant man separate objects. From the absolute point of view this objective (world) is the subject (the self) itself; it is not separate (from the self).
- The world is full of misery to an ignorant man and full of bliss to the wise one. The world is dark to a blind man

and bright to one who has eyes. The bliss of a man of discrimination, who has rejected saṃsāra and discarded all mental concepts, constantly increases.

- Like clouds which suddenly appear in a clear sky and as suddenly dissolve, the universe appears in the self and dissolves in it. He who reckons the rays as non-different from the sun and realizes that they are the sun itself is stated to be nirvikalpa (the undifferentiating man). Just as the cloth, when investigated, is seen to be nothing but thread, so also this world, when enquired into, is (seen to be) merely the self.
- This world rises like a wave in the ambrosial ocean of consciousness and dissolves in it. How then can it be different from it (i.e. consciousness) in the middle (i.e. when it appears)? Just as the foam, the waves, the dew and the bubbles are not different from water, even so this world which has come out of the self is not different from the self. Just as a tree consisting of fruits, leaves, creepers, flowers, branches, twigs and roots, exists in the seed of the tree, even so this manifest world exists in Brahman. Just as the pot (ultimately) goes back to mud, waves into water and ornaments into gold, so also this world which has come out of the self (ultimately) goes back to the self.
- The snake appears when one does not recognize the rope; it disappears when one recognizes the rope. In a similar manner, this world appears when the self is not recognized; it disappears when the self is recognized. Just as the dream becomes unreal in the waking state and the waking state in the dream, so also death becomes unreal in birth and birth in death. All these are thus neither real nor unreal. They are the effect of delusion, mere impression arising out of past experience.

3. Marks of a liberated person (jīvanmukta)

- The knowledge of the self is the fire that burns up the dry grass of desire and it leads to the state of samadhi. A mere abstention from speech is not samadhi.
- One who realizes that the whole universe is nothing but consciousness remains calm. One who reflects in his innermost heart upon the purport of the Upaniṣads and is not moved by joy and sorrow, is not tormented by saṃsāra.
- Just as birds and beasts do not take shelter on a mountain that is on fire, so also evil thoughts never occur to a knower of Brahman.
- Just as the trembling (of the body) caused by the (imaginary) snake persists (for some time) even after realizing that there is no snake, so also the effect of delusion persists (for some time) even after getting rid of it.
- Just as a crystal is not stained by what is reflected in it, so also a knower of truth is not affected by the result of his acts. Even intent on outward action, the knower of truth always remains calm.
- Firmly convinced of non-duality and enjoying perfect mental peace, the yogi goes about the work in serenity. Let death come today or at the end of aeons, the yogi remains untarnished like gold buried in mine. The desireless one is liberated at the very moment he attains knowledge (of Brahman).
- Like an empty vessel in space, the knower of truth is empty both within and without, while at the same time he is full within and without like a vessel immersed in the ocean.
- He who neither likes nor dislikes the objects seen by him and who acts with dispassion is said to be a liberated

person. He who is free from the knots (of desires) and whose doubts have been set at rest is liberated even when he is in the body, he is a jīvanmukta. He may appear to be bound, but he is free.

- He who has easily cast off all egoistic tendencies and has abandoned even the object of meditation, is said to be liberated.
- He who casts away from his mind all objects of perception and, attaining perfect quiescence, remains still as space, unaffected by sorrow, is a liberated person.
- The noble-hearted man whose desires of the heart have come to an end is a liberated man.
- The idea of self in the non-self is bondage, and abandonment of it is liberation. There is neither bondage nor liberation for the ever-free self. By perceiving that the objects of perception do not really exist, the mind is freed (from those objects).
- Liberation is not on the other side of the sky, nor is it in the nether world, nor the earth; it is the extinction of the mind based on the eradication of all desires. There is no intellect, no mind, and no individual soul (jīva).
- One who is established in infinite, pure consciousness, bliss and unqualified non-duality is already free. The mind has, by its own activity, bound itself; when it is calm it is free.

4. Dissolution of the mind

- When consciousness is attached to imagined objects, it is known as the mind.
- The power of imagining separate objects comes from consciousness.
- Just as fire fanned into a flame by the wind is extinguished by the same wind, so also that which is born of imagination is destroyed by imagination.

- The mind comes into existence through the imagination on account of forgetfulness. Like the experience of one's own death in a dream, it ceases to exist when scrutinized.
- The idea of self in what is not-self arises from incorrect understanding. The idea of reality in what is unreal is a characteristic of the mind. 'This is he', 'I am this', 'That is mine', such (ideas) constitute the mind, which disappears when one analyzes them logically.
- It is the nature of the mind to accept certain things and to reject others. The mind is the creator of the world; the mind is the individual (puruṣa); only that which is done by the mind is regarded as done, not that which is done by the body. The arm with which one embraces the wife is the very arm with which one embraces the daughter.
- The mind is the cause of the objects of perception. The three worlds depend upon it. When it is dissolved the world is also dissolved. It is to be cured (i.e. purified) with effort.
- The mind is bound by the latent impressions (vāsanās). When there are no impressions, it is free. Therefore, bring about quickly, through discrimination, the state in which there are no impressions.
- Just as a streak of cloud stains (i.e. appears to stain) the moon or a blotch of ink a lime-plastered wall, so also the evil spirit of desire stains the inner man. He who, with inturned mind, offers all the three worlds, like dried grass, as an oblation in the fire of knowledge, becomes free from the illusions of the mind.
- When one knows the real truth about acceptance and rejection and does not think of anything but abides in himself, abandoning everything, then the mind does not come into existence.

- The mind is terrible (ghoram) in the waking state, gentle (śāntam) in the dream state, dull (mūḍham) in deep sleep and dead when not in any of these three states.
- The mind is saṃsāra; the body is activated by the mind just as a tree is shaken by the wind.
- The only god to be conquered is the mind. Its conquest leads to the attainment of everything. Without its conquest all other efforts are fruitless. To human beings even the conquest of the three worlds, without the conquest of the mind, is pointless. Association with the wise, abandonment of latent impressions, self-enquiry, control of breathing—these are the means of conquering the mind.
- The mind becomes bound by thinking 'I am not Brahman'; it becomes free by the thought 'I am Brahman'. When the mind dissolves, everything that is dual or single is dissolved, and what remains after that is the Supreme Brahman. There is nothing to equal the joy felt by a person of pure mind who has attained the state of pure consciousness and overcome death.

5. **The destruction of latent impressions**

- This inquiry into the self is the fire which burns up the seeds of the evil tree which is the mind.
- Just as the wind does not affect the creepers in a picture, so also afflictions do not affect one whose understanding is fortified by firmness and (always) reflected in the mirror of inquiry.
- The wise declare that investigation into the truth of the self is knowledge. What is to be known is contained in it like sweetness in milk.
- One who has realized the self by investigation knows the meaning of Brahmā, Vishnu, and Śiva.

- For one who is fond of inquiring 'What is this vast universe?' and 'Who am I?' this world becomes unreal.
- Just as the thought of water does not occur to one who knows how a mirage arises, similarly latent impressions do not rise in one whose ignorance has been destroyed by realizing that everything is Brahman.
- By the abandonment of latent impressions or by the control of breathing, mind loses its negative powers.
- Cherishing the association of sages, one can attain the state of supreme consciousness quickly.
- Latent impressions cease to be active when one associates with sages, discards all thoughts of saṃsāra and remembers that the body has to die.
- Even ignorant persons convert by the firmness of their conviction poison into nectar and nectar into poison.
- When this body is taken to be real it serves the purpose of a body, but when it is seen to be unreal it becomes unsubstantial space.
- When the seeker thinks only of Brahman and remains calm and free from sorrows his egoity dies by itself.
- If one realizes the unity of things, one remains tranquil, inwardly cool and pure like space without the sense of 'I'.
- If inwardly one is cool the whole world will be cool, but if inwardly one is agitated the whole world will be a burning mess.

6. Meditation of the self

- I, the pure, stainless, and infinite consciousness beyond maya, look upon this body in action like the body of another.
- The mind, the intellect, and the senses are all the play of consciousness. They are unreal and seem to exist only due to lack of insight.

- Unmoved by adversity, a well-wisher to all, without ideas of existence and non-existence, I live free from misery.
- Inactive am I, desireless, clear as the sky, free from hankering, tranquil, formless, everlasting, and unmoving.
- I clearly understand that the five elements, the three worlds, and I are pure consciousness.
- I am above everything, I am present everywhere, I am like space, I am that which (really) exists, and I am nothing beyond this.
- Let imaginary waves of the universe rise or fall in me who is the ocean of infinite consciousness; there is no increase or decrease in me.
- How wonderful that in me, the infinite ocean of consciousness, waves of jīvas (individual souls) rise, sport for a while and disappear according to their nature.
- The world which has come into existence on account of my ignorance has dissolved likewise in me. I now directly experience the world as supreme bliss of consciousness.
- I prostrate to myself who am within all beings, the ever-free self abiding as inner consciousness.

7. **Method of purification**

- Be outwardly active but inwardly inactive, outwardly a doer but inwardly a non-doer, and thus play your part in the world.
- Abandon all desires inwardly, be free from attachments and latent impressions, do everything outwardly and thus play your role.
- Abandon all objects of contemplation, live in your innate self, liberated even while alive (jīvanmukta), and thus be one with the world.

- Burn the forest of duality with the fire of the conviction, 'I am the one pure consciousness'.
- You are bound firmly on all sides by the idea, 'I am the body'. Cut that bond by the sword of knowledge: 'I am consciousness'.
- Discarding the attachment to non-self, regarding the world as whole, attention turned inward, be pure consciousness.
- Be in consciousness which is your constant (i.e. true) nature beyond the states of waking, dream, and deep sleep.
- Do not be that which is understood, nor the one who understands. Abandon all concepts and be in your nature.
- Eliminate one concept by another and the mind by the mind and abide in the self.
- Replace the mind, which has on account of its cares become red hot, with one that is like iron sharpened by the study of scriptures.
- Your true self is not the body. Don't feel helpless and miserable by joys and sorrows on account of it.
- There is a vast difference between the body and you, the embodiment of consciousness. Even after knowing this why do you not abandon the idea of self in this body? The mere knowledge that this body is like a piece of wood, or a clod of earth enables one to realize the supreme self.
- It is strange that, while the real Brahman is forgotten by men, the transitory state called avidyā appears very real to them.
- When you do your work do it without attachment even as a crystal which reflects the objects before it (but is not affected by them). The conviction that everything is Brahman leads one to liberation. Therefore, reject entirely the idea of duality which is ignorance. Reject it entirely.

3. Worship of the self

- If you separate yourself from the body and abide at ease in consciousness you will become one with the reality.
- After knowing that by which you know this (world), turn the mind inward and then you will see clearly (i.e. realize) the effulgence of the self.
- That by which you recognize sound, taste, form, and smell, know that as your self, the supreme Brahman.
- That in which beings vibrate, that which creates them, know that self to be your real self.
- After rejecting, through reasoning, all that may be known as 'non-truth', take what remains, that is pure consciousness, as your real self.
- Knowledge is not separate from you and that which is known is not separate from knowledge. Hence there is nothing other than the self.
- All that Brahmā, Vishnu, Śiva, Indra, and others do is done by me, the embodiment of consciousness.
- I am the whole universe, I am the undecaying supreme self, and there is neither past nor future apart from me.
- Everything is the one Brahman, pure consciousness, the self of all, indivisible and immutable.
- There is neither I, nor any other thing. Only Brahman exists, full of bliss everywhere.
- The sense of perceiver and perceived is common to all embodied beings, but the yogi worships the one self.

4. Exposition of the self

- When this assemblage of body, and senses acts of its own accord there arises an idea 'I am this.' This is the jīva (ego) stained by the impurity of ignorance.
- When the conviction that everything is all pervasive consciousness becomes firm, the jīva comes to an end like a lamp without oil.

- Just as a child sees an apparition, so also the delusional jīva creates this unreal body and sees it as separate from him.
- A child superimposes a real elephant on the clay image and plays with it; likewise, the ignorant man superimposes the body on the self.
- The image of a snake does not terrify when it is realized to be only a picture, so similarly for the jīva-snake.
- Although bracelets may appear to be many, as gold they are one. Similarly, the adjuncts are many, the self is one.
- Like the organs of the body and modifications of clay, non-duality appears as multiplicity in the form of moving and unmoving objects.
- Just as a single face is reflected as many in a crystal or in a mirror, so also the one self is reflected in the many intellects or minds. Just as the sky appears to be stained by dust, smoke, and clouds, so also the pure self in contact with the qualities of maya appears to be soiled by them.
- Just as metal in contact with fire acquires the quality of fire (namely heat), so also the senses in contact with the self acquire the quality of the self.
- When water and fire come together, they acquire the qualities of each other. Similarly, when the self and the inert body come together the self looks like the non-self and the non-self looks like the self.
- Just as fire thrown into a large pool of water loses its quality, so also consciousness in contact with the inert seems to lose its real nature and becomes inert.
- The self is realized in the body only with effort, like extracting sugar from the sugar cane, oil from sesame seeds, and fire from wood. Like the sky seen in an unbroken crystal, consciousness exists in all objects. Just as a big lamp kept inside a vessel made of precious stones

illumines by its light both outside and inside, so also the one self illumines everything. Just as the sun's reflection in a mirror illumines other things, so also the reflection of the self in pure intellect illumines other things.

- The self is without beginning or end. It manifests space, it is the source of the jīva and is higher than the highest. The self is pure consciousness, eternal, omnipresent, immutable, and self-effulgent like the light of the sun. The omnipresent self, the substratum of all, is non-different from the effulgent consciousness like heat from fire. It can only be experienced, and not known.
- The self is absolute consciousness. It is pure awareness, undecaying, free from all ideas of acceptance or rejection and not limited by space, time, or genus. Just as the air in the universe pervades everything, so also the self abides bodiless in everything.
- There is neither bondage nor liberation, neither duality nor non-duality, there is only Brahman always shining as consciousness. The idea of consciousness as an object of consciousness is bondage; freedom from it is liberation. That which exists and which shines is the self; anything else which seems to shine does not exist. Consciousness alone shines by itself.

5. Nirvāṇa

- Supreme bliss cannot be experienced through contact of the senses with their objects. The supreme state is that in which the mind is annihilated through one-pointed inquiry. Contact with the sense-objects is bondage, freedom from it is liberation.
- Attain the pure state between existence and non-existence and hold on to it, do not accept or reject either the inner or the outer world. Depend always on that true reality

between the sentient and the inert which is the infinite space-like heart.

- The belief in a knower and the known is bondage. The knower is bound by the known. Abandoning the ideas of seer, seen, and sight along with latent desires (vāsanās), one meditates on that self which is the light that illuminates the mind.
- The light of lights lies between the two ideas of existence and non-existence. The firm state in which all thoughts are still and which is different from the waking and dream states is one's supreme state.
- The self shines by itself as the one boundless ocean of consciousness agitated by waves of thought. Just as the ocean is nothing but water the entire world of things is nothing but consciousness filling the quarters like the infinite space.
- Brahman and space are alike as to their invisibility, pervasiveness, and indestructibility, but Brahman is also consciousness. All this is truly Brahman; all this is ātman.
- One who has the firm conviction 'I am the supreme self called the undecaying Vāsudeva' is liberated. After eliminating everything as 'not this', 'not this', what remains is the supreme self. Know always that the self is Brahman, one and whole. One that is indivisible cannot be divided into the meditator and the object of meditation.
- The thought that one is pure consciousness is meditation, and when even the idea of meditation is forgotten, it is samadhi.
- The constant flow of mental concepts relating to Brahman without the sense of 'I' achieved through intense practice of self-inquiry (jñāna) is the samprajñāta samādhi (meditation with concepts).

- No harm befalls one whose mind is extinct. That consciousness which is the witness of the rise and fall of all beings, know that to be the immortal state of supreme bliss.
- Every moving or unmoving thing is only an object visualized by the mind. When the mind is annihilated, duality (i.e. multiplicity) is not perceived. That which is immutable, auspicious, and tranquil, that in which this world exists, that which manifests itself as the mutable and immutable objects, that is the sole consciousness.
- Before discarding the slough, the snake regards it as itself, but when discarded, it becomes an external thing. He who has transcended both good and evil does not, like a child, refrain from prohibited acts from a sense of sin, nor does he do what is prescribed from a sense of merit.
- Just as a statue is contained in a pillar (i.e. block) even if it is not actually carved out, so also the world exists in Brahman. The supreme state is not a void.
- Just as a pillar is said to be devoid of the statue before the latter is carved out, so also Brahman is said to be void when it is devoid of the impression of the world. Just as still water may be said to contain or not contain ripples, so also Brahman may be said to contain or not contain the world. It is neither void nor existence.

8

Lalitāditya and His Campaigns

Lalitāditya Muktāpīḍa (r. 724–757 or 760 CE), 'Pearl-crowned tremulous Sun', of Kashmir's Kārkoṭa dynasty was called a 'world conqueror' and *universal monarch* by Kalhaṇa in the *Rājataraṅginī*. Lalitāditya defeated the central Indian king Yashovarman, and then marched to eastern and southern lands, subjugating several more rulers on his way back. Later his campaigns towards the north and the west brought him further victories, and he conquered lands in the region of the Taklamakan Desert. Many scholars believe that Lalitāditya created an empire that included major parts of India as well as present-day Afghanistan and Central Asia.[1]

Lalitāditya was also a great builder of cities such as the new capital Parihāsapura, temples, and vihāras. Many of his temples were dedicated to Vishnu, Rāma, Krishna, and Śiva, and there were stupas and vihāras to the Buddha. The great Sun-temple of Mārtanḍ, although in ruins now, is a testament to the grandness and beauty of his conceptions.

Apart from Kalhaṇa's account, Lalitāditya also finds mention in the *New Book of Tang* (Xin Tang shu), a record of the Tang dynasty of China. This text mentions him as 'Mu-to-pi' or 'Muduobi' (a variation of Muktāpīḍa). The 11th century Iranian chronicler Al-Biruni mentions a king called Muttai, who was most certainly Lalitāditya (from 'Muktāpīḍa'), further claiming that the people of Kashmir organized an annual festival on the second day of the Chaitra month to celebrate Muktāpīḍa's famous victory over the Turks.

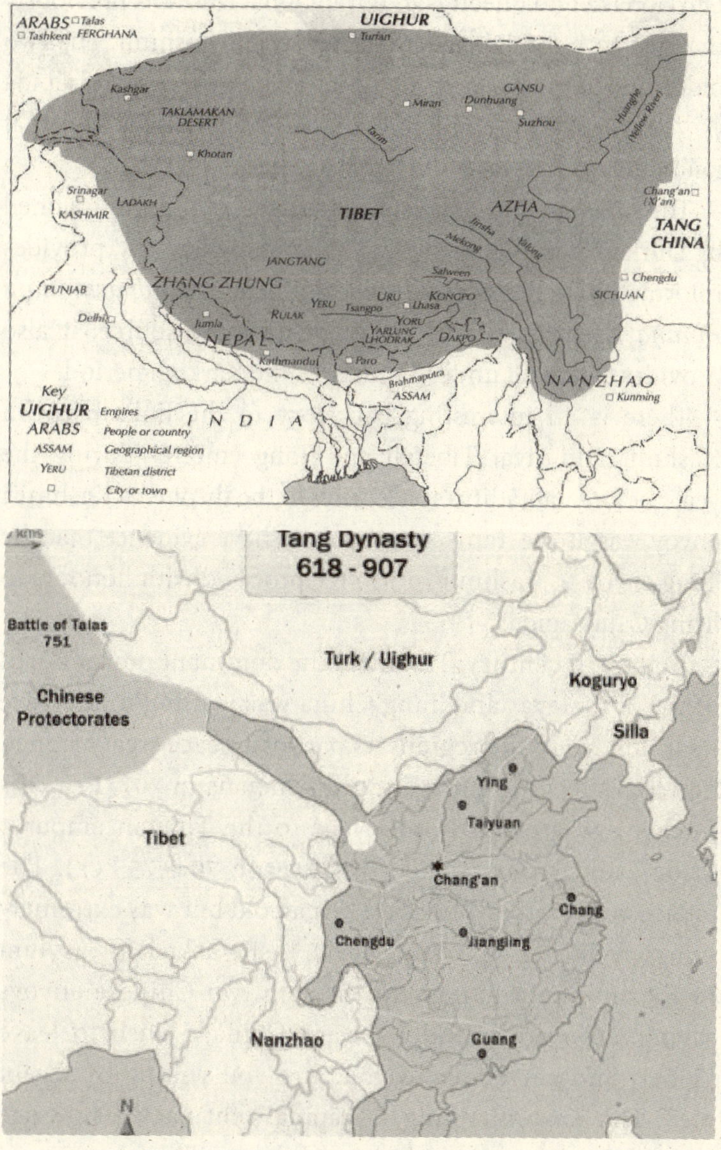

8.1 Tibetan empire at its greatest (late 8th century) and Tang empire protectorates north of Tibetan empire

The Kārkoṭa Dynasty

Lalitāditya was the youngest son of the Kārkoṭa king Durlabhaka and queen Narendraprabhā, who was previously married to a foreign merchant settled in Kashmir. His two older brothers who preceded him as king were Candrāpīḍa (r. 712/3–720) and Tārāpīḍa (r. 720–724). Kalhaṇa says that Lalitāditya's reign lasted for over 36 years.

The *Nīlamata Purāṇa*, believed to have been commissioned by Durlabhavardhana, the first ruler of the dynasty, provides information on contemporary affairs. The *Viṣṇudharmottara Purāṇa* is another local and contemporary source; it also provides a general understanding of the Kārkoṭa period.

There is an interesting backstory to the links between Kashmir and rival Tibetan and Tang empires during the years before Lalitāditya's ascension to the throne. A Kashmiri envoy was at the Tang court, and we have evidence that the Tang envoy to Kashmir in 720 reciprocated with honours to 'King Candrāpīḍa'.

In the 8th century, Tibet was the dominant power north of the Himalayas and Tang China was jostling to increase its influence in the region. As part of a peace treaty signed between the Tang court and the Tibetans in 707, Princess Jincheng was given in marriage to the Tibetan emperor Tridé Tsuktsen (Tibetan: ཁྲི་ལྡེ་གཙུག་བཙན, r. 704–755 CE). The princess arrived in 710 as a 12-year-old but was extremely unhappy in her marriage. In 723, she asked for asylum in Kashmir in a letter sent through two Chinese envoys saying, 'You are friendly toward China; I wish to leave [Tibet] and surrender to you. Are you willing to accept me?' The Kashmiri king, Tārāpīḍa, sent back a message saying, 'Princess, do come here and we will do our utmost to attend [to your needs].'[2]

The intermediary in this exchange was the king of Zābulistān (southern Afghanistan) and a military alliance between him and Kashmir was proposed to counter any Tibetan attack. The Tang Emperor Xuanzong approved of this plan.

The Princess's plan for asylum in Kashmir, however, never materialized, perhaps due to Tārāpīḍa's death shortly after he had received the secret communication. Was he killed by Tibetan agents? We don't know. Princess Jincheng stayed on as empress consort of Tibet although she was to die young in 739 at the age of 41.

Lalitāditya's Campaigns according to Kalhaṇa

Kalhaṇa gives the following account of Lalitāditya's campaigns.

Lalitāditya invaded the Antarvedi country, whose capital was located at Gadhipura (between Ganga and Yamuna, Kanyakubja or Kannauj), where the king was Yashovarman, who was known for a glittering court that included the poet Vākpatirāja, famous for the Prakrit epic poem *Gauḍavaho*, and the dramatist Bhavabhūti, rated by some as equal to Kālidāsa and author of plays such as *Mālatī-Mādhava.*

After initial skirmishes, Yashovarman offered a peace treaty, drawing up a document titled *The treaty of Yashovarman and Lalitāditya*. Lalitāditya's foreign minister, Mitrasharman, objected to this title, insisting that his king's name be first in the document. Lalitāditya, in agreement with Mitrasharman's advice, broke off the peace negotiations, resumed the battle and soundly defeated Yashovarman.

Lalitāditya's invasion of Kannauj has been dated to August 733 CE, based on a reference in the Gauḍavaho to an inauspicious solar eclipse as an allusion to Yashovarman's defeat. It is believed that Lalitāditya conquered Punjab, Afghanistan, and western part of the Central Asian highlands before embarking upon his campaign in central India. His conquest of Afghanistan is supported by the presence of a gigantic gilt copper Buddha statue beside his chaitya at Parihāsapura that appears to be inspired by the Bamiyan Buddhas.

Before Lalitāditya, Afghanistan was controlled by Turkic Shahi kings who were under nominal Chinese control after the fall of the Sasanian Empire. But with Lalitāditya, Afghanistan came under the control of the Hindu Shahi dynasty and Shahi princes served as his ministers when he reorganized the administration.

Lalitāditya instituted five new offices, in addition to the eighteen that were part of the traditional system, which was important in governance in a state of continual war. These bore the designations: office of high chamberlain, chief minister of foreign affairs, chief master of the horse, high keeper of the treasury, and chief executive officer (*mahāsādhanabhāga*).

According to the historian Hermann Goetz, Lalitāditya conquered present-day Bihar, Bengal and Odisha by 735–736 CE, and he marched to Gauḍa (Bengal) where he defeated the Later Gupta ruler Jīvitagupta, and then advanced up to the Bay of Bengal through present-day Odisha.[3]

Next in his digvijaya was the southern region. The sovereign of Dakshinapatha at this time was a Karṇāṭa queen named Raṭṭā. She submitted to his force, and he was able to go on to Kaveri River further south and then wheel his army to Malaya mountains (Chandanādri, Chanderi?) to Avanti and then to Dvārakā on the Western Sea. He proceeded from Avanti to Uttarapatha (the northern region), where he defeated several kings, returning to Kashmir with immense wealth obtained from his conquests.

It has been estimated that the march to Kanyakubja began in 733 CE, with return to Kashmir in 747 CE. This period of 14 years is longer than the 11-year military campaign of Alexander.

Other Accounts

Lalitāditya's campaign against Yashovarman is understandable as the two kings were immediate neighbours: Lalitāditya's empire extended up to present-day Punjab in the south-east, while Yashovarman's north-eastern frontier included parts of present-day Haryana. The discovery of coins bearing the legend Śri-Pratāpa (Lalitāditya's father) in present-day Uttar Pradesh is evidence in support of his campaign. Abhinavagupta's ancestor Atrigupta, a scholar who originally lived in Yashovarman's territory, was brought to Kashmir by Lalitāditya.

The Kārkoṭa kingdom's peaceful relations with neighbours in Afghanistan is consistent with the story about Princess Jincheng and the intersession by the king of Zābulistān. These friendly relations made it possible for Lalitāditya to leave Kashmir and lead troops to central and eastern India.

Lalitāditya's military victories in faraway lands led many foreigners to join his court. One of these was the Tokharian named Caṅkuna, who was to support many monasteries and build the great monument called Caṅkunakunavihāra.

Lalitāditya and the Tang Empire

The first few decades of the 8th century were extremely fluid in the history of the Hindukush-Pamir region. From the west, Turkic forces had made significant inroads, and the Tibetans asserted their power by occupying strategic locations in the area. From further northeast, the Tang court tried to defend its garrisons in the Taklamakan, which were under pressure from the Tibetans, while trying to extend its western borders. Taking the Tibetans as a serious threat to its vassals in the region, the Tang court established diplomatic relations with kingdoms located in the southern Hindukush region.

This explains the friendly relations between the Tang emperor of China and Lalitāditya. It appears that Lalitāditya saw the Tibetan empire as the greater threat and formed strategic alliance with the Tang Empire.

In 733, Lalitāditya wrote to the Chinese that he, together with an ally in central India, had defeated the Tibetans in north India. He now offered military help to the Chinese to reduce the sway of Tibet in the north and supply of provisions to an army even as large as 200,000 strong. In 737, Little Palūr (Gilgit valley) capitulated to the Tibetans. To secure their position in the Gilgit valley, the Tibetans gave Princess Khri-ma-lod in marriage to Sushilizhi, the pro-Tibetan leader of Little Palūr. The Tang forces and Lalitāditya, with his formidable cavalry and infantry, continued to battle the Tibetans for control of the region and after three-failed attempts captured it in 747 CE.

Two years later (in 749 CE), the Tang court was visited by an envoy from Tokharistan (Bactria), with a request to renew the alliance with Kashmir for a campaign against Tibet's ally Kashgar. The Chinese acted on the envoy's recommendation and sent precious gifts to Lalitāditya. The next year Kashgar was conquered by Tang general Gao Xianzhi in alliance with Lalitāditya's forces. Considering that the Chinese approached Lalitāditya for support, this victory could be seen as an extension of Kashmir's dominions.

The Tibetan invasion of Kashmir in 747 by Emperor Tridé Tsuktsen forced Lalitāditya to return to the Himalayas. He repelled the Tibetans, and invaded the Tarim Basin, and appears to have conquered the kingdoms of Kucha and Turfan. The Turkic kingdom of Tukharistan and the Darad kingdom in the Kishanganga valley were also invaded.

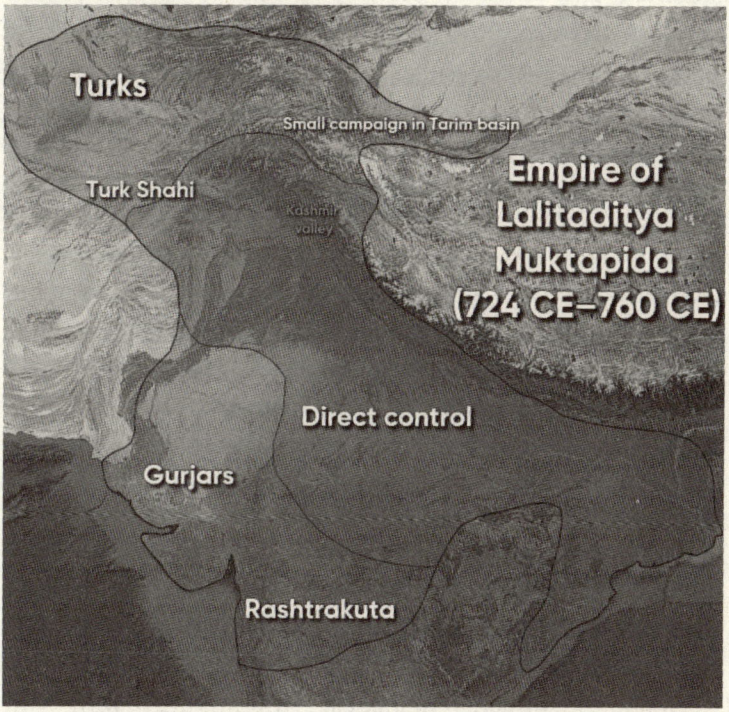

8.2 The estimated extent of Lalitāditya's empire

Kalhaṇa's account speaks of Lalitāditya's victory over a kingdom ruled by women (strī-rājya). The background to this is a mention by Xuanzang of a 'Land of Gold', Suvarṇagotra, that was ruled by women where the male king had no authority and all affairs were directed by the queen: 'The men manage the wars and sow the land, that is all.' This strī-rājya mentioned appears to be the Shigar valley of Baltistan, famous for gold-washing and as temporary home of migrants arriving from the north as described in the Buddhist 'Inquiry of Vimalaprabhā'.

Some say that the threat of advancing Muslim armies made it easy for Lalitāditya to absorb the neighbouring Turkic kingdoms and in the process he acquired their superior Sasanian and Chinese military technologies. It was this 'modernized army' of Lalitāditya that mounted successful attacks on the rest of India.

South and West India

The name 'Raṭṭa' in Kalhaṇa's account appears to be a reference to the Rāṣṭrakūṭas, who ruled the Karṇāṭa region. Goetz identified Kalhaṇa's Queen Raṭṭa with Bhavagana, who was a wife of the Raṣṭrakūṭa king Indra I. He speculates that she acted as a queen regent for her son Dantidurga after Indra's death, but her rule was threatened by her brother-in-law Krishna I. As a result, she appealed to Lalitāditya for help, who arrived in Deccan and fought on her side.

Bhavagana was a Chalukya princess before marriage, and therefore, her Chalukya relatives could have allowed Lalitāditya to pass through northern Deccan, enabling him to easily invade the territory controlled by Krishna.

Goetz identified Kalhaṇa's 'Mummuni' with the contemporary Shīlahāra ruler of Konkan. Although no contemporary Shīlahāra king by this name is known, there was an 11th-century Shīlahāra king with the same name and it is possible the Kalhaṇa erroneously used the name of a king that was closer to his times.

Kalhaṇa mentions that Kayya, the king of Lāṭa (south Gujarat), built a temple in Kashmir during Lalitāditya's reign. Goetz identifies Kayya with the Rāṣṭrakūṭa Karka, who succeeded the Chālukyas in Southern Gujarat, and whose name occurs in the Āntroli-Chhāroli grant inscription of 757.

According to Goetz, Lalitāditya invaded Kathiawar (in present-day Gujarat) between 740 and 746 CE. By this time, the local Maitraka kings had already been subjugated by the Chālukyas, which would have allowed Lalitāditya to establish his hegemony in the region.

Return to Kashmir

Hermann Goetz speculated that the legendary Guhila ruler Bappa Rawal of Chittorgarh served Lalitāditya as a vassal and died fighting in the Kashmiri king's Central Asian campaign. Goetz goes on to connect Lalitāditya to the mythological Agnikula legend, according to which some later regional dynasties originated from a fire pit during a sacrificial ceremony at Mount Abu.

After returning to Kashmir, Lalitāditya not only repulsed the Tibetans but also invaded the Tarim Basin through Sikatā-sindhu (Ocean of Sand) and marched to Kuc̣ha and Turfan after the Tang power ḍeclined as a result of the An Lushan Rebellion.

There are many versions of Lalitāditya's death and they all are about an unsuccessful military expedition in the northern lands. In one version, he perished due to excessive snow in a northern land called Āryānaka. In another version, when his army was annihilated, and his way blocked on a difficult mountainous route, the 'great conqueror burned himself on a pyre with his ministers and generals.' He had marched towards the 'boundless regions of the north', because he was curious to visit places where no one had reached before.

The Later Kārkoṭas

The rulers that immediately followed Lalitāditya were not noteworthy. The next prominent ruler was Lalitāditya's grandson Jayāpīḍa who ruled for 31 years during 776–807 CE. (This has a discrepancy of 25 years from Kalhaṇa's dates because he appears to have confusingly used the Kali Era rather than the purported Saptarshi or Laukika Era).

After becoming king, Jayāpīḍa began preparations for a campaign of world conquest like his grandfather's. But soon after he marched out of the valley with his army, he was deposed by his brother-in-law Jajja and his army melted away. He now found himself in Prayāga and later in the Gauḍa country where the local king gave his daughter, Kalyāṇadevī, in marriage to him. Next, he helped his father-in-law defeat other Gauḍa chiefs.

He was now able to rebuild his army, and on his way back home, he defeated the king of Kanyakubja. Once he arrived in Kashmir, he engaged Jajja and won the kingdom back after three years.

Jayāpīḍa was a patron of arts who invited scholars from abroad. Two literary theorists were installed in his office: Vāmana as a minister and Udbhaṭa as the chief scholar; other scholars included the poet Manoratha and the Buddhist scholar Dharmottara. Udbhaṭa wrote four works—Kumārasambhava, a poem on the theme of the marriage of Śiva and Pārvatī; Kāvyālaṃkārasaṃgraha, a short commentary on Bhāmaha's Kāvyālaṃkāra; a commentary on the Nāṭya Śāstra; and a mostly-lost but extensive Vivaraṇa on Bhāmaha. Vāmana composed sūtra texts. Both aimed at an audience of literary scholars and engaged (for the first time) in critical discussions surrounding poetic theory, praxis and semantic cognition using tools from mīmāṃsā. Udbhaṭa was installed as sabhāpati at a salary of one lakh dinnaras per day. It was an excellent salary but not extravagant since the value of dinnara had fallen considerably. Another scholar was the grammarian Kṣīrasvāmin from whom the king took personal lessons.

9

Vasugupta and the *Śiva Sūtra*

Vasugupta (c. 800–850 CE) is the author of the *Śiva Sutra,*[1] a foundational text of the Advaita tradition of Kashmir Śaivism. Little is known about his life, other than that he lived in Kashmir in the first half of the 9th century. This dating is based on the reference to his work in other texts, and the biography of his students Kallaṭa and Somānanda, both of whom are dated to have actively composed philosophical texts sometime between 825 and 900 CE.

According to one account, Vasugupta found the sutras inscribed on a rock called Sankaropala. The accounts of the immediate students of Vasugupta say that the sutras were received in a dream. Vasugupta also wrote the *Spanda Kārikas*[2] as a commentary on the *Śiva Sūtra.*

The Universal and the Individual

The *Ṛgveda* speaks of two birds sitting on a tree where one of them eats the sweet fruit and the other looks on without eating; one of the birds is the universal consciousness (paramātman), the other the individual consciousness (jīvātman). In truth, there is only one bird; the other is just the image of the first as reflected in the fruit.

We cannot explain consciousness using science, but we can intuitively grasp it. It is the self-shining light (prakāśa) that both creates the world and makes it understandable. Consciousness has free will (svātantrya) and its reflection on itself is vimarśa, which represents the Goddess. The light of consciousness illuminates the associations in the mind by the power of the will or icchā śakti. The process of reflection is bliss (*ānanda*) and it is equivalent to vimarśa and svātantrya.

Awareness requires the idea of succession of cognitions or saṃvit that is 'awareness-reality'; so another name for consciousness is saṃvitti. The awareness (saṃvit) occurs across the unfoldment of time (samaya) and, therefore, the mystery of Śiva can be resolved through meditation on samaya, where Śiva (Prakāśa or Light) and Śakti (Vimarśa or Knowledge) are one. Indeed, this forms the basis of a powerful spiritual practice called Samayācāra.

If people are not creative, it is because the lamp of consciousness is obscured by coverings created by habits and saṃskāras, by education and culture. To obtain knowledge, one must remove these coverings of the mind. Sometimes, some light streams in spontaneously through a crack into the mind, and that can be a life-changing epiphany.

The creativity of the mind springs from direct light, pratibhā, and although this intuition springs from outside the mind, it is eventually manifested in terms of a sequence, krama, associated with time and space. This sequence is represented in terms of conceptual schema or sacred images.

The self (Śiva) is shown as a dot, bindu, in the centre of artistic maṇḍalas, where the rest of the diagram denotes evolutes of Śakti in expansion.[3] But how does the process begin? In the individual it starts with desire, which can operate at many different levels, not just the personal. In this unfolding, Śiva is addressed as Kāmeśvara, and together with Śakti the conjoined form is Kāmakalā.

The individual who wishes to be creative must become a yogi, and move the focus away from the gross elements, that constitute the body, to pure sensations (tanmātra), then to the senses, and finally to the source of awareness. The yogi endeavours to reach the fourth state (turīya) beyond the ordinary states of waking, dreaming, and deep sleep; turīya is the real source of creativity.

There is a paradox in yogic practice: While its purpose is to unite one's personal self with universal consciousness, the union promised by yoga can only be achieved by disuniting oneself from the earlier self. It is the act (kriya) of removing traces (vāsanā) of discrete perceptions (vikalpa) born out of misconceptions (impurities, mala) that contract consciousness.

The Bound and the Free

The cranial vault has no light: it's totally dark and there is no projection of images in the theatre of the mind. Yet the sensory information is bound (paś = to bind) in our perception, and we can say that the binding, pāśa, is the working of Śiva. Remember that paśu (domesticated animals) are bound, *paśum aśvyam gavyam* (RV 5.61.5), and can be pulled by even a child. Humans are paśu for they too are led by simple stories like that of paradise or revolution or glory.

This explains why paśya is 'to see' and Paśupati is another name of Śiva, for the binding of sense-impressions comes from consciousness, which also provides capacity for freedom.

Rudra-Śiva is called the 'best of physicians', *bheṣaja śiromaṇi* or Vaidyanātha (RV 2.33.4). The eight names of Śiva given in Śivapurāṇa 1.20 are Hara (Destroyer), Maheśvara (Great Lord), Śambhu (Source of Bliss), Śūlapāṇi (Carrier of

Triśūla), Pinākin (Archer), Śiva, Paśupati (Lord of beings), and Mahādeva (Great God).

Of these, the triśūla signifies the overarching connections between the three aspects of reality, that is, body, mind, and consciousness, as well as the three guṇas. Śiva as Pinākin, the archer, sends out the flaming arrow that shines light in the dark chamber of the mind.

The great sage Yājñavalkya in the *Bṛhadāraṇyaka Upaniṣad* speaks of the 11 Rudras as different aspects of consciousness. These 11 find systematic representation in the categories of Kashmir Śaivism, by getting added to the 25 tattvas of Sāṅkhya for the total of 36. In our perspective the system is an emanation of the categories in the Vedas.

Let us return to the mind. It can be in states that do not provide clarity. But if mind is the problem, it is also the only instrument that one has. The practitioner must leverage the perceptions of the mind, which are recounted in language, to transcend its limitations. Also, since the mind is situated in the body, one must also address bodily states to be calm and focused. A primal sound is a mantra that can open doorways to innate knowledge that lies beyond material associations.

The *Śiva Sutra* has three movements:

- The first movement is about universal consciousness (Śiva)
- The second movement is about the emergence of innate knowledge (Śakti)
- The third movement is about self-transformation (the individual)

These movements begin with the question of who we are. We couldn't be just our life-history, our memories, and our desires and aspirations. A lot of that is the accident of our birth and our social experience.

When we strip off layer upon layer of the social self, we come to the essential being. The process of the stripping of the social self is painful but it is liberating. It is this process that transforms the individual. It is this process that is the greatest sacrifice.

1. Śāmbhavopāya, Śiva's path

1.1 *caitanyamātmā*

Consciousness is the self.

Note: This is fundamentally the same as the Upaniṣadic mahāvākyas *aham brahmāsmi,* 'I am Brahman', or *prajñānam brahma,* 'Consciousness is Brahman'. But using the term *caitanya*, 'awareness', makes it more accessible to the reader. There is no mysterious 'soul' in the body; awareness is the self. Śiva as universal consciousness makes it possible for the material associations of the physical world to have meaning.

1.2 *jñānam bandhaḥ*

(Ordinary) knowledge is bondage.

Note: The associations or mundane knowledge become bondage for they suggest that embodiments exhaust all reality. In other words, this surface knowledge becomes accepted and considered sufficient in lieu of deeper knowledge.

1.3 *yonivarga kalāśarīram*

The multitude of emanations are the various parts of the body.

Note: Physical emanations are parts of the embodied activity.

1.4 *jñānādhiṣṭhāna mātṛkā*

The ground of knowledge is *mātṛkā* (the set of elemental sounds).

Note: One obtains knowledge from the senses. Of these the origins of touch, taste, smell, and sight are direct, whereas that of sound is indirect. Since one is able to describe reality in terms of concatenations of elements of sound, or likewise by the alphabet of letters, this forms the basis of our deeper perception of reality.

Our phenomenal knowledge can only be in terms of the associations of the outer world. But the associations in themselves need something to bind them together. The binding is the mātṛkā, the womb of elementary sounds or phonemes associated with the resonances of the mind, which are components of the spoken language. It is the binding that makes it possible to understand words or symbols when they are strung together.

1.5 *udyamo bhairavaḥ*
The upsurge (of consciousness) is Bhairava.

Note: Bhairava is the name given to awareness as it registers in the mind. In that moment one feels alone, and therefore this awareness (also called Rudra in Vedic texts) is overpowering.

1.6 *śakticakrasandhāne viśvasaṃhāraḥ*
By union with the energy centres one withdraws from the universe.

Note: When absorbed in the sensation emanating from the cakras, there exists no sense of the outer universe. It is in that withdrawal that one is near to the Ātman.

1.7 *jāgrat-svapna-suṣupta-bhede turyābhogasambhavaḥ*
Even during waking, sleep, and deep sleep one can experience the fourth state (*turīya*, which transcends ordinary consciousness).

Note: This means that extraordinary knowledge can be obtained in all states, including the waking state. This is significant because it demystifies the process of obtaining acute insight.

1.8 *jñānam jāgrat*

(Mundane) knowledge is [obtained] in the waking state.

Note: This sets up an interesting duality in that sensory or associative knowledge is the foundation of mundane knowledge, and of transcending turīya at the same time.

1.9 *svapno vikalpāḥ*

Dreaming is free ranging of thoughts.

Note: In a dream one is not governed by the constraints or rules of the ordinary world of senses, and therefore the mind has access to a broader range of possibilities.

1.10 *aviveko māyāsauṣuptam*

Deep sleep is *māyā*, the (state of) non-distinction.

Note: Deep sleep is where the manas and buddhi are dormant and so no distinctions are made about the world.

1.11 *tritayabhoktā vīreśaḥ*

The experiencer of the three states is the lord of the senses.

Note: The experiencer of the three states is Śiva, who is behind the intellect and the manas.

1.12 *vismayo yogabhūmikāḥ*

The stages of Yoga are astonishing, *vismaya*.

Note: The union of the three is when one has access to the light of Śiva, which takes one beyond mundane experience.

1.13 *icchā śaktirumā kumārī*

The power of the will is the playful Umā.

Note: The will (*icchā*) works in terms of embodiments, physical, emotional, or abstract and is represented by Umā, the consort of Śiva.

1.14 *dṛśyam śarīram*
The observed is embodied.

Note: Ordinary reality is in terms of embodiments.

1.15 *hṛdaye cittasaṅghaṭṭād dṛśyasvāpadarśanam*
By fixing the mind on its heart one can comprehend the perceivable and emptiness.

Note: At the heart of one's experience, one is in a constant movement between embodiment and awareness, which is the Dance of Śiva.

1.16 *śuddhatattvasandhānād vā apaśuśaktiḥ*
Or by contemplating the pure principle one is free of the power that binds animal instincts.

Note: The pure (śuddha) tattva is the consciousness tattvas, and by getting absorbed in it on gets free of one's bondage to the body.

1.17 *vitarka ātmajñānam*
Reflection is the knowledge of the self.

Note: Meditation on the nature of meaning itself takes one to the knowledge of the Ātmā.

1.18 *lokānandaḥ samādhisukham*
The bliss of perceived world is the joy of *samādhi.*
Note: At samādhi the world makes sense and that fills one up with joy.

1.19 *śaktisandhāne śarīrotpattiḥ*
In the union of power, the body emerges.

Note: The power of māyā makes embodiments (which are separated) emerge from the interconnected state of undifferentiated reality.

1.20 *bhūtasandhāna bhūtapṛthaktva viśvasaṅghaṭṭāḥ*
Elements are united and elements are separated, and the universe is assembled.

Note: The universe feels the way it is owing to the capacity in the mind to separate and unite tattvas (elements).

1.21 *śuddhavidyodayāccakreśatva siddhiḥ*
The tattvas of lordship arises from the wheel that leads to pure knowledge.

Note: The knowledge of consciousness states (śuddha vidyā) leads to a mastery of energy centres.

1.22 *mahāhradānusandhānānmantravīryānubhavaḥ*
The great lake (of mind) is experienced through the power of mantra.

Note: The deepest knowledge is attained through the elements of sound that go on to create the language in which one contemplates.

2. Śāktopāya, the Process, the path of Śakti

2.1 *cittam mantraḥ*
The mind is a measure (mantra).

Note: The mind is a measure of reality.

2.2 *prayatnaḥ sādhakaḥ*
Effort leads to attainment.

Note: Knowledge is attainable for one can see one's progress in the path.

2.3 *vidyāśarīrasattā mantrarahasyam*
The secret of mantra is in the being of the body of knowledge.

Note: The embodiment of knowledge takes one to the secret of the mantra. In other words, it reveals aspects of our reality that are accessed by primal sound.

2.4 *garbhe cittavikāso'viśistavidyāsvapnaḥ*
The emergence of the mind in the womb is like a dream based on indistinct knowledge.

Note: The mind is an embodiment based on the senses projecting in the brain, and its very foundation is limited, associative knowledge.

2.5 *vidyāsamutthāne svābhāvike khecarī śivāvasthā*
When the knowledge of one's self arises, one moves in the sky of consciousness, which is Śiva's state.

Note: With the rise of the knowledge of oneself, one can have a measure of the space in which consciousness moves.

2.6 *gururupāyaḥ*
The guru is the means.

Note: The teacher can help in overcoming the obstacles (associated with implicit assumptions about the world that lie in the Kāraṇa Śarīra).

2.7 *mātrkācakrasambodhaḥ*
[In] the awakening of the wheel of *mātṛkā* (the elemental sounds).

Note: The mastery of the wheel of sounds makes the understanding of the world possible.

2.8 *śarīram haviḥ*
The body is the oblation.

Note: In this process one must get rid of one's attachment to the idea that one is just one's body; it is in this sense that the body is to be sacrificed.

2.9 *jñānam annam*
Knowledge is food.

Note: To complement the physical body, one must create a body (*annam*) of knowledge.

2.10 *vidyāsamhāre taduttha svapna darśanam*
With the extinction of knowledge emerges the vision of That.

Note: This body of knowledge leads to a domain of That, which is the sky of consciousness.

3. Āṇavopāya, the individual's path

3.1 *ātmā cittam*
The mind is the self.

Note: Although the mind is a part of the body, yet from a practical point of view it is only through it that one can see the light of the Ātman, and thus is effectively the Ātman.

3.2 *jñānam bandhaḥ*
(Material) knowledge is bondage (association).

Note: All ordinary knowledge is bondage for it makes one believe that all there is to reality is materiality, and this knowledge itself makes one become a prisoner to the idea.

3.3 *kalādīnām tattvānām aviveko māyā*
Māyā is the lack of discernment of the beginnings of transformation (*kalā*).

Note: Māyā makes one feel secure in the logic of outer associations, which makes one misunderstand the transformations that need to be analyzed.

3.4 *śarīre samhāraḥ kalānām*
The destruction on the transformation is in the body.

Note: Whereas one may consider the plausibility of the outer reality as being separated and disconnected, this is not possible when considering one's own body.

3.5 *nāḍī saṃhāra bhūtajaya bhūtakaivalya bhūta-pṛthaktvāni*
The quieting of the vital channels, the mastery of the elements, the withdrawal from the elements, and the separation of the elements.

Note: To understand the limitations of māyā, one needs to go within to control one's inner processes.

3.6 *mohāvaranāt siddhiḥ*
Perfection is through the concealment of delusion (of the mind).

Note: It is possible to pierce the normal state of existence which is that of delusion.

3.7 *mohajayād anantābhogāt sahajavidyājayaḥ*
Overcoming delusion while enjoying the world innate knowledge is obtained.

Note: The idea is to be of the world and contribute to it while recognizing its true nature.

3.8 *jāgrad dvitīyakaraḥ*
Waking is the second doing.

Note: The waking state is the second aspect of reality as experienced by us.

3.9 *nartaka ātmā*
The self is the dancer.

Note: The self is aware that he is not the body, which is obvious in statements such as 'my body is in pain' that make it clear that for the self the body is only a garment. So the self is dancing wearing different masks.

3.10 *rango'ntarātmā*
The inner self is the stage.

Note: The dialogue with the Witness takes place on the inner stage.

3.11 *prekśakāṇīndriyāṇi*
The senses are the spectators.

Note: One observes this dialogue through the senses.

3.12 *dhīvaśāt sattvasiddhiḥ*
The pure state is achieved by the power of the intellect.

Note: One must rise from the mind to the intellect to reach the pure state.

3.13 *siddhaḥ svatantrabhāvaḥ*
The siddha (who has achieved highest knowledge) has freedom.

Note: When one is in the pure state, one is free.

3.14 *yathā tatra tathānyatra*
As here, so elsewhere.

Note: Since the same order exists throughout the universe, one can know about the greater truth by knowing one's own truth. This means the same as the equivalence of the part and the whole, or the microcosm and the macrocosm.

3.15 *visargasvābhāvyād abahiḥ sthitestatsthitiḥ*
Flow (of consciousness) is the way [of nature] and so what is not external is seen as external.

Note: Consciousness as it operates through the senses makes what is connected to be outside of the body.

3.16 *bījāvadhānam*
Attention to the seed.

Note: The path of dhyāna is to pay attention to a seed sound.

3.17 *āsanasthaḥ sukham hrade nimajjati*
Seated one sinks effortlessly in the lake (of consciousness).

Note: When seated in an āsana, and doing dhyāna, one loses sense of one's own body.

3.18 *svamātrā nirmānam āpādayati*
One creates one's own measure of consciousness.

Note: It is clear that consciousness creates the world as it is experienced.

3.19 *vidyā avināśe janma vināśaḥ*
As (limited) knowledge is transcended, birth is transcended.

Note: Going beyond limited associations one is free of the karmic chain, which governs our thoughts and our life.

3.20 *kavargādisu māheśvaryādyāḥ paśumātaraḥ*
Māheśvarī and other mothers (sources) of beings reside in the "k" sound elements.

Note: The syllable 'k' is the seed sound for several reasons. The consonants of the Sanskrit alphabet begin with it, and because many interrogative words start with this syllable, as here: kim (what), kasmin (in what), kutra (where), kati (how many), katham (how), kutah (from where), kena (by what), kistih (whose), kada (when), kutra (where), kim (is it so), kasya (of whom/to whom), kena (by whom).

3.21 *triṣu caturtham tailavadāsecyam*
The fourth (state of consciousness) should be used to oil the (other) three (states of consciousness).

Note: The fourth state interpenetrates the other three, namely, waking, dreaming, and dreamless sleeping.

3.22 *magnaḥ svacittena praviśet*
Absorbed (in his nature), one penetrates (by the phonemes) one's mind.

Note: This addresses the question of how the mind obtains meaning from sounds.

3.23 *prāṇa samācāre samadarśanam*
Balanced breathing leads to a balanced vision.

Note: Balanced breathing implies a harmony in the body that facilitates concentration.

3.24 *madhye'vara prasavaḥ*
The lower plane arises in the middle (of the phoneme).

Note: The process of obtaining meaning from the phonemes is a dance in which the lower plane thrusts itself up in the middle.

3.25 *mātrāsvapratyaya sandhāne naṣṭasya punarutthānam*
What was destroyed rises again by the joining (*sandhāne*) of perceptions (*svapratyaya*) with the objects (*mātrā*) of experience.

Note: This dance leads to the joining of perceptions with the object.

3.26 *śivatulyo jāyate*
One becomes like Śiva.

Note: At the point of obtaining the meaning, one is like Śiva.

3.27 *śarīravṛttirvratam*
The activity of the body is the vow.
Note: The body is now the medium.

3.28 *kathā japaḥ*
The recitation is the discourse.
Note: The actions serve the ends of consciousness.

3.29 *dānam ātmajñānam*
Self-knowledge is the gift.
Note: One has arrived at self-knowledge.

3.30 *yo'vipastho jñāhetuśca*
He who is established is the means and knowledge.
Note: It is the coming together of means and ends.

3.31 *svaśakti pracayo'sya viśvam*
The universe is the aggregate of his powers.
Note: All things are interconnected.

3.32 *stithilayau*
Maintenance and absorption.
Note: Things go through transformation phases.

3.33 *tat pravṛttāvapyanirāsaḥ samvettṛbhāvāt*
Even when this (maintenance and dissolution) occurs, there is no break (*anirāsaḥ*, in awareness) due to the perceiving subjectivity.

3.34 *sukha duḥkhayorbahirmananam*
The feeling of pleasure and pain is external.
Note: The witness within remains detached.

3.35 *tadvimuktastu kevalī*

The one who is free of that is alone (with consciousness).

Note: The witness is aware of pleasure and pain but does not experience them.

3.36 *mohapratisaṃhatastu karmātmā*

A mass of delusion, the mind is subject to activity.

Note: The activity is going from one thing to another.

3.37 *bheda tiraskāre sargāntara karmatvam*

When separateness is gone, action leads to creation.

3.38 *karaṇaśaktiḥ svato'nubhavāt*

The power to create is from one's own experience.

3.39 *tripadādyanuprāṇanam*

That which precedes the three (states of consciousness) vitalizes them.

3.40 *cittasthitivat śarīra karaṇa bāhyeṣu*

The same stability of mind (permeates) the body, senses, and external world.

Note: At enlightenment, everything is in harmony.

3.41 *abhilāṣādbahirgatiḥ samvāhyasya*

Declaration leads to the extroversion of the inner process.

Note: This is how the Kāraṇa Śarīra operates through a declaration in the mind that then becomes the driver of future action.

3.42 *tadārūḍhapramitestatkśayājjīvasaṅkṣayaḥ*

When established in pure awareness, the process is destroyed and the (empirical) personhood ceases to exist.

3.43 *bhūtakañcukī tadā vimukto bhūyaḥ patisamaḥ paraḥ*
Although cloaked in the elements that are not free, like the Lord, one is supreme.

3.44 *naisargikaḥ prāṇasambandhaḥ*
The link with the vital breath is natural.

3.45 *nāsikāntarmadhya saṃyamāt kimatra savyāpasavya sauṣumneṣu*
Concentrating on the centre within the nose, what use are the left and the right channels or suṣumnā?

3.46 *bhūyaḥ syāt pratimīlanam*
May (the individual) merge (in the Lord) once again.

10

The Age of Avantivarman

Avantivarman, the founder of the Utpala dynasty, ruled Kashmir from 855 to 883 CE, provided peace and prosperity, patronized the arts, and built the Avantisvāmī Temples in Avantipura and other monuments.

The story of his ascension is interesting. After Lalitāditya, his grandson, Jayāpīḍa ruled during 776–807 (we have mentioned him in an earlier chapter). He, in turn, was followed by Jayāpīḍa's son Lalitāpīḍa, who had a concubine named Jayādevī who was the daughter of a spirit-distiller. Lalitāpīḍa ruled for 12 years, and he was followed by his half-brother Saṅgrāmāpīḍa who ruled for 7 years.

The real power was exercised by Jayādevī's brothers Padma, Utpal, Kalyāṇa, Mamma, and Dharma. After Saṅgrāmāpīḍa they placed on the throne Lalitāpīḍa and Jayādevī's son Cippaṭajayāpīḍa who was still a child. His nominal rule lasted for 12 years, 826–838, until his early death.

A power play now developed between the brothers of Jayādevī. Her brother, Utpal, used force to put on the throne a great-grandson of Lalitāditya, named Ajitāpīḍa, who ruled until 850/851. The struggle between the brothers had by now spilled over into a violent contest in which the younger brother Mamma triumphed over Utpal, leading to the deposing of Ajitāpīḍa.

A nominee of Mamma ruled for three years and then Utpal died and his son Sukhavarman challenged his uncle and won, and put Ajitāpīḍa's son, Utpalāpīḍa, on the throne. In two years, Sukhavarman felt bold enough to take the kingship for himself but was killed by a treacherous relative.

At this point, the influential minister Śūra stepped in, deposed Utpalāpīḍa, and placed Sukhavarman's son Avantivarman on the throne. This was the beginning of the new dynasty in 855.

The Utpal Dynasty

Avantivarman was consecrated with fresh water from the mouth of a golden jug, as was the custom. He soon won over the powerful people in the kingdom with his mild disposition, and soon after his consecration he distributed money to the public, winning goodwill.

Avantivarman and his chief minister Śūra develolped a great partnership. They were towards each other both (equally) masters in giving orders, and (equally) servants in receiving them. Thus, they acted as check and balance on each other. The king was grateful, the minister loyal and without vanity. Kalhaṇa had the king reflect thus:

> Lakshmi (Goddess of Fortune) creates violent desires and spoils the (once) high-minded. There is none who was favoured once does not meet misery. Fortune has no affection and has followed no king to the other world. The stores of golden drinking vessels of departed kings no longer belong to them. Why do not kings feel ashamed to eat from plates from which others have eaten before them? Who does not have misgiving when seeing the names of bygone kings on silver bowls that look like skulls? Who can delight in necklaces that have been taken from the backs of dying kings? And who does not feel the heart shrink touching ornaments left behind and marked by the death struggle and

tears of misfortune. Fortune is purified when bestowed on worthy persons.

Avantivarman's reign is devoid of conquests and acquisition of fresh territories. His fame and glory rests primarily on a series of administrative reforms assisted by Śūra. The second person of consequence was the minister Suyya, who was the architect of several works of irrigation and civil works. It was based on these works that Avantivarman established order, stability, peace, and prosperity in Kashmir.

Soon after accession, Avantivarman faced challenges to his authority from his brothers and cousins, but he suppressed all of them with the help of Śūra.

The power of the ḍāmaras, landowners in the country, had been increasing over the years. Under the weak successors of Lalitāditya, they had managed to amass great wealth. Kalhaṇa tells us about a ḍāmara named Dhanva who had become so powerful that he appropriated land belonging to a temple. There was a chance that slowly things will go out of control and so Śūra had Dhanva killed.

Although Avantivarman was a Vaishnava, he built the temple of Śiva Avantīśvara after his accession.

Avantivarman's Reforms

The Mahāpadma Lake (now called Wular) often overflowed flooding rice paddies. During the reign of Lalitāditya, some channels had been made to drain it, but the later Kārkoṭa rulers did not upkeep the channels. Early in the reign of Avantivarman there was extensive flooding causing a famine in which the price of rice shot up to 1,050 dinnaras per Khari.

Avantivarman's reforms and civil works addressed drainage improvement for agriculture. At that time, it was hard to motivate villagers to do the channel cleaning work and remove boulders obstructing the flow of water. Suyya hit upon a clever scheme in which he had boat loads of coins dropped at two villages there were submerged due to the obstruction in the river. People thought he was mad, but soon 'the famine-stricken villagers searched for the money under the rocks, and thus cleared the bed of the river'.

A dam was constructed, and the confluence of Sindhu and Vitastā near Srinagar was properly engineered. Embankments were made to protect the waterways. He built a seven-yojana (42 miles) stone embankment to protect the Vitasta River and dammed the waters of the Mahapadma Lake.

Having reclaimed land from the waters, he founded new villages. The waters were kept out of the new villages by means of circular dykes. The soil of the villages was examined to see how much of water would be needed for irrigation and provisions made for that amount of water.

The *Rājataraṅginī* mentions that the price of rice that was 200 dinnaras in years of abundance dropped to just 36 dinnaras per Khari.

The economic prosperity ushered in by Avantivarman's reforms made it possible for him to establish new towns and temples. The king founded the town of Avantipura and built two magnificent temples in it. These temples were those of Avantisvāmī Vishnu and Śiva Avantisvāmī. Vishnu was worshipped in his Trailokyamohana form, wherein the central face was of Vasudeva, to the right was Nṛsiṃha, to the left was the Varāha and at the back side was the fierce face of Rishi Kapila.

Avantivarman died in 883 CE and his death was followed by another civil war among his descendants. The throne was finally seized by Śaṅkaravarman in 885 CE, who ruled till 902 CE.

Scholars

Śūra brought to Avantivarman's court (sabhā) many brilliant scholars such as Muktākaṇa, Śivasvāmin, Ānandavardhana, and Ratnākara. The poet Kṛtamandāra perhaps had a sense that things were going to change. He exhorted others in the sabhā, 'This is the time to do good, while fortune lasts, for fortune is fleeting. There may be no more time to do good deeds, for misfortune is always imminent.'

Bhaṭṭa Kallaṭa, pupil of Vasugupta, wrote the Spandasarvasva. Perhaps the most notable scholar of his time was Ānandavardhana (c. 820–890), the author of the Dhvanyāloka.

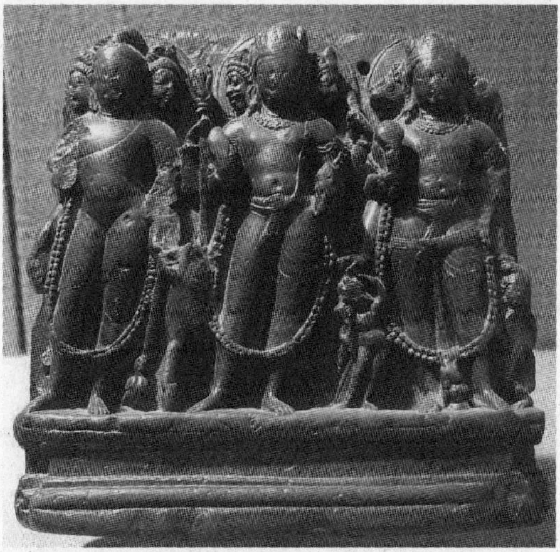

10.1 The triad of Brahmā, Śiva, Vishnu, 8th–9th century (Metropolitan Museum, New York). In this uniquely Kashmiri visualization, all three deities are represented in three-faced form.

The Poet Ratnākara

Ratnākara's Haravijaya[1] is the largest surviving mahākāvya in Sanskrit in 50 cantos and 4351 verses, it is based on the defeat of the demon Andhaka by Śiva. The mahākāvya genre is characterized by ornate and elaborate descriptions of scenery, love, battles and so on in a manner that tests a poet's skill at description. Ratnākara is also the author of a chronicle of the kings of Kashmir, but that is lost.

In the colophons of the Haravijaya's cantos, Ratnākara is referred to as a dependant of Bālabṛhaspati, 'young Bṛhaspati', which is generally assumed to be an epithet of the king Cippaṭajayāpīḍa, pointing to his learning and young age. Although the Haravijaya may have been written under the patronage of Cippaṭajayāpīḍa, Ratnākara's fame was established during Avantivarman's reign.

His contemporaries had a high opinion of him, expressed rather extravagantly thus[2]

> Thinking the four oceans were not enough,
> the creator
> made another ocean,
> the poet Ratnākara. (*Rājaśekhara*)

> Not a hundred lovely golden pots of nectar
> in Dhanvantari's hand,
> no, not a hundred thousand Merus,
> are worth the poem of the excellent poet Ratnākara. (*Kṣemendra*)

Apart from its literary value, the Haravijaya informs us about prevailing intellectual ideas. We will examine the Stotra to Siva in the Harivijaya that is particularly interesting in how it presents the understanding of Śiva as complementing physical reality as the Puruṣa of the Saṅkhya, and that its form is transcendent consciousness that interpenetrates physical reality.[3] Its parallels with the *Śiva Sūtra* are noteworthy.

Summary of the Śiva-Stotra of Ratnākara

1–13. Introduction

13–17. Śiva's omniscience

18–20. Sāṅkhya's Puruṣa is Śiva

21–31. Śiva as the Īśvara of Yoga

32–41. Upaniṣads, sacrifice, Pāñcarātra

42–50. Paradoxes

51–58. Limits to analysis, transcendence, and immanence

59–61. Śiva at the end of the oṃ-sound, reached via suṣumṇā after piercing four maṇḍalas

62–71. Śiva is the source of life, compared to the Sun, source of all knowledge.

72–85. Śiva as one without a beginning; as creator.

86–106. Sāṅkhya cosmology; identification of Puruṣa with Īśvara; other teachings.

107–121. Śaiva Siddhānta. Alphabet goddesses, six paddhatis.

122–123. Identity of the Vedic Dharma with Śiva's innate nature. The Aṣṭamūrti form of Śiva.

124–138. Śiva's Māyā as wish-fulfilling entity; his kañcukas are agents that make the jīva experience prakṛti. The jīva, always bound by kalā, does not perceive anything beyond its range. By bhakti, the malas are washed away. Śiva draws the jīva out of the well of prakṛti.

139–147. Two aspects of kalā: binding, and liberating; obtaining Śiva's grace, and finding Śiva within oneself.

148–157. The working of Śiva's śakti and becoming free from kalā or transformation.

158–166. Śiva fulfilling wishes, his grace, liberation when darkness is torn by Śiva's light of consciousness.

167–182. Reaching Śiva's abode, his cosmic form, burning of the three cities and of Kāmadeva, Kālakūṭa poison on Śiva's neck, Śiva dancing.

183–187. Śiva as the shelter of the world, unfathomable, astonishing.

188–195. Andhaka's story.

196–197. Prayer for grace.

I present a free translation of verses 13–28, of which the first few speak of Śiva's omniscience and his transcendental nature. This is followed by the equivalence with Sāṅkhya's Puruṣa, and Īśvara of Yoga.

Śiva's Omniscience and Transcendence

13. You preside over the lotus seat in the hearts, and you are the sole witness of the activities of the three worlds. Your consciousness transcends all and so there is nothing that is not known to you.
14. Your innate set of four [creation, wrath, auspiciousness, and ascetic self-discipline] starting with knowledge is perfection and nothing can surpass it.
    Note: According to commentators Alaka and Utpala, the four are knowledge, dispassion (vairagya), enjoyment (aiśvaryam), and dharma (morality).
15. You who is the light of unobstructed consciousness, you see furthest, and you know all better than the Āgamas.
    Note: The language of the Āgamas, being (aparā) will obviously be insufficient in communicating the transcendent (parā) experience.
16. Like the sun, who shines on all things, your mind reaches beyond all obstacles, and by it the darkness of delusion ceases.
17. You know all, but now in speaking with you I receive your grace.

Sāṅkhya and Puruṣa

18. Separate from Prakṛti, you are free of modifications (vikṛti); you are not material; thus you are actionless. You are called Puruṣa, the 25th element, known to us by the analysis of 10 topics.

19. You are detached from feelings and existence associated with multiplicity, beyond action, bodiless, without parts, you are a worthy lover of Prakṛti [as Puruṣa is its complement].
20. The analysis of the 10 elements reveals that you abide by the old sect of the Sāṅkhya, and the highest station of yours is without return.
Note: Once one has seen the light in its full intensity, there is no going back to one's previous state.

Yoga and Īśvara

21. According to the wise, you are 'Īśvara', who does not experience the fruits of action, and knows the real nature of everything.
22. The wise know of your faultless Īśvaratvam [lordship], which is free of existence and non-existence and is never diminished by the contact with what is in bondage.
23–24. The praṇava, oṃ, existed before the one arisen from the lotus [Brahmā]; it has five characteristics with 'many faces and feet'. Reaching it, people don't get born again; the praṇava is an expression of you.
Note: Not being born again implies breaking from the karmic chain in one's life.

25–26. O Śarva, you neither perish nor arise, you are the leader of the gods, devouring all that is moving and unmoving. Time, which is perceived by action, by its parts in sequence and by counting, its own characteristic, does not limit you. You are that time, which is without beginning, middle, and end, impelled by your own Māyā.
Note: Ordinary time is related to things and to change, whereas Śiva represents consciousness that transcends time.

27–28. Oh Śaṅkara, by your wish obtained samādhi without reasoning (vitarka), outside the realm of ideas (vicāra), without the experience of happiness and not connected to existence, a man does not experience saṃsāra. By the cultivation of indifference to forms, for they are opposite of that whose form is mental power, one who has self-control rejects even the state of seeing the difference.

Note: This samādhi is beyond viveka-darśana, which is analysis and ideation.

Ānandavardhana

The Dhvanyāloka, or 'Light on Suggestion', articulates the philosophy of dhvani or 'aesthetic suggestion' or 'resonance'. The philosopher Abhinavagupta wrote an important commentary on it, the 'Locana'. According to the American scholar Daniel H.H. Ingalls, 'there is nothing in the Western classical tradition of criticism that corresponds to rasa and nothing that corresponds to dhvani in the grand dimensions in which Ānanda and Abhinava conceived it'.[4]

Very little is known of Ānandavardhana's life excepting that he was the son of Noṇa, and he bore the title Rājānaka. He wrote several other works, both poetry and philosophy, but they are lost and known only in quotations.

The problem of understanding a poem or other literature is that often beneath the surface structure lurks a deeper meaning. In the Western tradition we speak of metaphor and simile as devices that help in communicating deeper experience. Sanskrit has similar devices with 'simile' called *upamā* and 'metaphor' called *utprekṣā* and *rūpaka*.

Kashmiri scholars set out to examine ever more subtle layers of meaning or rasa that do not lend to logical analysis. To the powers of abhidha (name) and lakṣaṇā (definition) of the śabda (word), they said one must add vyañjanā that adds the suggestive hint that takes one to deeper meaning.

Ānandavardhana discusses the relationship between vyañjankatva and guṇavṛtti, 'transfer of denotation' that covers only vācakatva, or direct definition. Guṇavṛtti provides abheda upacāra, which is its common experience, whereas dhvani touches upon a direct perception in one's consciousness. Beyond the ordinary meaning of words known to grammarians, a deeper meaning is accessible to readers who are knowledgeable in poetic and artistic appreciation.

Dhvani is the 'essence' (ātman) of poetry (kāvya). The poem creates a resonant field of emotions. To understand the poetry, the reader or hearer must be on the same 'wavelength' as the writer.

One may speak of vyañjakatva, the power of revelation, from the verbal root vyañj and its derivatives vyakti, and abhivyakti and further to the dhvani. In a literary text, what is vyakta is an artha. There can likewise be narrative or rhetorical meaning—vastudhvani, alaṅkāradhvani—and finally, rasadhvani, which the emotional content of the literary work.

11

Abhinavagupta on the Gītā

We have already spoken about Abhinavagupta (c. 950–1016 CE) in earlier chapters. He was a philosopher, mystic, aesthetician, musicologist, poet, dramatist, logician, and polymath who has strongly influenced Indian culture.

Abhinavagupta speaks of the importance of curiosity, eclectic education, eloquence, and universal knowledge. There is a need to cultivate aesthetic sensitivity by means of literature, drama, painting, and music, but also use logic and grammar for clarity. His guru Kallaṭa speaks of how he was the disciple of everyone (sarvaśiṣya). One had to learn through observation both the outside world and oneself.

Abhinavagupta was born in a family of scholars and mystics whose ancestors migrated from Kannauj with King Lalitāditya Muktāpīḍa. He studied philosophy and art under the guidance of many teachers and gurus. He completed 35 works, the most famous of which is the *Tantrāloka*, an encyclopaedic treatise on the philosophical and practical aspects of Kaula and Trika systems (Kashmir Śaivism). His contribution to aesthetics was in two famous commentaries: Abhinavabhāratī on the *Nāṭya Śāstra* and Locana on the *Dhvanyāloka.*

Abhinavagupta's literary creativity is well equilibrated between the branches of the triad: will (icchā), knowledge (jñāna), action (kriyā), and his works also include devotional songs, philosophical works and works describing yogic practices. As a systematizer, he organized the existing philosophical knowledge into a coherent form.

Abhinavagupta's mother, Vimalā (Vimalakalā) died when he was just two years old. After his wife's death, his father, Narasiṃhgupta, favoured an ascetic lifestyle. His father was devoted to Mahesvara (Śiva), and as the first teacher, instructed him in grammar and other subjects. His brother, Manoratha, and sister, Ambā, were also into spiritual practice. Ambā and her husband Karṇa had a son, Yogeśvaridatta, who was talented in yoga. His relatives included Kṣema, possibly the same as the illustrious disciple Kṣemarāja. His rich and learned friend, Mandra, hosted him in his residence, and Vatasikā, Mandra's aunt, cared for him with exceptional dedication and concern.

His family and friends were filled with spiritual fervour and had taken Abhinavagupta as their spiritual master. This support was essential for the completion of a work of the magnitude of Tantrāloka.

As mentioned earlier in the chapter on Lalitāditya, his most remote known ancestor was called Atrigupta, who was born in Madhyadeśa, and travelled to Kashmir around year 740 CE. Among the most prominent of his teachers, he enumerates four, two of whom were Vāmanātha, who instructed him in dualistic Śaivism, and Bhūtirāja in the dualist/nondualist school. Besides being the teacher of the famous Abhinavagupta, Bhūtirāja was also the father of two eminent scholars.

Lakṣmaṇagupta, a direct disciple of Utpaladeva, in the lineage of Tryambaka, taught him the schools of Shaivite thought: Krama, Trika, and Pratyabhijña, and Śambhunātha taught him the fourth school of Kaula (Ardha-tryambaka). He received Kaula initiation from Śambhunātha's wife, indicating the egalitarianism of the tradition.

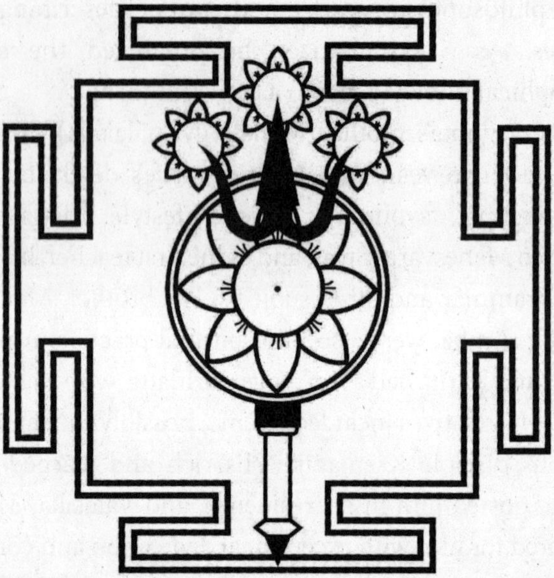

11.1 The yantra of Parama Śiva, showing energies of parā, parā-aparā, and aparā Śakti

Abhinavagupta's disciple Madhurāja made a sketch of his master in the Gurunātha Parāmarśa:[1]

> He sits in a pavilion in a garden of grapes, adorned with crystals and lovely paintings. Perfumed by flower garlands, incense sticks, and oil lamps, it is resounding with music, songs, and dancing with yoginīs and siddhas. In the centre of the pavilion is a golden seat decked with strings of pearls with the canopy stretched over. Here he sits attended by his numerous students, with Kṣemarāja at their head, who are writing down everything he says. Two dūtīs stand at his side holding boxes with betel leaves and jars of water. His eyes are rolling in ecstasy, and the centre of his forehead has three lines made with ashes. He has a rudrākṣa bead hanging from his ear, and his long hair is held by a garland of flowers. His beard is cropped and he has reddish skin. His neck, dark and glistening with musk and sandalwood paste, looks splendid. He wears a silken cloth, white like the rays of the moon, and he sits in the yogic posture known as vīrāsana. His right hand holds a japa-mālā

and his fingers make the mudrā that signifies his knowledge of the highest Śiva. With the tip of the nails of the lotus-like left hand, he is playing the vīṇā that can make nāda.

The Gītārtha

The *Gītārtha-Saṅgraha*, Abhinavagupta's gloss on the Bhagavad Gītā (BG), includes summatory verses called *saṅgraha* at the end of each chapter.[2]

There are some who claim that Advaita Vedānta takes the world to be unreal, whereas Kashmir Śaivism does not. They quote Śaṅkara's verse *brahma satyam jagan-mithyā jīvo-brahmaiva nāparaḥ* (*Brahmajñānāvalīmālā* 20), 'Brahman is real, the world is unreal; and the individual is Brahman, and no other.' But here *mithyā*, or the unreality of the world means its 'impermanence' and not 'illusion' as is sometimes claimed. Thus, the views of Vedānta and Kashmir Śaivism on reality of the world are identical.

As mentioned before, the 25 tattvas of Sāṅkhya mentioned in the BG together with the 11 Rudras (embodiments of the veiling and unveilings of consciousness), which may be associated with corresponding tattvas, equal the 36 tattvas of Kashmir Śaivism.

The one and non-dual absolute consciousness (*brahma-caitanya*), Parama Śiva may be viewed as cosmic consciousness (īśvara-caitanya), individual consciousness (*jīva-caitanya*), and indwelling consciousness (*sākṣī-caitanya*). Parama Śiva manifests himself by a process of descent to jīva by first manifesting Śiva and Śakti tattvas by means of a vibrant creative energy known as *spanda*, projected as *līlā* or divine play.

In this unveiling of consciousness, emerge the Sadāśiva-tattva (*icchā-śakti*, will), Īśvara-tattva (*jñāna-śakti*, knowledge), and Sad-vidyā (*kriyā*–śakti, action).

These unfold into the Pañcakṛtya (five acts) of creation, maintenance, destruction, concealment, and grace. Next comes the Māyā tattva, which manifests into five tattvas known as *kañcukas* that are the limitations or cloaks of *kalā, vidyā, rāga, kāla,* and *niyati* (specific manifestation, limitations of knowledge, attachment to the manifestation, specificity related to time, and necessity). Māyā hides the true nature of things in our minds for it creates a sense of separateness between consciousness and the mind of the limited being (jīva).

The waking world and the dream world, from the point of view of the jīva, are two aspects of the function of the mind. The mind projects itself in perception, both in waking and dream, and the complete cessation of the activity of the mind, due to exhaustion, is deep sleep, *suṣupti.*

With this as background, we now consider the Gītārtha Saṅgraha of Abhinavagupta.

The Gītārtha-Saṅgraha and Brief Notes

vidyāvidyobhayāghātasaṃghaṭṭa vivaśīkṛtah
yuktyā dvayamapi tyaktvā nirviveko bhavenmunih ||1||

Compelled into a troubled union between knowledge and ignorance, the sage, having analyzed and rejected both, enters a state beyond thought.

Note: Vidyā and avidyā are the knowledge of consciousness and materiality, respectively. Since we are also bodies and not just awareness, we constantly go from one to another. The term 'rejection' in the verse really means going away from either one or the other and transcending the notion of apartness.

aho nu cetasaścitrā gatistyāgena yatkila
ārohatyeva viṣayāñchrayaṃstāṃstu parityajet ||2||

Amazing is the movement of the mind. Giving up one [object of senses],
it jumps to others, getting absorbed in (new) objects that are to be given up.

Note: That the mind is not simply a product of the processes in the brain is obvious from the fact that it has this amazing facility to go from on subject to another. Many I's appear and disappear so that none of these could be the real self. In particular, the subject-object relationship necessary for perception is absent in deep sleep when ego consciousness is absent, yet the self does not cease to exist for one is retrospectively aware of having been in that state. The true I, the real self, must therefore transcend each of the conditional I's.

ghanāni dārāndehaṃ ca yo'nyatvenādhigacchati
kiṃ nāma tasya kurvanti krodhādyāścittavibhramāḥ ||3||

If one approaches wealth, wife, or body with a sense of detachment, what harm will be done to the mind by anger and other disturbances?

Note: The mind creates the sense of possessiveness, whereas consciousness leads to the sense of connection with all reality. One who possesses detachment will have equanimity to face life's ups and downs.

vidhatte karma yatkiñcidkṣecchāmātrapūrvakam
tenaiva śubhabhājaḥ syustṛptāḥ karaṇadevatāḥ ||4||

Actions arising from the will inherent in the sense organs
gratify the gods [cognitive centres] and spread auspiciousness.

Note: The Ātman has three characteristics: *ekatva* (oneness), ātmatva (selfhood) and *sāratva* (essentiality) and they are reflected in the jīvātman, who if left alone projects the icchā and kārya śakti of divinity. The yogi can tap into this inherent wisdom and achieve excellence in action (*karmasu kauśalam*).

sarvāṇyevātra bhūtāni samatvenānupasyataḥ
jaḍavadvayavahāro'pi mokṣāyaivāvakalpate ||5||

He who sees all beings with equanimity, even if he is simple-minded in practical affairs, is fit for mokṣa (freedom).

Note: Since the same Ātman dwells in all beings, it should not be difficult to see all in the same light.

bhagavannāmasaṃprāptimātrātsarvamavāpyte
phalitāḥ śālayaḥ samyagvṛṣṭimātre'valokite ||6||

By attaining God's name [absorption in Being] everything is attained, quite as rice plants flower when the rains come.

Note: Attaining of God's name is connection to the unfolding of the world mid-stream and not just being an eddy near the bank that goes nowhere.

sphuṭaṃ bhagavato bhaktirāhitā kalpamañjarī
sādhakecchāsamucitāṃ yenāśāṃ paripūrayet ||7||

The devotion to God is the wish-fulfilling sprout by which hope, in accord with the desires of the sādhaka (seeker), may be fulfilled.

Note: In the devotion to God, the sādhaka channels God's power and, therefore, his hope is the divinity's will. The contents of the three states of Viśva (waking), Taijasa (dreaming), and Prājña (deep sleep) that the *Māṇḍukya Upaniṣad* speaks about are entangled in different ways.

sarvatattvagatvena vijñāte parameśvare
antarbahirna sāvasthā na yasyāṃ bhāsate vibhuḥ ||8||

When the Lord is felt to pervade all tattvas, then [for the yogin] there is no place inside or outside, where Parameśvara is not present.

Note: Consciousness pervades all tattvas and it is for the yogin to attain that discrimination. Since the waking mind is primarily reactive, ordinary experience is incapable of delivering knowledge. For knowledge to emerge there must be a conscious factor other than experience that recognizes experience for what it is.

advaite brahmaṇi parā sarvānugrahaśālinī
śaktirvijṛmbhate tena yatanīyaṃ tadāptaye ||9||

The non-dual, transcendent Śakti who blesses all is expansive and one should strive to attain it.

Note: Śakti is to be found in all aspects of embodied reality. Indeed, whatever we behold is a process or ought to be reducible to one. Therefore, devotion to Śakti deepens understanding.

icchāyāmindriye vāpi yadevāyāti gocaram
haṭhādvilāpayaṃstattatpṛśāntaṃ brahma bhāvayet ||10||

Whatever the object of one's senses and whatever the range of one's desire, one should resolutely dissolve all that and meditate on Brahman, who is the highest peace.

Note: Brahman and Parama Śiva are identical. Whereas the jīvas are present only at one place at a time, Īśvara is present everywhere. Though we cognize objects outside, we don't have power over them.

śuddhāśuddhavimiśrotthasaṃvidaikyavimarśanāt
bhūrbhuvaḥ svastrayaṃ paśyansamatvena samo muniḥ ||11||

Since it is one single consciousness that illumines the three manifestations—pure, impure, or mixed—the steady sage dwells viewing the three worlds—bhū (earth), bhuvaḥ (atmosphere), and svaḥ (heavens)–with equanimity.

Note: An individual reacts to sensory input in accordance with learnt behaviour and, therefore, lives primarily in the tattvas closer to the mahābhūtas. To obtain freedom in action one must have access to the higher tattvas related to the unveiling of consciousness in which the individual is an instrument of prakṛti.

paramānandavaivaśyasañjātāveśasaṃpadaḥ
svayaṃ sarvāsvavasthāsu brahmasattā hyayatrataḥ ||12||

[The yogin] is overcome by (a sense of) supreme happiness, experiencing spontaneously the reality of Brahman in all states.

Note: The path guides the yogi to higher attainments. All intellectual experience is in the waking state of Viśva. This is circumscribed by the established patterns internalized by the mind. Therefore, creativity cannot come from the waking state. It comes from the Taijasa state where the light is not constrained by rules of everyday understanding. We normally see its workings in dreams that we generally remember only hazily, yet it has within it the potential to provide out-of-the-box insight in a dream at night or in a daydream.

pumānprakṛtirityeṣa bhedaḥ saṃmūḍhacetasām
paripūrṇāstu manyate nirmalātmamayaṃ jagat ||13||

The distinction between Puruṣa and Prakṛti is only for the simple-minded. The perfect ones regard the world as pervaded by one pure Ātman.

Note: This is because the two are intertwined in each tattva.

lasadbhaktirasāveśahīnāhaṃkāravibhramaḥ
sthite'pi guṇasaṃmarde guṇātītaṇ samo yatiḥ ||14||

One who is freed from ahaṅkāra (egoism) and delusion under the influence of the nectar of devotion, overcomes the influence of the guṇas, even though living through them.

Note: To think it's the mind that does things becomes a psychological obstacle.

hṛtvā dvaitamahāmohaṃ kṛtvā brahmamayīṃ citim
laukike vyavahāre'pi munirnityaṃ samāviśet ||15||

Abandoning the great delusion of duality, and letting the mind be pervaded by *Brahman*, the sage, even in worldly dealings always remains merged [in highest reality].

Note: The delusion of duality is very hard to overcome. Consciousness is transcendental so it is beyond space and time, whereas material knowledge is about transitory phenomena, and one needs to go beyond this duality.

abodhe svātmabuddhyaiva kāryaṃ naiva vicāryet
kintu śāstroktavidhinā śāstraṃ bodhavivardhanam ||16||

When things are unclear, one must not use one's own mind to decide what to do, but rather choose in accordance with what is in the śāstras forthe śāstras promote understanding.

Note: While the jīva's knowledge cannot be identified with the existence of its objects, Īśvara's knowledge is identical with the existence of everything. While 'sat' and 'cit' unite in the Being of Īśvara, they get separated in the case of the jīva. The jīva's existence is separated from its knowledge, and the knowledge is separated from power, while all these are one in the case of Īśvara.

sa eva kārakāveśaḥ kriyā saivāviśeṣiṇī
tathāpi vijñānavatāṃ mokṣārthe paryavasyati ||17||

He [Śiva] alone becomes various instruments; his Śakti, free of all attributes is action. Therefore, those who possess knowledge perform action to achieve mokṣa [freedom].

Note: Tattvas mapping various states of cognition are divided into three groups: *śuddha* (pure tattvas); *śuddhāśuddha* (pure-impure tattvas); and *aśuddha* (impure tattvas), where pure and impure refer to consciousness and prakṛti, respectively. The pure tattvas describe internally felt aspects of consciousness related to freedom; the pure-impure tattvas describe the limitations of consciousness in the phenomenal world; while the impure tattvas include the universe and living beings that assist in the experience of consciousness.

bhaṅktvā jñānavimohamantharamayīṃ sattvādibhinnāṃ dhiyaṃ
prāpya svātmavibhūtasundaratayā viṣṇūṃ vikalpātigam
yaktiṃcitsvarasodyadindriyanijavyāpāramātrasthiter
helātaḥ kurute tadasya sakalaṃ saṃpadyate śaṅkaram ||18||

Having freed the mind perplexed by qualities of sattva etc., and through the beauty of realization of one's own Ātman having attained to Viṣṇu, who is [existence] beyond thought, action performed effortlessly and playfully reaches to Śaṅkara.

Note: Viṣṇu is existence and Siva is consciousness. The perspective that all is existence is the normal Vaiṣṇava position, whereas Abhinavagupta's position is that existence itself is contained in consciousness and therefore one can see the movement as reaching Śiva or Śaṅkara.

12

Somadeva and the *Kathā-sarit-sāgara*

The *Kathā-sarit-sāgara* is an abridgement of the *Bṛhatkathā*, or 'Great Story' written earlier by Guṇāḍhya. Somadeva wrote the book sometime between 1063 and 1081 CE for the amusement of Sūryamatī, wife of King Ananta of Kashmir, at whose court Somadeva was a poet.[1]

Ananta's coronation came in difficult circumstances. His father had died suddenly after passing the crown to the young prince Harirāja, who died after only 22 days. Now the queen mother Śrilekhā wanted the throne for herself but as she waited for the consecration, the assembly placed the crown on the boy Ananta in 1028.

The boy king got into bad company and his mother Śrilekhā continued to exercise real power until Ananta married princess Sūryamatī. Ananta's profligacy necessitated the pawning of the royal diadem, and eventually queen Sūryamatī intervened using her own wealth and she oversaw the appointment of ministers with ability to stabilize the government. In 1063, she forced Ananta to abdicate in favour of their son, Kalaśa, but it was soon clear that Kalaśa was not yet ready, and it was then arranged that Ananta will continue to rule even though the son held the title. This led to a feud between father and son that went on for nearly 20 years.

Kalaśa freed himself from the effective rule of his father in 1076, causing Ananta to leave the capital along with many loyal courtiers. Kalaśa now laid siege to his father in his new abode. On the verge of being pushed into exile and faced with a wife who even at this stage doted on her son, Ananta in 1081 committed suicide and queen Sūryamatī immolated herself. Kalaśa was king until 1089.

Kṣemendra (c. 990–1070), the Sanskrit polymath also made an abridgement of the *Bṛhatkathā*, called *Bṛhatkathāmañjarī*, a couple of decades before Somadeva's version, but his is only one-third as long.

The stories of *Katha-sarit-sagara* cover a variety of topics.[2] In Book 1, historical events are interwoven with a background of happenings at Kailāsa, the abode of Śiva and Pārvatī, and tales are spun about how their Vidyādharas (aerial creatures) come to be born on earth and what happens to them. These stories are multilayered that touch upon the idea of life as a random game that is nevertheless held together by a higher logic.

These stories are also about grace and camatkāra, which is central to Kashsmir Śaivism. The resolution to our difficulties occurs suddenly when we discover our true nature. The characters in the stories below are famous grammarians, and the intent is also to gently mock them for, as we know, grammarians take their work too seriously. The stories should not be taken as literal history, but rather as the genre that is now called magic realism.

Book 1: Kathāpīṭha

On the Himavat Mountain reside semi-divine beings called Kinnaras, Gandharvas, and Vidyādharas. The northernmost summit of the mountain is Kailāsa, which towers many thousand yojanas in the air. There dwells Śiva, the beloved of Pārvatī, the chief of things animate and inanimate, attended upon by Gaṇas, Vidyādharas, and Siddhas. In the upstanding yellow tufts of Śiva's matted hair, the new moon enjoys the delight of touching the yellow of the eastern mountain in the evening twilight.

Once upon a time Śiva, gratified with praises from Pārvatī, said, 'What can I do to please you?' The daughter of the mountain answered, 'My Lord, tell me a delightful new story.' Śiva said to her, 'What can there be in the world, present, past, or future that you don't know?' But the goddess insisted.

So Śiva began telling her a short story to flatter her, for it recalled her own divine power.

Once upon a time Brahmā and Nārāyaṇa (Vishnu) came to the foot of Himavat to see me. They beheld there a great flame-liṅga. To discover the end of it, one of them went up, and the other down; and when they could not find the end of it, they proceeded to propitiate me by means of austerities. I bade them ask for some boon. Hearing that, Brahmā asked me to become his son; on that account he ceased to be worthy of worship, for he had disgraced himself by his pompous effrontery.

For his boon, Nārāyaṇa wished to become devoted to my service. This is how he became incarnate and was born as mine in your form: 'for you are the same as Nārāyaṇa, the all-powerful within me. Moreover, you were my wife in a former birth.'

Pārvatī asked, 'How could I have been your wife in a former birth?'

Śiva said, 'Long ago, to Prajāpati Dakṣa were born many daughters, of whom you were one. He gave you in marriage to me, and the others to Dharma and the rest of the gods. Once he invited all his sons-in-law to a sacrifice. But I alone was not included and when you asked him why, he said: "Your husband wears a necklace of skulls; how can he be invited to a sacrifice?" And then you in anger abandoned your body.'

'And thereupon in wrath I destroyed that sacrifice of Dakṣa. Then you were born as the daughter to the mountain of snow. When I came to the Himālaya to perform austerities; your father asked you to serve me as his guest. I was won by your severe austerities in this life.'

When Śiva ceased speaking, the goddess, knowing this story already, exclaimed in anger, 'You are a deceiver! You will not tell me a pleasing tale even though I ask you.' Hearing that, Śiva proceeded to placate her and promised to tell her a wonderful new tale. Pārvatī ordered that no one was to enter their room.

Nandi was assigned to guard the door, and Śiva began by saying, 'The gods are supremely blessed, men are ever miserable, the actions of demigods are exceedingly charming. Therefore, I now proceed to relate the history of the Vidyādharas.'

While Śiva was thus speaking to his consort, there arrived a favourite companion of Śiva's, Puṣpadanta, the best of Gaṇas. His entrance was barred by Nandi at the door. Curious to know why even as ardent a servant as he had been forbidden to enter without any apparent reason, Puṣpadanta slipped in using his magic power that made him invisible.

Puṣpadanta thus heard the extraordinary and wonderful adventures of the seven Vidyādharas. Once home, he, in turn, narrated them to his wife Jayā, for who can hide wealth or a secret from women?

Jayā the doorkeeper recited it to her friends in the presence of Pārvatī, for how can women be expected to restrain their speech. And then Pārvatī flew into a passion, and said to her husband, 'You did not tell me any extraordinary tale, for Jayā knows it too.'

Śiva, through his powers, knowing what had transpired and said, 'Puṣpadanta used his magic to come into the room to hear the story. He told it to Jayā, and no one else knows it.'

The goddess summoned Puṣpadanta and cursed him, saying, 'Become a mortal, you disobedient servant.' She cursed also the Gaṇa Mālyavān who was interceding on behalf of Puṣpadanta.

The two, along with Jayā, fell at Pārvatī's feet and entreated her to say when the curse would end, and Pārvatī said, 'A Yaksha named Supratīka, who has been made a Piśācha by the curse of Kubera is residing in the Vindhya Forest under the name of Kāṇabhūti. When you see him, tell him this tale, and Puṣpadanta, you shall be released from this curse. When Mālyavān shall hear this tale from Kāṇabhūti, then Kāṇabhūti shall be released, and you, Mālyavān, when you have published it abroad, shall be free also.'

As soon as Pārvatī finished speaking, the Gaṇas disappeared like flashes of lightning. Then it came to pass that Pārvatī full of pity for the now departed servants asked Śiva, 'My lord, where have those excellent servants whom I cursed, been born?' And the moon-diademed god answered, 'My beloved, Puṣpadanta has been born under the name of Vararuci [Vararuci] in that great city which is called Kauśāmbī. Mál-yaván has been born in the splendid city called Supratiṣṭhita under the name of Guṇāḍhya.'

Book 2

Puṣpadanta, wandering the earth in the form of a man, was known by the names of Vararuci and Kātyāyana. He had attained perfection in the sciences and was serving King Nanda as minister. Wearied, he went once to visit the shrine of Durgā, and that goddess, being pleased with his devotion, told him in a dream to go to the forest of Vindhya to meet Kāṇabhūti. There in a waterless and savage forest, full of tigers and apes, he saw a lofty Nyagrodha tree near which, surrounded by hundreds of Piśāchas, sat Piśācha Kāṇabhūti.

When Kāṇabhūti had seen him and respectfully clasped his feet, Kātyāyana said, 'You, so knowledgeable of the ways of the world, how have you come into this state?'

Kāṇabhūti said, 'I know not of myself, but listen to what I heard from Śiva at Ujjayiní in the cremation ground.' The adoring God was asked by Durgā, 'Whence, my lord, comes your delight in skulls and cremation grounds?'

Śiva said, 'Long ago when all things had been destroyed at the end of a Kalpa, the universe became water. I then clefted my thigh and let fall a drop of blood. That drop falling into the water turned into an egg, from that sprang Puruṣa, and from him arose Prakṛti, brought forth for the purpose of further creation. From their action was born the lord of beings, Prajāpati (Brahmā). For this reason he is called the grandfather of the world.

'Having thus created the world, animate and inanimate, Brahmā became arrogant. Thereupon I cut off his head. Through regret for what I had done, I undertook a difficult vow. Thus, I carry skulls in my hand, and love the places where corpses are burned. Moreover, this world resembling a skull, rests in my hand; for the two skull-shaped halves of the egg I mentioned before are called heaven and earth.'

When Śiva had thus spoken, Pārvatī asked her husband, 'After how long will Puṣpadanta return to us?' Hearing that, Śiva pointed me out to the goddess and said, 'That Piśācha was once a Yaksha, a servant of Kubera, the god of wealth, and he had for a friend a Rākshasa and the lord of wealth perceiving that he associated with that evil one, banished him to the wilds of the Vindhya Mountains. But his brother fell at the feet of the god, and humbly asked when the curse would end. Kubera said, 'After your brother has heard the great tale from Puṣpadanta, who has been born into this world in consequence of a curse, and after he has in turn told it to Mālyavān, who owing to a curse has become a human being, he together with those two Gaṇas shall be released from the effects of the curse.'

When I heard that speech of Śiva, I came here overjoyed, knowing that the calamity of my curse would be terminated by the arrival of Puṣpadanta. When Kāṇabhūti was done telling this story, Vararuci remembered his origin, and exclaimed like one aroused from sleep, 'I am that very Puṣpadanta, hear that tale from me.' Thereupon he narrated the seven great tales in seven hundred thousand verses, and then Kāṇabhūti said to him, 'Through your favour that curse has almost left my body. Therefore, tell me your own history from your birth.' Then Vararuci, to gratify Kāṇabhūti, told his history from his birth at full length.

The Story of Vararuci, His Teacher Varṣa, and His Fellow-Pupils Vyāḍi and Indradatta

'I was born in the city of Kauśāmbí to Somadatta and his wife Vasudattā. While I was still a child my father died. My mother raised me through severe hardship. One day, two Brāhmin travellers came to our house to stop for the night, and while they were there sounds of drum and speeches were heard coming from a far place. Hearing that, my mother began to sob for she was thinking of her husband and said, "This is your father's friend giving a dramatic performance."

'I said, "Let me go and see it, and then I will repeat it all for you." On hearing me speak thus, the Brāhmins were astonished, but my mother said to them, "There is no doubt about the truth of what he says; this boy remembers by heart everything that he has heard once."

'To test me, they recited a Prātiśākhya, and I repeated the whole thing in their presence. Then I went with the two Brāhmins and saw that play, and when I came home, I went through the whole of it in front of my mother. One of the Brāhmins, named Vyāḍi, having confirmed that I can recollect a thing on hearing it once, told with submissive reverence this tale to my mother.

'"Mother, in the city of Vetasa there were two Brāhmin brothers, Devasvāmin and Karambaka, who loved one another very dearly. This Indradatta here is the son of one of them, and I am the son of the other, and my name is Vyāḍi. It came to pass that my father died. Owing to grief for his loss, the father of Indradatta went on the long journey, and then the hearts of our two mothers broke with grief. Being orphans thus, though we had wealth and desiring to acquire learning, we went to the southern region to supplicate the lord Kārtikeya."

'While we were engaged in austerities there, the god gave us the following revelation in a dream: "There is a city called Pāṭaliputra, the capital of king Nanda, and in it there is a brāhmin, named Varṣa, from him you shall learn all knowledge. Go there." We went to that city, and when we made inquiries, people said, "There is a blockhead of a Brāhmin in this town, of the name of Varṣa." Immediately, we went and saw the house of Varṣa in a miserable condition, made a very anthill by mice, dilapidated by the cracking of the walls, untidy, deprived of eaves, looking like the very birthplace of misery.

'Seeing Varṣa plunged in meditation within the house, we approached his wife, who showed us proper hospitality. Her body was emaciated and begrimed, her dress tattered and dirty, she looked like the incarnation of poverty. Bending humbly before her, we told her of our circumstances, and that we had heard in the city the report of her husband's imbecility. She exclaimed, "My children, I am not ashamed to tell you the truth. Listen! I will relate the whole story," and then she proceeded to tell us the tale which follows.

'"There lived in this city an excellent Brāhmin who had two sons, my husband Varṣa, and Upavarṣa. My husband was stupid and poor, and his younger brother was just the opposite, and Upavarṣa appointed his own wife to manage the elder brother's affairs. Then in the course of time, the rainy season came on, and at this time the women have a custom of making a cake of flour mixed with molasses, of an unbecoming and disgusting shape, and giving it to any Brāhmin who is thought to be a blockhead, and all self-respecting people refuse it.

'"This cake was presented by my sister-in-law to my husband, together with a sacrificial fee. He took it, and brought it home with him, and got a severe scolding from me. Then he began to be inwardly consumed with grief at his own stupidity, and went on to worship god Kārtikeya, and the god, pleased with his austerities, bestowed on him the knowledge of all the sciences, and told him, 'When you find a brāhmin who can recollect what he has heard only once, then you may reveal these.' Thereupon my husband returned home delighted and told the whole story to me. From that time forth, he has remained continually muttering prayers and meditating. So please find someone who can remember anything after hearing it once, and bring him here. If you do so, you both will undoubtedly obtain all that you desire."

'When we heard this from the wife of Varṣa, we immediately gave her a hundred gold pieces to relieve her poverty, and then we set out looking for a person with such a memory and now we have found this boy, your son, who can recollect anything after once hearing it. Therefore, give him to us and let us go forth to acquire the thing called knowledge.

'Having heard this speech of Vyāḍi, my mother said with respect, "All this tallies completely. I believe you, for long ago at the birth of this my only son, a distinct voice was heard from heaven that a boy has been born who shall be able to remember what he has heard once; he shall acquire knowledge from Varṣa and shall make the science of grammar famous in the world, and he shall be called Vararuci."

'Consequently, ever since this boy grew up, I have been thinking where that teacher Varṣa might be, and today I am exceedingly gratified at hearing it from you. Therefore, take him with you. What harm can there be in it; he is your brother?' When they heard this speech of my mother's, those two, Vyāḍi and Indradatta, became very happy. Then Vyāḍi quickly gave his own wealth to my mother and desiring that I should be qualified to read the Vedas, he invested me with the sacred thread.

'My mother and I, full of grief and tears at the parting, said goodbye to each other, and the three of us—Vyāḍi. Indradatta, and I—set out rapidly from that city. In course of time, we arrived at the house of the teacher Varṣa.

'The next day as we three sat in front of him on a consecrated spot, Varṣa began to recite the syllable Oṃ. Immediately the Vedas with the six supplementary sciences rushed into his mind, and he began to speak without stopping. I retained what the teacher told us after hearing it once, Vyāḍi after hearing it twice, and Indradatta after hearing it three times.

'Then the brāhmins of the city, hearing these divine sounds, came at once from all quarters to hear this knowledge, and they honoured Varṣa with deep bows. Beholding that wonderful miracle, Upavarṣa and the citizens of Páṭaliputra began to celebrate. King Nanda, of exalted fortune, was delighted, and immediately filled the house of Varṣa with wealth, showing him every mark of respect.

'While dwelling there with Vyāḍi and Indradatta, I gradually attained perfection in all sciences. Once when we went out to witness the festival of Indra, we saw a maiden looking like some weapon of Kāmadeva. Indradatta, on my asking him who that girl might be, replied, "She is the daughter of Upavarṣa, and her name is Upakośā." Meanwhile, Upakośā found out by means of her handmaids who I was, and drawing my soul after her with a loving, tender glance, she with difficulty managed to return to her own house. She had a face like the full moon, eyes like a blue lotus, she had arms graceful like the stalk of a lotus, and a lovely full bosom; she had a neck marked with three lines like a shell, and magnificent coral lips; in short, she was a second Lakshmī.

'My heart was cleft by the stroke of love's arrow, and I could not rest that night through my desire to kiss her *bimba* lips. Having at last with difficulty gone off to sleep, I saw, at the close of night, a celestial woman in white garments who said to me, "Upakośā was your wife in a former birth; she desires no one but you, therefore, my son, you ought not to feel anxious about this matter. I am Sarasvatī that dwells continually in thy frame, I cannot bear to behold your grief.' When she had said this, she disappeared."

'Then I woke up and somewhat encouraged I went slowly and stood under a young mango tree near the house of my beloved; then her confidante came and told me of the ardent and passionate attachment of Upakośā to me. Then I, with my pain doubled, said to her, "How can I obtain Upakośā, unless her natural protectors willingly bestow her upon me? For death is better than dishonour; so if by any means your friend's heart became known to her parents, that might lead to a good end." When she heard this, she went and told all to her friend's mother, who immediately told it to her husband Upavarṣa, he to Varṣa his brother, and Varṣa approved of the match. Then, my marriage having been decided, Vyāḍi brought my mother from Kauśāmbī; so Upakośā was bestowed upon me by her father with all due ceremonies, and I lived happily in Pāṭaliputra with my mother and my wife.

'In course of time, Varṣa got a great number of pupils, and among them there was one rather stupid pupil by name Pāṇini; he, being wearied out with service, was sent away by the preceptor's wife, and being unhappy and longing for learning, he went to the Himālaya to perform austerities. Then he obtained from Śiva a new grammar, which is the source of all learning.

'He came and challenged me to a disputation, and seven days passed away in the debate and on the eighth day he was fairly conquered by me, but immediately afterwards a terrible menacing sound was uttered by Śiva in the firmament. Owing to that, our Aindra grammar exploded in the world, and all of us, being conquered by Pāṇini, were called fools. Accordingly, full of despondency I deposited in the hand of the merchant Hiraṇyadatta my wealth for the maintenance of my house, and after informing Upakośā of it, went fasting to Mount Himālaya to propitiate Śiva with austerities.'

The Story of Upakośā and Her Four Suitors

'Upakośā, on her part, anxious for my success, remained in her own house, bathing every day in the Ganga, strictly observing her vow. One day, when spring had come, she being still beautiful, thin, and slightly pale and charming to the eyes of men, like the streak of the new moon, was seen by the king's domestic purohita while going to bathe in the Ganga, and also by the head magistrate, and by the prince's minister; and immediately they all of them became a target for the arrows of love.

'It so happened that she took a long time bathing that day, and as she was returning in the evening, the prince's minister laid violent hands on her, but she with great presence of mind said to him, "Dear Sir, I desire this as much as you, but I am of respectable family, and my husband is away from home. How can I act thus? Some one might perhaps see us, and then misfortune would befall you as well as me. Therefore, you must come to my house in the first watch of the night of the spring festival when the citizens are all excited."

'When she had said this and pledged herself, he let her go, but as chance would have it, she had not gone many steps further before she was stopped by the king's domestic purohita. She made a similar assignation with him for the second watch of the same night; and so he too was, though with difficulty, induced to let her go; but after she had gone a little further, up comes a third person, the head magistrate, and detains the trembling lady.

'She made a similar assignation with him too for the third watch of the same night, and having by great good fortune to be released, she went home all trembling, and of her own accord told her handmaids the arrangements she had made, reflecting, "Death is better for a woman of good family when her husband is away, than to meet the eyes of people who lust after beauty." Full of these thoughts and feeling sorry for me, the virtuous lady spent that night in fasting, lamenting her own beauty.

'Early, the next morning, she sent a maidservant to the merchant Hiraṇyagupta to ask for some money in order that she might honour the brāhmins. Then that merchant came and said to her in private, "Show me love, and then I will give you what your husband deposited." When she heard that, she reflected that she had no witness to prove the deposit of her husband's wealth, and perceived that the merchant was a villain, and so tortured with sorrow and grief, she made a fourth and last assignation with him for the last watch of the same night and the merchant went away.

'In the meanwhile, she had prepared by her handmaids in a large vat lamp-black mixed with oil and scented with musk and other perfumes, and she made ready four pieces of rag anointed with it, and she caused to be made a large trunk with a fastening outside. On that day of the spring-festival, the prince's minister came in the first watch of the night in gorgeous clothes. When he had entered without being observed, Upakośā said to him, "I will not receive you until you have bathed, so go in and bathe."

'The simpleton agreed and was taken by the handmaids into a secret dark inner apartment. There they took off his under-garments and his jewels and gave him by way of an under-garment a single piece of rag, and they smeared the rascal from head to foot with a thick coating of that lamp-black and oil, pretending it was an unguent. While they continued rubbing it into every limb, the second watch of the night came and the purohita arrived, the handmaids said to the minister, "Here is the king's purohita, a great friend of Vararuci's, so creep into this box." They bundled him into the trunk, just as he was, all naked, and then they fastened it outside with a bolt.

'The priest too was brought inside into the dark room on the pretence of a bath, and was in the same way stripped of his garments and ornaments, and made a fool of by the handmaids by being rubbed with lamp-black and oil, with nothing but the piece of rag on him, until in the third watch the chief magistrate arrived.

'The handmaids immediately terrified the priest with the news of his arrival and pushed him into the trunk like his predecessor. After they had bolted him in, they brought in the magistrate on the pretext of giving him a bath, and so he, like his fellows, with the piece of rag for his only garment, was bamboozled by being continually anointed with lamp-black, until in the last watch of the night the merchant arrived.

'The handmaids made use of his arrival to alarm the magistrate and bundled him also into the trunk and fastened it on the outside. So those three, being shut up inside the box, were like accustoming themselves to live in the hell of blind darkness, dared not speak on account of fear, though they touched one another.

'Upakośā brought a lamp into the room, and making the merchant enter it said to him, "Give me that money which my husband deposited with you." When he heard that, the rascal said, observing that the room was empty, "I told you that I would give you the money your husband deposited with me."

'Upakośā calling the attention of the people in the trunk, said, "Hear, O ye gods this speech of Hiraṇyagupta." When she had said this, she blew out the light, and the merchant, like the others, on the pretext of a bath was anointed by the handmaids for a long time with lamp-black. Then they told him to go, for the darkness was over, and at the close of the night they took him by the neck and pushed him out of the door much against his will.

'He made the best of his way home, with only the piece of rag to cover his nakedness, and since he was smeared with the black dye, the dogs bit him at every step, and thoroughly ashamed of himself, he at last reached his own house; and when he got there he did not dare to look his servants in the face while they were washing off that black dye. The path of vice is indeed a painful one.

'In the morning Upakośā accompanied by her handmaids went, without informing her parents, to the palace of king Nanda, and there she stated to the king that the merchant Hiraṇyagupta was endeavouring to deprive her of money deposited with him by her husband. The king immediately had the merchant summoned, who said, "I have nothing in my keeping belonging to this lady." Upakośā replied, "I have witnesses, my Lord; before he went, my husband put the household gods into a box, and this merchant with his own lips admitted the deposit in their presence. Let the box be brought here and you may ask the gods yourself." Having heard this the king in astonishment ordered the box to be brought.

'That trunk was carried in by many men. Upakośā said, "Relate truly, O gods, what that merchant said and then go to your own houses. If you do not, I will burn you or open the box in court." Hearing that, the men in the box, beside themselves with fear, said, "It is true, the merchant admitted the deposit in our presence."

'The merchant, being utterly confounded, confessed to his guilt. But the king, unable to restrain his curiosity, after asking permission of Upakośā, opened the chest there in court by breaking the fastening, and those three men were dragged out, looking like three lumps of solid darkness, and were with difficulty recognized by the king and his ministers.

'The whole assembly burst out laughing, and the king in his curiosity asked Upakośā, what was the meaning of all this; so the virtuous lady told the whole story. All present in court expressed their commendation of Upakośā's conduct, observing, "The virtuous behaviour of women of good family, who are protected by their own excellent disposition, is incredible."

'All those coveters of their neighbour's wife were deprived of their living and banished from the country. Upakośā was dismissed by the king, who showed his great regard for her by a present of much wealth, and said to her, "Henceforth you are my sister." So she returned home. Varṣa and Upavarṣa when they heard it, congratulated that chaste lady, and there was a smile of admiration on the face of every single person in that city.'

The Return of Vararuci

'Meanwhile, performing a very severe penance on the snowy mountain, I propitiated the god, the husband of Pārvatī, the great giver of all good things. He revealed to me that same treatise of Pāṇini; and in accordance with his wish, I completed it. Then I returned home without feeling the fatigue of the journey and was full of the nectar of the favour of that god who wears on his crest a digit of the moon. I worshipped the feet of my mother and of my spiritual teachers and heard from them the wonderful achievement of Upakośā. Joy and astonishment swelled in my breast, along with natural affection and great respect for my wife.

'Now Varṣa expressed a desire to hear from my lips the new grammar, and thereupon the god Kārtikeya himself revealed it to him. And it came to pass that Vyāḍi and Indradatta asked their preceptor, Varṣa, what fee they should give him. He replied, "Give me ten million of gold pieces."

'The three resolved to go to Nanda who was the only one with this kind of money. Meanwhile, King Nanda had just died and so Indradatta entered the body of the dead king briefly so that the award could be made. Many complications followed after Indradatta's own body was cremated, and so ultimately Nanda lived on with Indradatta's jīvātaman and he was now known as Yogānanda.

'Yogānanda took firm control of the kingdom. After many years, Vyāḍi approached him after giving the present to his teacher, saying, "May your rule, my friend, last long. I take my leave, I must go to perform austerities elsewhere." Hearing that, Yogānanda's voice choking with tears, said to him, "Stop, and enjoy pleasures in my kingdom, do not desert me."

'Vyāḍi answered, "King, life comes to an end in a moment. What wise man, I pray you, drowns himself in these hollow and fleeting enjoyments? Prosperity is like a desert mirage, and it does not turn the head of the wise man." Saying this he went away, having resolved to mortify his flesh with austerities. Yogānanda went to his metropolis Pāṭaliputra for the purpose of enjoyment accompanied by me and surrounded with his whole army.

'So I, having attained prosperity, lived for a long time in that state, waited upon by Upakośā, bearing the burden of the office of prime-minister to the king, enjoying the company of my mother and my preceptors. There the Ganga, propitiated by my austerities, gave me every day much wealth, and Sarasvatī advised me continually on what measures to adopt.'

13

Representation of Divinity

The Kashmiri approach to the world is uniquely positive. It celebrates natural beauty for it considers the objective world to be an embodiment of Śiva. This approach, in both its strands of Śaivism and Vaishnavism, is infused with the worship of the Goddess. The Tantras stress the equivalence of the universe and the body and look for divinity within the person. If the transcendent is represented by Śiva and Vishnu, the ruler of the embodied world is the Goddess as proclaimed in the *Ṛgveda* 10.125 (Devīsūkta).

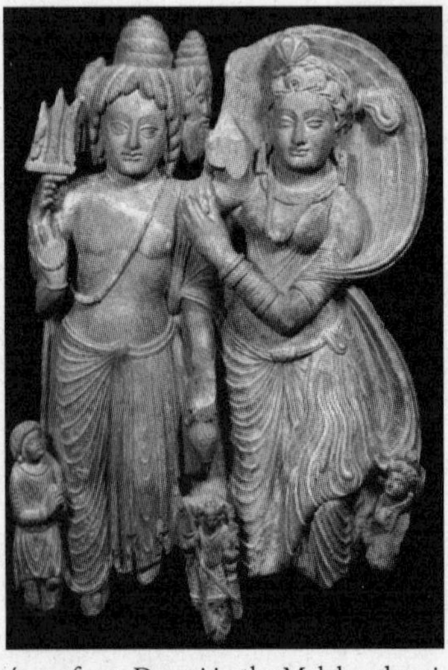

13.1 Umā-Maheśvara from Dargai in the Malakand region in Gandhāra/ Bopearachchi

Many of the rituals of the Vaishnavite Pāñcarātra ontology, which is quite old and mentioned in the *Taittirīya Samhita*, the *Śatapatha Brāhmaṇa*, and the Mahābhārata, are described in the *Viṣṇudharmottara Purāṇa*. The *Nīlamata Purāṇa*[1] names the four emanations of Viṣṇu amongst the deities that the Nāgas worshiped in the remote past in Kashmir. This theology informs that the king was enjoined to build a temple to perform the celebratory rites of victory over his opponents. These rites marked his symbolic union with Vishnu and represented an important milestone in the conceptualization of the role of the king.

Kalhaṇa says that the worship of Śiva in Kashmir dates prior to the Mauryan King Aśoka.[2] The Tantras were enshrined in texts known as the Āgamas, which speak of how to become one with Śiva to transcend oppositions and polarities. The jīvanmukta (the liberated person) experiences the freedom of Śiva in a blissful and unitary vision of the all-pervasiveness of the Absolute.

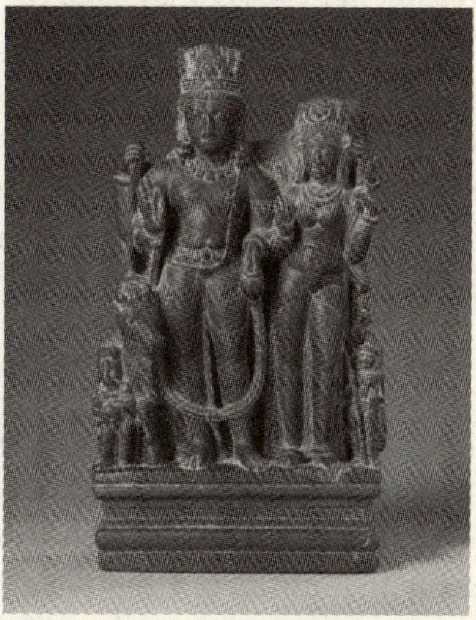

13.2 Śiva and Pārvatī with their sons Kārtikeya and Ganesha and the calf bull Nandi, 9th century (Metropolitan Museum, New York)

Two very interesting ideas in Kashmir Śaivism are that of recognition and of vibration. In the philosophy of recognition, it is proposed that the ultimate experience of enlightenment consists of a profound and irreversible recognition of one's own identity as Śiva. By this recognition the individual transcends the paśu (animal) condition by shaking off the fetters (pāśa) that bind to instincts and the causal chain and becomes the master (pati). The doctrine of Vibration speaks of the importance of experiencing *spanda*, the vibration or pulse of consciousness.[3] Every activity in the universe, as well as sensations, cognitions, and emotion, ebbs and flows are part of the universal rhythm of the singular reality. This rhythm is in the space of consciousness, and the vibrations spread into the multiplicity of becoming. In the unfolding of time, both being and becoming come together. This also opens many subtle practices and rituals for obtaining the understanding of the self of which Śrī Vidyā is the most famous.[4]

In Kashmir Śaivism, activity is ascribed to the ātman, who is not inert, but in possession of the five-fold actions of creation, maintenance, dissolution, occultation, and grace.[5]

Krishna, in Bhagavad Gītā 15.15 speaks of how universal consciousness resides in each sentient being and it is associated with memory (smṛti), knowledge (jñāna), and forgetting (apohana), which means that knowledge emerges on the foundation of memory. In his commentary on the Īśvara-pratyabhijñā-kārikā by Utpaladeva, Abhinavagupta speaks of the Shaivite view as jñāna-smṛti-apohana, implying that jñāna can arise spontaneously and is a consequence of the workings of Śiva who resides within everyone. Intuition is associated with camatkāra, but it is not really that different from the grace (prasāda) in Vaishnavism.

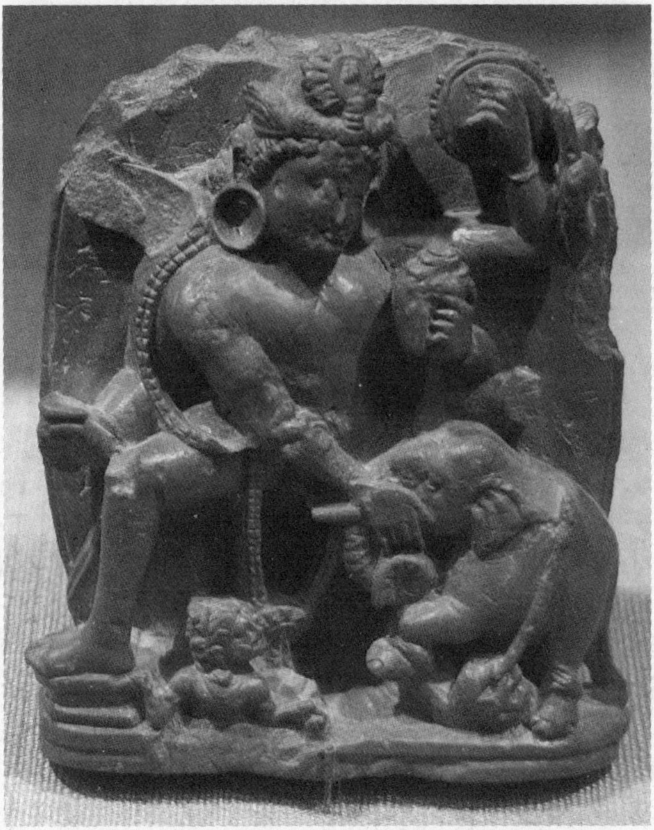

13.3 Vishnu rescuing Gajendra. 8th–9th century (Metropolitan Museum, New York)

The founder of the Kushan Empire was Kujula Kadphises, who was a devotee of Śiva although he also patronized Iranian and Buddhist divinities. In the first century, the Kushan emperor Kanishka chose Kashmir as the venue of a major Buddhist Council. At this meeting the previously uncodified portions of Buddha's discourses and the theoretical portions of the canon were codified. The entire canon (the Tripiṭaka) was inscribed on copper plates and deposited in a stupa. This Council also helped in the recognition and propagation of Kashmiri approach to the representation of divninty.

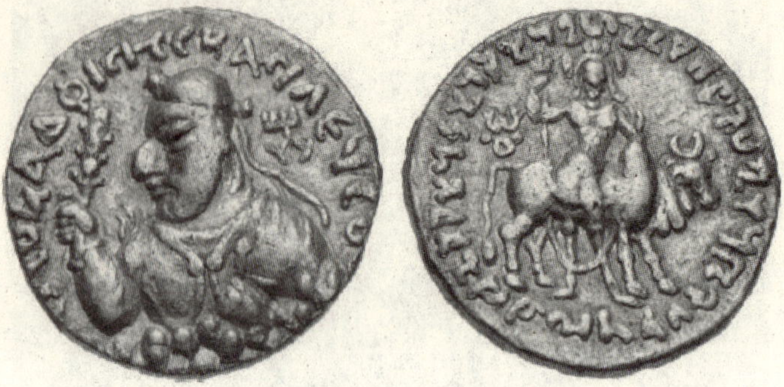

13.4 A coin issued by the Kushan Vima Kadphises (c. 100) showing Śiva with Nandi

Kashmiris were tireless in the spread of these ideas to Central Asia. Attracted by Kashmir's reputation as a great centre of scholarship, many Buddhists came from distant lands to learn Sanskrit and train as translators and teachers. The evolution of the image of Śiva and Vishnu beyond Kashmir is an interesting story on which much new information has emerged in recent years.[6]

According to some Tibetan sources, Padmasambhava (who introduced Tantric Buddhism into Tibet) was from the Kashmiri region, perhaps from Swat. The Tibetan script was invented by Thonmi Sambhota, who was sent to Kashmir during the reign of Duralabhavardhana (7th century) to study with Devatītasiṃha.

The currency of Hinduism in Sogdia (Western Central Asia) is seen in the worship of Brahmā, Indra, Mahādeva (Śiva), Nārāyaṇa, and Vaiśravaṇa (Kubera). It is remarkable that Sogdian Buddhist and Manichaean texts mimic the Vedic trinity and use Hindu symbols. Zurvan (who symbolizes Time from Sanskrit *Śravaṇa)* is depicted in the form of Brahmā, Adbag (Ādibhaga, the first God) is in the form of Indra (Śakra), and Veśparkar (Vāyu) in the form of Śiva (Mahādeva).

Images of Maheśvara have been found in Khotan, Sogdia and China, and the Zoroastrian wind god Vāyu-Vāta took on the iconographic appearance of Śiva.[7] In a depiction on a wall painting from Penjikent in Tajikistan, Śiva is portrayed in tiger skin with sacred thread and trishul. In Japan, Daikokuten is evolved from Śiva.

The representation of divinities with many faces is a unique feature of Hinduism. As comparison, Greek divinities only have one face. The many faces of Hindu divinities stress the cosmic and transformative power of consciousness. The Greek outer religion was Apollonian, and the mystery of consciousness was kept apart in the worship of Dionysus.

Brahmā is shown with four faces and Śiva with five. Vishnu is normally shown with one face for he represents the moral law although in his universal form he has an infinity of faces. In Kashmir, Vaikuṇṭha Vishnu is shown with three faces.

Śiva's dance of creation, preservation, dissolution, concealing grace, and revealing grace occurs at both personal and cosmic levels. In the first three, Śiva is Sadyojāta, Vāmadeva, and Aghora with equivalence with Brahmā, Vishnu and Rudra (Bhairava). The fourth and the fifth are Tatpuruṣa and Īśāna, where the first represents the hidden light within Prakṛti (Goddess) and the second represents the unveiling grace.

The five faces of Śiva are associated in various texts with the five elements, the five senses, the five organs of perception, and the five organs of action.

The first four represent the directions west, north, south, and east respectively, while Īśāna represent ākāśa, space. A four-faced liṅgam is said also to represent the five aspects of Śiva, the fifth aspect is assumed to be emerging from the top of the shaft and denotes the formless Absolute. The sculpted liṅgam has three parts: the Brahma-bhaga, the lowest part of the liṅga which is a square platform; the Vishnu-bhaga, the middle section of the liṅga with a pedestal or pītha, and the Rudra-bhaga, the topmost part of the central shaft with a rounded top.

The iconography of Śiva and his son Kārtikeya (the general of the gods), with five and six faces, in China (most commonly in the Six Dynasties Period) follows formulas that were part of the canon. Given the primacy of Śiva worship in Kashmir, and the fact that there is attested interaction between the two areas during this period, one may speculate that Kashmir was the source.[8]

Svetovid

In the Slavic world, the Vedic Parjanya, which is a name of Indra, is the principal deity; he is also mentioned in the Bhagavad Gītā and the *Nīlamata Purāṇa*. The Slavic divinity Zhibog (Śiva-bhaga) directly invokes Śiva.

Svetovid (Skt. Śvetavid, Knower of Light) is the four-faced highest Slavic divinity.[9] To make sense of the name here, remember that Śiva is also called Prakāśa (light). Svetovid's nickname is Beli (or Byali) Vid (Beli = white, bright, shining) which is quite accurate although the word '*svet*' is sometimes translated as 'sacred' in modern Slavic languages.

Svetovid's white northward head is Svarog (Skt. Svarga), the red westward head is Perun (Skt. Parjanya), the black southward head is Lada (Earth Goddess, Skt. Laḍaha, meaning beautiful, written more compactly as Laḍa), and the green eastward head is Mokosh (Skt. Mokṣa).

It is significant that the Śāradā Māhātmya that was composed in the same centuries when there was great interaction between Kashmir and Central Asia speaks of Śāradā, Kashmir's version of Sarasvatī, as having three colours of Śveta (white), Rakta (red), and Śyāmā (black) corresponding to the three guṇas that constitute all Nature. The name of the goddess is from the word *śāri*, meaning variegated.

The image of Svetovid then represents a natural fusion of the three colours of the Goddess with the fourth that is Light. The mystery of the green colour associated with it comes from the fact that Sanskrit uses the same word *hari* for both green and golden. This double use is from the fact that the plants in the field turn from green to golden when they ripen.

That the names are all identical in Sanskrit and the wrong colour that got associated with Mokṣa in the popular imagination indicates that the synthesis arrived from a Sanskritic land. The visualization with multiple faces with a count that agrees with the three colours for the Goddess and the golden colour for Śiva, who represents freedom in the inner world and the sun in the outer, is consistent with the Indian conception.

Śiva and Vishnu continue to be worshiped all over Asia. To get the background, the 25th chapter of the *Lotus Sūtra* describes Avalokiteśvara as a bodhisattva who embodies the compassion of all Buddhas. But bodhisattvahood itself requires worship of the Self within. The Nīlakaṇṭha Dhāraṇī, a chant popular throughout East Asia, is said to have been recited by Avalokiteśvara in praise of the compassion shown by Harihara (Vishnu and Śiva), especially as Śiva who drank *halāhala* poison at the churning of the ocean to save the world which made his neck blue (*nīlakaṇṭha* in Sanskrit),

> *siddhāya svāhā | mahāsiddhāya svāhā | siddha-yogeśvarāya svāhā | Nīlakaṇṭhāya svāhā | Varāha-mukhāya svāhā | Narasiṃha-mukhāya svāhā | padma-hastāya svāhā | cakra-hastāya svāhā | padma-hastāya svāhā | Nīlakaṇṭha-vyāghrāya svāhā | Mahābali-Śaṅkarāya svāhā ||*

Note that this worship covers both Śiva and Nīlakaṇṭha and Vishnu is invoked as Varāha and Narasiṃha.

In the *Kāraṇḍavyūha Sūtra*, an adaptation of the Ṛgvedic Puruṣa Sūkta that most likely originated in Kashmir in the 4th or 5th century, the sun and moon are said to be born from Avalokiteśvara's eyes, Śiva from the brow, Brahmā from the shoulders, Nārāyaṇa from the heart, and Sarasvatī from the teeth. The mantra *Oṃ maṇi padme hūṃ* about the 'jewel in the lotus' which is the heart of practice in many Asian traditions is to be found here.

Scholars have argued that the intense activity of translation of Sanskrit texts into Chinese lasting over a thousand years was to influence the Chinese language in fundamental ways. This activity introduced Indian philosophical and abstract concepts for which new Chinese words had to be coined. According to the American scholar Victor Mair, this led to the enlargement of the Chinese lexicon by at least 35,000 words.[10]

14

Art and Music

The ancient temple ruins in Kashmir are some of the oldest standing temples in India (7th–9th centuries). The *Viṣṇudharmottara Purāṇa* chapters on the arts give us a peek into the theoretical framework of the creative arts. The third khaṇḍa addresses the origin of image making and the interdependence of arts; it has further material on vocal and instrumental music, dance and dramaturgy, methods and ideals of painting, iconography, and temple construction.

Lalitāditya's Mārtaṇḍa temple is one of the earliest and yet largest stone temples to have been built in Kashmir. The temple is rectangular in plan, consisting of a maṇḍapa and a shrine. Two other shrines flank the maṇḍapa. It is enclosed by a vast courtyard by a peristyle wall with 84 secondary shrines in it. The columns of the peristyle are fluted. Each of the 84 niches originally contained an image of a form of Sūrya. The number 84, as 214, appears to have been derived from the numerical association of 21 with the sun.

Lalitāditya also built an enormous chaitya in the town of Parihāsapura which housed an enormous Buddha.[1] Only the plinth of this huge monument survives, although one of the paintings at Alchi is believed to be its representation. There was also an enormous stupa in Parihāsapura built by Lalitāditya's minister Caṅkuna, which may have even been larger than the chaitya. The Parihāsapura monuments became models for Buddhist architecture from Afghanistan to Japan.[2]

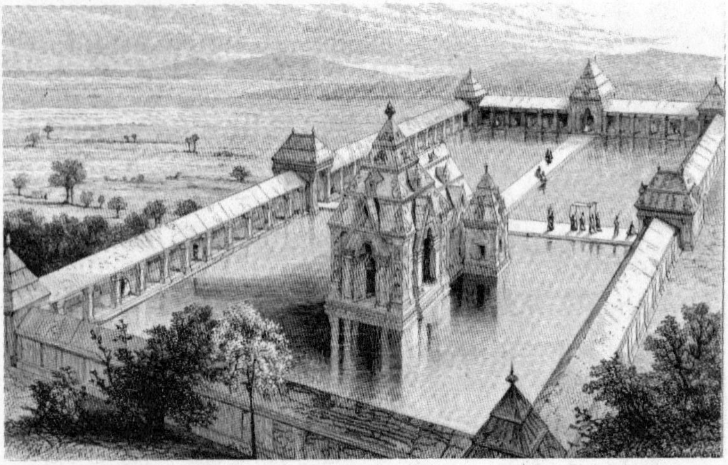

14.1 The restored impression of Mārtaṇḍa in *Letters from India and Kashmir* by J. Duguid, 1870–1873

Paintings were made to decorate books, horoscopes, temples walls, and made on rolls of canvas. The Viṣṇudharmottara speaks of thousand-fold mixture of colours and drawing with decrease (kṣaya) and increase (vṛddhi) for perspective. The life movement of the scene should be captured by the work of the painter, and it should have rhythm and expression. Paintings could be natural (dṛṣṭa, such as landscape) or use classical abstractions (adṛṣṭa).

The earliest surviving examples of these painting come from Gilgit and date from about 8th century. Representing a highly developed style, these paintings must be seen as belonging to a very old tradition. Kashmiri craftsmen were long famed for their work and their hand can be seen in many works of art in Central Asia and Tibet.

Although references to paintings in ancient Kashmiri literature are scattered, and because all records of painting in the Valley were destroyed after the advent of Islam, it is possible to piece together this tradition from the paintings that are preserved in the Buddhist temples of Ladakh and Western Himalayas. We mentioned earlier that Tibetan scholar Rinchen Zangpo claimed to have visited Kashmir thrice to obtain the services of 75 Kashmiri craftsmen, painters, and teachers to build and decorate one 108 temples in Western Tibet. According to the Tibetan scholar Lama Tārānātha (c. 1575–1634), author of a history of Buddhism in India, there existed in the 9th century India four principal school of art: eastern, middle country, Marwar, and the Kashmiri.

The discovery of Gilgit manuscript paintings has deepened our understanding of Kashmiri painting. Discovered in a wooden box in a circular chamber inside a Buddhist stupa by cattle grazers in 1931, the manuscripts[3] are one of the earliest surviving Indian documents. Gilgit was an important city on the Silk Road, along which Buddhism was spread from Bharat to the rest of Asia.

Although usually assigned to the Kashmir school of the 9th century, on stylistic grounds they may date even earlier as their nearest parallels are found in the 8th century stone sculpture of Pandrethan. Painted figures of Bodhisattva Padmapāṇi demonstrate the mingling of the Gandharan and the Gupta Indian conventions with local elements.

The Gilgit manuscripts were produced and dedicated due to the generosity and the religious zeal of Patola Shahis who ruled Gilgit and Baltistan until early 8th century CE. With just a few exceptions, the manuscripts were written on birch bark in Buddhist hybrid Sanskrit in the Gupta Brahmi and post-Gupta Brahmi scripts. The manuscripts deciphered thus far cover a wide range of subjects such as religion, ritual, philosophy, iconometry, monastic discipline, folk tales, medicine, and culinary art.

After Lalitāditya, Kashmiri style appears to have changed somewhat and it endured till the 10th–11th centuries. This phase is the most developed stage of Kashmiri art with its fame spreading into the remote Himalayas.

The 9th century complex of Avantipura built by King Avantivarman is an amalgam of earlier prevalent forms of India and regions beyond. The best example of this style is found in the bronzes dated to the 9th–11th centuries cast by Kashmiri craftsmen for Tibetan patrons. The style of such bronzes presents a remarkable affinity to the wall-paintings dating to 10th–11th centuries decorated in the Buddhist temples of Western Tibet.

The Pandrethan temple as well as the Avantipura complex provide us further examples of the excellence of Kashmiri architecture and art. Kashmiri ivories and metal images are outstanding and are generally considered to be among the best anywhere in the world.

The wall paintings of Mangnang and manuscript painting discovered in Western Tibet are generally accepted to have been created by Kashmiri painters. Stylistically, they are a pictorial translation of contemporary Kashmiri bronzes. In the treatment of costumes and ornaments, the artists have meticulously executed the finest details of diaphanous and embroidered garments and intricate design. These wall paintings present a final stage of the progression of the Kashmiri style that bears elements of resemblance with distant Ajanta.

One of the best sites to see the Kashmiri painting style is in the five temples comprising the dharma-mandala at

Alchi in Ladakh,[4] which escaped destruction that other Ladakhi temples suffered at the hands of a Ladakhi king who embraced Islam. The earliest of these buildings is the Du-Khang where one can see astonishingly well-preserved mandalas that document the Kashmiri Buddhist pantheon as well as the Buddhist representation of the Hindu pantheon.

The creation of the Alchi complex is attributed to the scholar-translator Rinchen Zangpo (958–1055). Also known as Mahaguru, Zangpo built many monasteries in the trans-Himalayan region,[5] and was the principal translator of Sanskrit texts into Tibetan during the second diffusion of Buddhism in Tibet.

The story goes that Zangpo, after spending 17 years in Kashmir, brought with him a group of scholars, craftsmen, and monks. Seventy-five craftsmen and painters of Kashmir introduced the art of wall painting and sculpture of their own style and period into Ladakh and western Tibet. His biographers confirm that he paid three visits to Kashmir to get artists for the project. Tabo Monastery, located in the Tabo village of Spiti Valley, Himachal Pradesh, was also founded by Rinchen Zangpo in 996, and its ancient paintings also appear to be connected to the Kashmiri tradition.

Among the Alchi paintings is the six-armed Green Tārā as Prajñāpāramitā, the personification of wisdom and transcendental knowledge. She has Kashmiri features, she wears a blue blouse, with an ornate head scarf. Perched in her celestial abode, she is surrounded by apsaras, snow lions, elephants, and other mythical creatures. Two of her hands hold blue lotus flowers that represent wisdom and intelligence, and in another hand she holds a scroll, indicating the transcendence of knowledge.

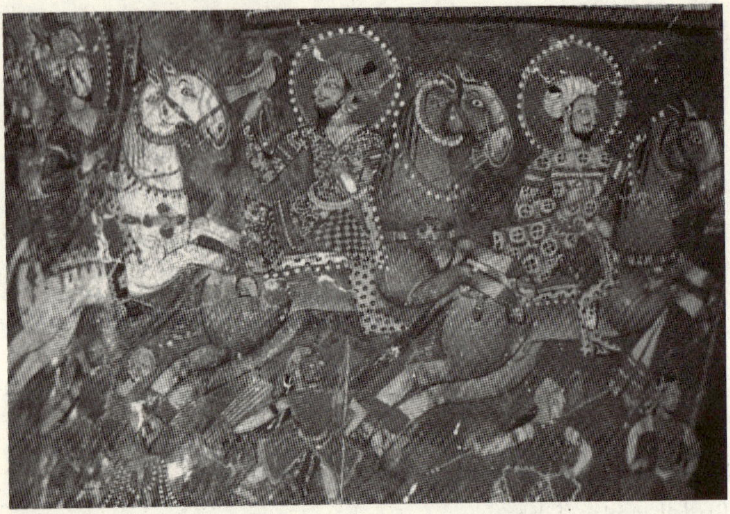

14.2 Soldiers depicted on mural paintings in Alchi Monastery

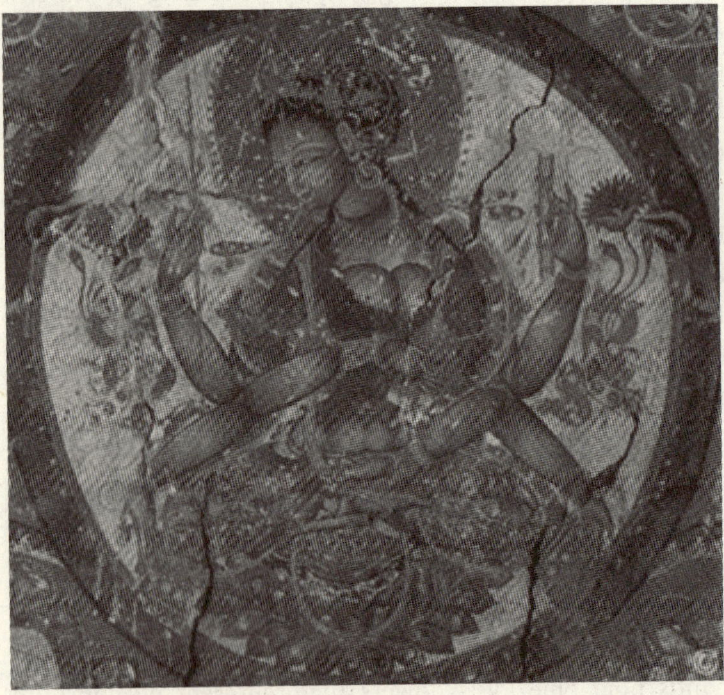

14.3 Goddess Tārā, Alchi

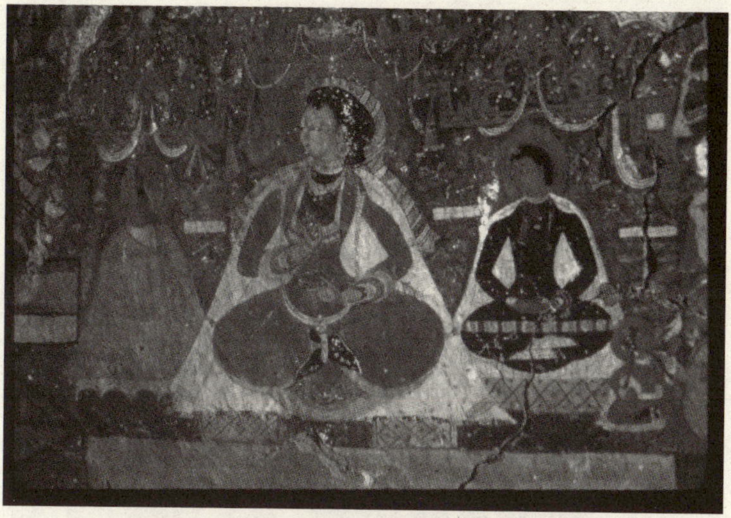

14.4 Woman holding a conch shell with seated monk at the back, Alchi

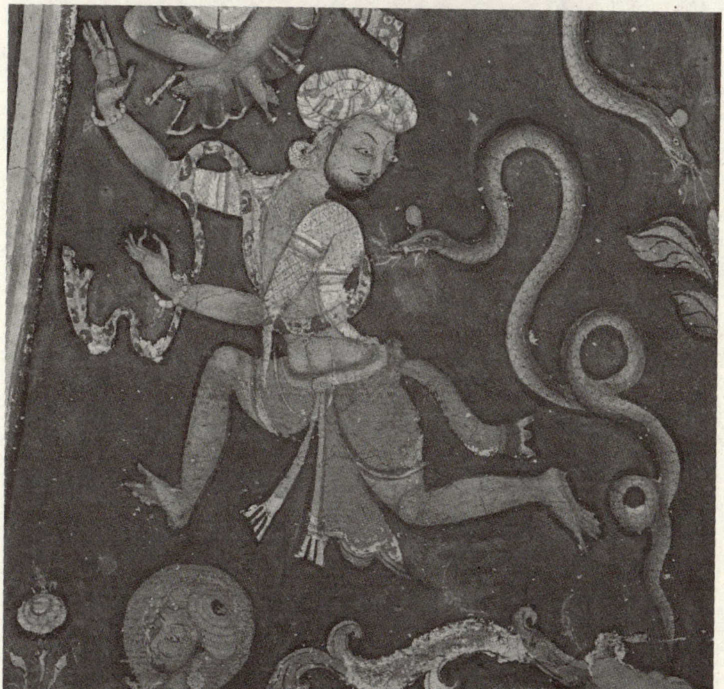

14.5 Man running away from snakes. Alchi

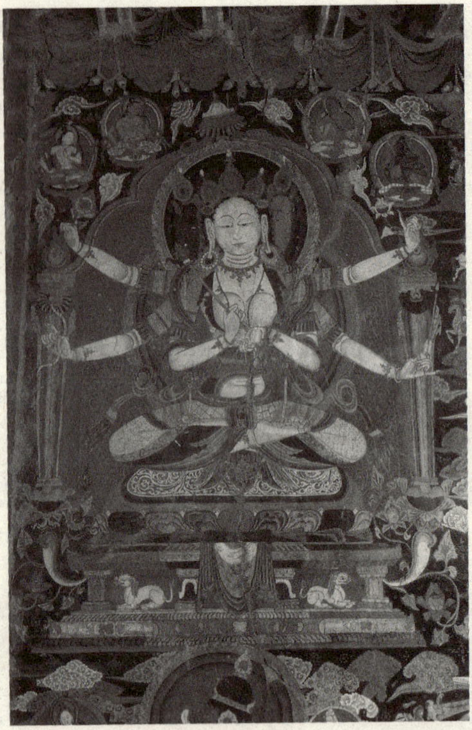

14.6 Sitātapatrā Aparājitā, 'the invincible Goddess with the white parasol', at Tabo

According to the art historian Susan Huntington,[6]

> Kashmir served as a source of imagery and influence for the northern and eastern movements of Buddhist art. The Yunkang caves in China, the wall paintings from several sites in Inner Asia, especially Qizil and Tun-huang, the paintings from the cache at Tun-huang, and some iconographic manuscripts from Japan, for example, should be evaluated with Kashmir in mind as a possible source. A full understanding of the transmission of Buddhist art through Asia is dependent on developing a greater knowledge of Kashmiri art.

The Kashmiri family of Shiv Raina in Kangra in Himachal produced several generations of outstanding painters in the

Pahari tradition. His younger son Nainsukh (1710–1778) has been called one of India's most brilliant and original artists, whose work represents the pinnacle of the miniature style.[7]

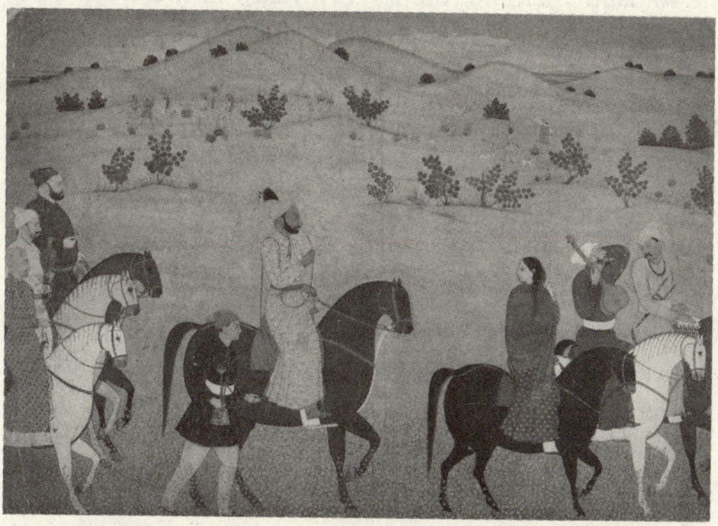

14.7 Mukund Dev of Jasrota out on a ride, ascribed to Nainsukh (Victoria & Albert Museum, London)

The paintings in Kashmiri style are suggestive of the temple dances that prevailed in Kashmir at the time these paintings were made (10th–11th centuries). Indian classical dance in its different forms was born out of the tradition of dancing before the temple deity. Kalhaṇa mentions many kings who were interested in dance and music.

Since modern Bharatanāṭyam conforms to the description of the 108 karaṇas (dances poses) of the *Nāṭya Śāstra*, one can imagine that ancient Kashmiri dance may have been quite like it in some ways, although it could also have been a more flowing form like the modern Kathak.

The *Nāṭya Śāstra*, mentioned in an earlier chapter, introduced the theory of bhāva and rasa, where bhāva means an emotional state or mood, portrayed by the dancer-actor.

According to this theory, one of these permanent sentiments should govern any good work of art.

Later literature describes the eight different moods of the romantic heroine (the *Aṣṭa-Nāyikā*). In these eight, the heroine is: dressed up for union, distressed by separation, having one's husband in subjection, separated by quarrel, enraged with her lover, deceived by her lover, missing her husband who has gone away on business and not returned, and going to meet her lover.

The *Aṣṭa-Nāyikā* have been illustrated in Indian painting, literature, sculpture as well as classical dance. In dance, Rādhā is presented as experiencing each of the eight moods in turn until she is assured by Krishna that he loves her and no one else.

Music and Imagery

The relationship between melodic patterns and visual imagery is part of the music tradition. Many rāgas, musical melodies that evode specific mood and emotion, are named after deities, and this association helps guide the musician in the interpretation. The musician visualizes a rāga to draw a sound-picture of it.

The ancestary of the rāgamala can be traced to the Bṛhaddeśī, which states:[8] 'A rāga is called by the learned that kind of composition which is adorned with musical notes . . . which have the effect of colouring the hearts of men.' Often, the mood, or rāga, is also written as poetry on the margins of the painting. These works thus evocatively express the intersections of painting, poetry, and music in Indian court art.

The unifying subject of a rāgamālā painting is love, which is evoked as a range of specific rasa that has a corresponding musical form. In paintings these are typically the trials and passions of lovers, which are explored in both sound (rāga) and analogous imagery, with a rāga generally understood to denote the male protagonist and a ragini the female. These musical modes are also linked to six seasons—summer, monsoon, autumn, early winter, winter, and spring—and times of the day, dawn, dusk, night, and so on.

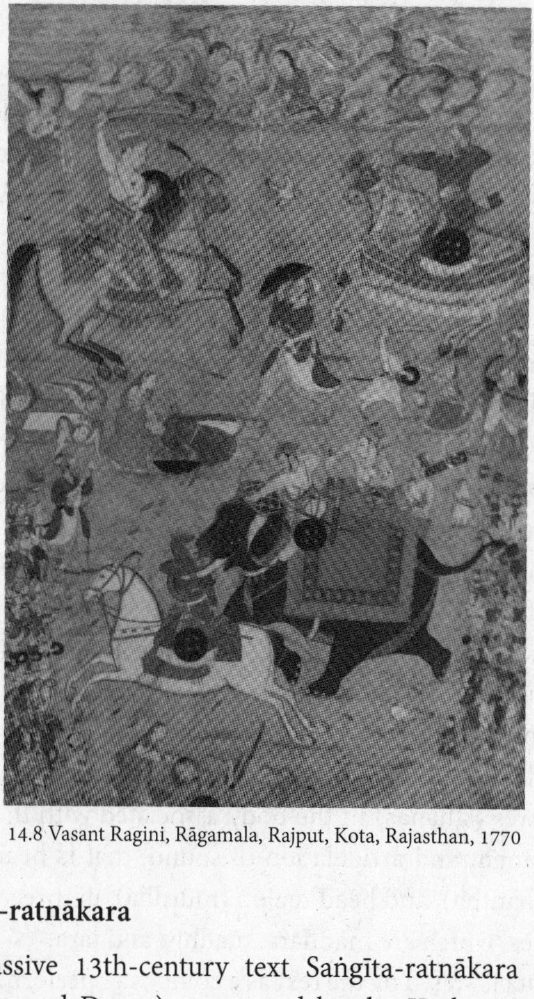

14.8 Vasant Ragini, Rāgamala, Rajput, Kota, Rajasthan, 1770

Saṅgīta-ratnākara

The massive 13th-century text Saṅgīta-ratnākara (Ocean of Music and Dance), composed by the Kashmiri theorist Śārṅgadeva, is one of the most important landmarks in

Indian music history.[9] A large part of this work is devoted to *mārga*, the ancient music that includes the system of jātis and grāma-rāgas.

Both Karnāṭaka saṅgītam and Hindustani music traditions of Indian classical music regard it as a definitive text. The author was a part of the court of King Siṃhana (r. 1200–1247) of the Yādava dynasty whose capital was Devagiri, Maharashtra.

Śārṅgadeva's grandfather, Bhaskara, an Ayurveda physician, moved from Kashmir into the newly founded Yādava capital Devagiri (Maharashtra) in the Deccan region at the invitation of King Bhillanna V (1173–1192). After the death of Bhillanna, his son Jaitrapala or Jaitugi ascended the throne and ruled for a short period. He was succeeded in 1200 by Siṃhana, who was a powerful king and also a patron of the arts, literature, and science. It is during his reign that Śārṅgadeva was appointed in his father's post as the Royal Accountant (Śrī-karaṇa-agraṇī). Along with his work at the King's offices, Śārṅgadeva continued to practice the family profession of Ayurveda.

The Saṅgīta-ratnākara not only provides materials for the study of the ancient music, but also on social practices. In general, he follows the ideas of Abhinavagupta as found in his commentary the Abhinavabharatī.

Given that he was also a doctor, it is not surprising that Śārṅgadeva presents elaborate details of human anatomy, the centres (sthānas) in the body associated with the origin, development and articulation of sound, that is heart (hṛd), throat (kaṇṭha), and head region (mūrdha), in three varieties of pitches, which are mandara, madhya and tāra.

Saṅgīta is stated by the text as a composite performance art consisting of gīta (melodic forms, song), vādya (instrumental music), and nṛtta (dance, movement). It classifies music into two kinds: mārga-saṅgīta and deśi-saṅgīta. Mārga refers to the classical techniques taught by Bharata in Nāṭya Shastra. Deśi Saṅgīta refers to regional improvizations that may not follow the classical rules and structure for the music and performance arts.

The text has seven chapters:

Svarāgatādhyāya (sound system)
Rāgavivekādhyāya (rāga)
Prakīrṇakādhyāya (performing practice)
Prabandhādhyāya (compositions, poetic meter)
Tālādhyāya (tāla)
Vādyādhyāya (musical instruments)
Nartanādhyāya (dance)

According to Śārṅgadeva, song is everywhere, in the cry of a baby, in the beats of nature, in the pulse of life, in every human act of dharma, artha, kāma, and mokṣa. He describes nāda (sound), svara (tone), śruti (microinterval), grāmas (primary scales), mūrcchanās (derivative scales), varṇa (colour or class), jāti (mode), alaṅkāra (embellishment), gīti (singing styles), meters and other basic musical concepts.

The text describes 253 rāgas and presents all classical (mārga) and regional tālas. It summarizes the saṅgīta practice in the Vedic literature, then presents the post-Vedic developments. It includes a description of theatre design, make up and decoration of the artists, performance standards for instrumentalists and singers, as well as methods for improvising on a musical theme.

Śārṅgadeva also describes the ancient and pre-13th century musical instruments of India into four class: chordophones, aerophones, membranophones, and idiophones. He mentions physical description of the instruments, how to play them,

ॐ

शिवाभ्यां नमः

श्री-निःशङ्कशार्ङ्गदेव-प्रणीतः

संगीतरत्नाकरः

चतुरकल्लिनाथ-विरचितया कलानिध्याख्यटीकया सिंहभूपाल-
विरचितया संगीतसुधाकराख्यटीकया च समेतः

प्रथमः स्वरगताध्यायः

तत्रादिमं पदार्थसंग्रहाख्यं प्रकरणम्

ब्रह्मग्रन्थिजमारुतानुगतिना चित्तेन हृत्पङ्कजे
सूरीणामनु रञ्जकः श्रुतिपदं यो ऽयं स्वयं राजते ।
यस्माद् ग्रामविभागवर्णरचनाऽलंकारजातिक्रमो
वन्दे नादतनुं तमुद्धुरजगद्गीतं मुदे शंकरम् ॥ १ ॥

(कलानिधिः)

कर्णालम्बितकम्बलाश्वतरयोर्गीतामृतास्वादना-
दान्दोलीकृतमौलिनिर्जरनदीतारङ्गपाटश्रिया ।

14.9 The title page of the Saṅgīta-ratnākara

and the repertoire that best flows with each. Next is is a relatively brief description of classical and regional dance forms of India, including Kathak. Its dance chapter describes expressive styles, posture, and body language as a form of silent communication of ideas, the rasa theory categorized through nine emotions, and the art of individual movements of a dancer.

The Saṅgīta-ratnākara mentions the presiding deity of each rāga. From the 14th century onwards, they were described in short verses in Sanskrit, for dhyāna, "contemplation", and later depicted in a series of paintings, called the Rāgamālā paintings. Some of the best available works of Rāgamālā are from the 16th and 17th centuries, when the form flourished under royal patronage.

An ancient musical form that has survived in Kashmir is *henzae,* which preserves in a folk-music form *Sāmaveda*'s three tones: uddāta (accented), anuddāta (unaccented), and svarita (circumflex).

15

Epilogue

Sharada Peeth was a great centre of learning in ancient India. The earliest Indian astronomical text called Vedāṅga Jyotiṣa (1300 BCE) gives the ratio of longest day to shortest day of the year as 1.5, which is almost exact for Shāradā Peeth. In most likelihood, Kashmir Smast, halfway between Taxila and Peshawar and a Shaivite monastery, was an extension of this centre of learning.

Thonmi Sambhota (7th century CE) was sent to Kashmir to procure an alphabet for the Tibetan language, and he devised the script based largely on the Shāradā alphabet. The peeth played a key role in the popularization of the Shāradā script in North India, causing the script to be named after it, and Kashmir to acquire the name 'Shāradā Desh'.

Al-Biruni, the scholar who accompanied Mahmud of Ghazni on his many military campaigns into India and wrote the Tārīkh al-Hind, declared Shāradā to be one of the four most significant temples of northwest India, with the other three being that of Sūrya in Multan, Viṣṇu Cakrasvāmin in Thanesar, and Śiva in Somanath.

The persistence of the influence of Shāradā Peeth is clear from the accounts in the Dravida country of the travels of the great sages Śaṅkara and Rāmānuja to Kashmir to debate and consult texts.

Mādhavīya Śaṅkara Digvijayam mentions Śaṅkara's visit to the ancient temple of Śaradā. This is how it is described:[1]

> On earth Jambudvīpa is best, and in Jambudvīpa Bhārata is best, and in Kashmir resides Śaradā, the Goddess of speech. In there is the Throne of Transcendental Knowledge with its four gates that shine in splendour. No one, except the greatest scholar has the right to sit on the seat. The scholars from east, north, and west have attempted to open the gates, but none from the south has tried to open the gate.

So Śaṅkara approaches the south gate and is challenged by numerous scholars who are the best in their fields and after defeating them becomes entitled to sit on the seat.

In the 11th century, Rāmānuja travelled here from Srirangam to consult Bodhāyana's Vṛtti on the *Brahma Sūtras*, which was apparently not available elsewhere in the country. He needed this before writing his own commentary, the Śrī Bhāṣya. The story goes that he and his disciple Kuresan were not permitted to copy the book, but thanks to Kuresan's prodigious memory, this did not prove a hindrance. It is fascinating that Rāmānuja's insistence on the reality of the embodied world is consistent with the Kashmir Śaivism understanding of it.

The 13th century text *Prabhāvakacarita* contains the story of the scholar and polymath Hemacandra (1088–1173) who visited Shāradā Peeth to study eight Sanskrit grammatical texts preserved there. After this, he wrote his Sanskrit grammar, the *Siddha-Hema-Śabdanuśāśana*. Although this account may not be the literal truth, it attests to the fame of Shāradā as centre of learning.

Today, Shāradā Peeth continues to figure in South Indian traditions. At the beginning of formal education, some sects ritually prostrate in the direction of Shāradā Peeth. The Sārasvat communities in Karnataka, who trace their origin to Kashmir, perform a ritual of walking seven steps towards Kashmir during the Yajñopavīta ceremony, and include the Shāradā stotram in their morning prayers.

namaste śārade devī kāśmīrapuravāsini
tvāmahaṃ prārthaye nityaṃ vidyādānaṃ ca dehi me

Salutations to Devi Shāradā, who resides in the abode of Kashmir
To you, O Devi, I always pray; bestow on me the gift of knowledge.

The extraordinary brilliance and creativity of Kashmir in various arts and sciences was sustained for over a thousand years. Its ideas and innovations were influential not only in the ancient world but through its powerful approach to consciousness in the philosophy of Kashmir Śaivism they retain contemporary relevance.

The classic arts and the sciences of Kashmir ended abruptly when Islam became the dominant power in Kashmir in the 14th century. Sculpture, painting, dance, music could no longer be practised. After the political situation became stable, the creative arts were largely confined within a religious context on devotion and its expression through the Kashmiri language as in the poetry of Lalleśvarī.[2] The creative urges at the folk level found expression in the works of the craftsmen of wood and textiles.

However, Kashmiri ideas lived on through the arts that transformed expression in Central and East Asia, and through Tantra and aesthetics that shaped attitudes in Bharat and beyond. Many Kashmiris, notably the musicologist Śārṅgadeva and the poet Bilhaṇa, left for other parts of India. Although Kashmir had sunk to a state of misery, outsiders continued to pay homage to the memory of Kashmir as the land of learning, and Shāradā, the presiding goddess of Kashmir, became synonymous with Sarasvatī.

Notes

Chapter 1: Introduction

1 Abhinavagupta, Tantrāloka 37.46.

2 M.A. Stein, *Kalhaṇa's Rājataraṅginī: A Chronicle of the Kings of Kashmir*, Motilal Banarsidass, 1900.

3 R. Kanjilal and J. Zadoo, *Nīlamatapurāṇam*, Motilal Banarsidass, 1924; Ved Kumari, *The Nīlamata Purāṇa*, J&K Academy of Art, Culture and Languages and Motilal Banarsidass, 1968.

4 S.B. Majumdar and Kashmir Smast, *Proceedings of the Indian History Congress*, vol. 66, 2005–2006.

5 S. Kak, *The Idea of India*, Garuda Prakashan, 2023.

6 B.N. Puri, *Buddhism in Central Asia*, Motilal Banarsidass, 1987; V. Hansen, *The Silk Road: A New History*, Oxford University Press, 2015.

7 J.C. Dutt, *The Rājataraṅginī of Jonarāja*, Delhi: Gian Publishing, 1898.

8 S. Jagchid and P. Hyer, *Mongolia's Culture and Society*, Westview Press, 1979.

9 K.N. Pandit, *Baharistan-i-shahi: A Chronicle of Mediaeval Kashmir*, Gulshan Books, Srinagar, 2013.

10 P.N.K. Bamzai, *Culture and Political History of Kashmir*, vol. 1, M.D. Publications, 1994.

11 S. Kak, *The Astronomical Code of the Ṛgveda* (3rd edition), Delhi, Aditya Prakashan, 2016a.

12 A. Aklujkar, 'Patañjali: A Kashmirian', in Mrinal Kaul and Ashok Aklujkar (eds), *Linguistic Traditions of Kashmir*, D.K. Printworld, 2008.

13 P.V. Sharma, *Caraka-Saṃhitā*, Agniveśa's Treatise Refined and Annotated by Caraka and Redacted by Dṛḍhabala, Chaukhambha Prakashan, 1981–1994.

14 J.E. Mitchiner, *Traditions of the Seven Ṛṣis*, Motilal Banarsidass, 2000; S. Kak, *The Astronomical Code of the Ṛgveda* (3rd edition), Delhi, Aditya Prakashan, 2016a.

Chapter 2: Charaka and Ayurveda

1 P.V. Sharma, *History of Medicine in India*, Indian National Academy of Science, 1992.

2 Sharma, 1981-1994.

3 P.V. Sharma, *History of Medicine in India*, Indian National Academy of Science, 1992.

4 *Caraka Saṃhitā*, Sūtra Sthāna, 30/12.

5 *Caraka Saṃhitā*, Cikitsā Sthāna, 15/21.

6 *Caraka Saṃhitā*, Vimāna Sthāna, 5/7.

7 For reference see S. Kak, *The Idea of India*, Garuda Prakashan, 2023.

8 S. Kak, 'Ayurveda', in Stanley Wolpert (ed.), *Encyclopedia of India*, Charles Scribners & Sons, 2005. The book also presents a general summary of Ayurveda.

Chapter 3: Drama And The Arts

1 M. Ghosh, *The Nāṭyaśāstra*, Calcutta: Asiatic Society of Bengal, 1951. See also A. Rangacharya, *Introduction to Bharata's Nāṭyaśāstra*, Munshiram Manoharlal Publishers, 1998, and S. Nair, *The Natyashastra and the Body in Performance*, McFarland, 2015.

2 G. Cardona, *Pāṇini: His Work and Its Traditions*, Delhi: Motilal Banarsidass, 1997; R.N. Sharma, *Aṣṭādhyāyī of Pāṇini*, New Delhi: Munshiram Manoharlal, 2001.

3 V.S. Agrawala, *India as Known to Pāṇini*, University of Lucknow, 1953.

4 E. Te Nijenhuis, *Indian Music: History and Structure*, Brill Academic, 1974; R. Widdess, *The Ragas of Early Indian Music*, Oxford University Press, 1996; S. Kak, 'Early Indian music', in Jose S. Buenconsejo (ed.), *A Search in Asia for a New Theory of Music*, Center for Ethnomusicology, University of Philippines, 2003; R. Widdess and R. Sanyal, *Dhrupad: Tradition and Performance in Indian Music*, Farnham, 2004.

5 P.D. Mukherji, *The Citrasūtra of the Viṣṇudharmottara Purāṇa*, IGNCA, 2001; Citraśikhaṇḍa, Khaṇḍa III, Adhyāyas 35–43.

6 P. Pal, 'A Painted Book Cover from Ancient Kashmir', *Asian Art*, 2008.

7 P. Pal, *The Arts of Kashmir*, Asia Society, 2007.

8 R.C. Kak, *Ancient Monuments of Kashmir*, London: India Society, 1933; J. Siudmak, 'Early Stone and Terracotta Sculpture', in P. Pal (ed.), *The Art and Architecture of Ancient Kashmir*, Mumbai: Marg, 1989.

9 R.C. Kak, *Ancient Monuments of Kashmir*, India Society, London, 1933; P. Pal, *Bronzes of Kashmir*, Hacker, 1978; Huntington, 2016

10 S. Kramrisch, *The Vishnudharmottara*, Calcutta University Press, 1928.

Chapter 4: The *Panchatantra*

1 M.R. Kale, *Pañcatantra of Viṣṇuśarman*, Motilal Banarsidass, 1986.

2 A.W. Ryder, *The Panchatantra*, Bombay: Jaico Publishing House, 1925.

3 I.K. Falconer, *Kalilah and Dimnah or the Fables of Bidpai*, Philo Press, 1970.

4 I have used the version of the stories as given in the *Kathā-sarit-sāgara*: C.H. Tawney, *The Kathā-sarit-sāgara Or Ocean of the Streams of Story* by Somadeva Bhatta, Calcutta: Baptist Mission Press, 1880.

Chapter 5: Patañjali, Sage of Grammar and Yoga

1 For a fictionalization of the lives of these grammarians, see C.H. Tawney, *The Kathā-sarit-sāgara Or Ocean of the Streams of Story* by Somadeva Bhatta, Calcutta: Baptist Mission Press, 1880, and Chapter 12 of the book.

2 A. Aklujkar, 'Patañjali: A Kashmirian', in Mrinal Kaul and Ashok Aklujkar (eds), *Linguistic Traditions of Kashmir*, D.K. Printworld, 2008.

3 Ved Kumari, *The Nīlamata Purāṇa*, J&K Academy of Art, Culture and Languages and Motilal Banarsidass, 1968, 651.

4 S. Kak, *Mind and Self*, Mt. Meru, 2016b.

Chapter 6: Kumārajīva and the Middle Way

1 S. Kak, *Saka Verbs and Sanskrit*, Academia, 2022a; S. Kak, *Kuchean Language and Sanskrit*, Academia, 2022b.

2 Xuanzang, *Record of the Western Regions*, Translated by Samuel Beal, 1884; M. Chandra, *Trade and Trade Routes in Ancient India*, Abhinav Publications, 1977; V. Hansen, *The Silk Road: A New History*, Oxford University Press, 2015.

3 H. Nakamura, *Indian Buddhism*, Motilal Banarsidass, 1980.

4 R.H. Robinson, *Early Mādhyamika in China and India*, Madison: University of Wisconsin Press, 1967; B.N. Puri, *Buddhism in Central Asia*, Motilal Banarsidass, 1987.

Chapter 7: Cosmology and Consciousness: The *Yoga Vāsiṣṭha*

1 S. Venkatesananda, *Vasiṣṭha's Yoga*, State University of New York Press, 1993.

2 K.N. Aiyer, *Laghu Yoga Vasistha*, Theosophical Publishing House, 1975.

3 S. Sureshananda (tr.), *Yoga Vāsiṣṭha Sāra*, Ramana Ashram, 1973.

4 The preceding texts have been used for the abridgements.

Chapter 8: Lalitāditya's Military Campaigns

1 For example, H. Goetz, 'The Conquest of Northern and Western India by Lalitāditya-Muktāpīḍa of Kashmir', in

Hermann Goetz, *Studies in the History and Art of Kashmir and the Indian Himalaya*, Wiesbaden: Otto Harrassowitz, 1969; A. Wink, *Al-Hind: The Making of the Indo-Islamic World*, Brill, 2002.

2 C. Beckwith, *The Tibetan Empire in Central Asia*, Princeton, 1987.

3 Goetz, 1969.

Chapter 9: Vasugupta and the *Śiva Sutra*

1 J. Singh, *Śiva Sutras*, Motilal Banarsidass, 1979; S. Lakshmanjoo, *Kashmir Shaivism: The Secret Supreme*, 1st Books Library, 2003.

2 J. Singh, *Spanda-Kārikas*, Motilal Banarsidass, 1980; M. Dyczkowski, *The Doctrine of Vibration*, SUNY Press, 1987.

3 S. Kak, 'The Great Goddess Lalitā and the Śrī Cakra', *Brahmavidyā: The Adyar Library Bulletin*, 72–73, 155–172, 2008–2009.

Chapter 10: The Age of Avantivarman

1 D. Smith, *Ratnākara's Haravijaya*, Oxford University Press, 1985.

2 D. Smith, *Ratnākara's Haravijaya*, Oxford University Press, 1985.

3 P. Pasedach, *Bhagavatstutivarṇana or the Description of the Praise of the Divine*, A Critical Edition of Text and Commentaries, and Annotated Translation of the Sixth Canto of Ratnākara's Haravijaya, University of Hamburg, 2017.

4 D.H.H. Ingalls, *The Dhvanyaloka of Anandavardhana with the Locana of Abhinavagupta*, Harvard University Press, 1990.

Chapter 11: Abhinavagupta on the Bhagavad Gita

1 P.N. Pushp, *Gurunātha Parāmarśa of Madhurāja*, Research and Publication Department, J&K Government, 1960.

2 A. Sharma, *Abhinavagupta Gitārtha Saṅgraha*, E.J. Brill, 1983.

Chapter 12: Somadeva and Stories from the *Kathā-sarit-sāgara*

1 *Rājataraṅginī*, Book 7.
2 C.H. Tawney, *The Kathā-sarit-sāgara Or Ocean of the Streams of Story* by Somadeva Bhatta, Calcutta: Baptist Mission Press, 1880.

Chapter 13: Representations of Divinity

1 Ved Kumari, *The Nīlamata Purāṇa*, J&K Academy of Art, Culture and Languages and Motilal Banarsidass, 1968.
2 *Rājataraṅginī*, Book 1.
3 M. Dyczkowski, *The Doctrine of Vibration*, SUNY Press, 1987.
4 S. Kak, 'The Great Goddess Lalitā and the Śrī Cakra', *Brahmavidyā: The Adyar Library Bulletin*, 72–73, 155–172, 2008–2009.
5 Lakshmanjoo, 2015.
6 R. Gallo, *The Image of Maheśvara*, London: SOAS, 2013; Luczantis, 2014; O. Bopearachchi, *Emergence of Viṣṇu and Śiva Images in India*, San Francisco, Asian Art Museum, 2016.
7 S. Kak, *The Idea of India*, Garuda Prakashan, 2023.
8 S.L. Huntington, *The Art of Ancient India*, Motilal Banarsidass, 2016.
9 S. Kak, *The Idea of India*, Garuda Prakashan, 2023.
10 V. Mair, 'Language and Script and Buddhist Literature', in Victor H. Mair (ed.), *The Columbia History of Chinese Literature*, Columbia University Press, 2001.

Chapter 14: Art and Music

1 R.C. Kak, *Ancient Monuments of Kashmir*, India Society, London, 1933.
2 S.L. Huntington, *The Art of Ancient India*, Motilal Banarsidass, 2016.
3 N. Dutt, *Gilgit Manuscripts*, Srinagar, 1939–1943.
4 C. Luczanits, 'From Kashmir to Western Tibet: The Many Faces of a Regional Style', in Rob Linrothe (ed.), *Collecting*

Paradise: Buddhist Art of Kashmir and Its Legacies, Rubin Museum of Art, Northwestern University, 2014; Y. Chandra, 'The Religious Iconography and Stylistic Analysis of the Alchi Group of Monuments', Sahapedia, 2017.

5 C. Luczanits, 'From Kashmir to Western Tibet: The Many Faces of a Regional Style', in Rob Linrothe (ed.), *Collecting Paradise: Buddhist Art of Kashmir and Its Legacies*, Rubin Museum of Art, Northwestern University, 2014.

6 S.L. Huntington, *The Art of Ancient India*, Motilal Banarsidass, 2016.

7 B.N. Goswamy and Eberhard Fischer, 'Nainsukh of Guler', in Milo C. Beach, Eberhard Fischer and B.N. Goswamy (eds), *Masters of Indian Painting*, Zürich: Artibus Asiae Publishers, 2011.

8 E. Te Nijenhuis, *Indian Music: History and Structure*, Brill Academic, 1974

9 K. Vatsyayan, *Aesthetic Theories and Forms in Indian Tradition*, Munshiram Manoharlal, 2008.

Chapter 15: Epilogue

1 Mādhavācārya, K.R. Venkataraman and K.V. Subbaratnam, MādhavīyaŚrīmacchaṅkaradigvijayaḥ,Śrīvāṇīvilāsamudraṇālaya, 1972.

2 J. Kak, *Mystical Verses of Lalla*, Motilal Banarsidass, 2007.

References

Agrawala, V.S. *India as Known to Pāṇini*. University of Lucknow, 1953.

Aiyer, K.N. *Laghu Yoga Vasistha*. Theosophical Publishing House, 1975.

Aklujkar, A. 'Patañjali: A Kashmirian'. In Mrinal Kaul and Ashok Aklujkar (eds), *Linguistic Traditions of Kashmir*. D.K. Printworld, 2008.

Bamzai, P.N.K. *Culture and Political History of Kashmir*, vol. 1. M D Publications, 1994.

Beckwith, C. *The Tibetan empire in Central Asia*. Princeton, 1987.

Bopearachchi, O. *Emergence of Viṣṇu and Śiva Images in India*. San Fransisco: Asian Art Museum, 2016.

Cardona, G. *Pāṇini: His Work and Its Traditions*. Delhi: Motilal Banarsidass, 1997.

Chandra, M. *Trade and Trade Routes in Ancient India*. Abhinav Publications, 1977.

Chandra, Y. 'The Religious Iconography and Stylistic Analysis of the Alchi Group of Monuments'. *Sahapedia*, 2017.

Dutt, J.C. *The Rājataraṅginī of Jonarāja*. Delhi: Gian Publishing, 1898.

Dutt, N. *Gilgit Manuscripts*. Srinagar, 1939–1943.

Dyczkowski, M. *The Doctrine of Vibration*. SUNY Press, 1987.

Falconer, I.K. *Kalilah and Dimnah or The Fables of Bidpai*. Philo Press, 1970.

Gallo, R. *The Image of Maheśvara*. London: SOAS, 2013.

Ghosh, M. *The Nāṭyaśāstra*. Calcutta: Asiatic Society of Bengal, 1951.

Goetz, H. 'The Conquest of Northern and Western India by Lalitāditya-Muktāpīḍa of Kashmir'. In Hermann Goetz (ed.), *Studies in the History and Art of Kashmir and the Indian Himalaya*. Wiesbaden: Otto Harrassowitz, 1969.

Goswamy, B.N. and E. Fischer, 'Nainsukh of Guler'. In Milo C. Beach, Eberhard Fischer and B.N. Goswamy (eds), *Masters of Indian Painting*. Zürich: Artibus Asiae Publishers, 2011.

Hansen, V. *The Silk Road: A New History*. Oxford University Press, 2015.

Huntington, S.L. *The Art of Ancient India*. Motilal Banarsidass, 2016.

Ingalls, D.H.H. *The Dhvanyaloka of Anandavardhana with the Locana of Abhinavagupta*. Harvard University Press, 1990.

Jagchid, S., and P. Hyer. *Mongolia's Culture and Society*. Westview Press, 1979.

Jettmar, K. 'The Paṭolas, Their Governors and Their Successors'. In *Antiquities of Northern Pakistan*, vol. 2. Mainz: Verlag Philipp von Zabern, 1993.

Kak, J. *Mystical Verses of Lalla*. Motilal Banarsidass, 2007.

Kak, R.C. *Ancient Monuments of Kashmir*. London: India Society, 1933.

Kak, S. 'Early Indian Music'. In Jose S. Buenconsejo (ed.), *A Search in Asia for a New Theory of Music*. Center for Ethnomusicology, Univ of Philippines, 2003.

———. 'Ayurveda'. In Stanley Wolpert (ed.), *Encyclopedia of India*. Charles Scribners & Sons, 2005.

———. 'The Great Goddess Lalitā and the Śrī Cakra'. *Brahmavidyā: The Adyar Library Bulletin*, 72–73, 155–172, 2008–2009.

———. *The Astronomical Code of the Ṛgveda* (3rd edition). Delhi: Aditya Prakashan, 2016a.

———. *Mind and Self*. Mt. Meru, 2016b.

———. *Saka Verbs and Sanskrit*. Academia, 2022a.

———. *Kuchean Language and Sanskrit*. Academia, 2022b.

———. *The Idea of India*. Garuda Prakashan, 2023.

Kale, M.R. *Pañcatantra of Viṣṇuśarman*. Motilal Banarsidass, 1986.

Kanjilal, R., and J. Zadoo, *Nīlamatapurāṇam*. Motilal Banarsidass, 1924.

Kramrisch, S. *The Vishnudharmottara*. Calcutta University Press, 1928.

Kumari, Ved. *The Nīlamata Purāṇa*. J&K Academy of Art, Culture and Languages & Motilal Banarsidass, 1968.

Lakshmanjoo, S. *Kashmir Shaivism: The Secret Supreme*. 1st Books Library, 2003.

Luczanits, C. 'From Kashmir to Western Tibet: The Many Faces of a Regional Style'. In Rob Linrothe (ed.), *Collecting Paradise. Buddhist Art of Kashmir and Its Legacies*. Rubin Museum of Art, Northwestern University, 2014.

Mādhavācārya, K.R. Venkataraman and K.V. Subbaratnam. *Mādhavīya Śrīmacchaṅkaradigvijayaḥ*. Śrīvāṇīvilāsamudraṇālaya, 1972.

Mair, V. 'Language and Script and Buddhist Literature'. In Victor H. Mair (ed.), *The Columbia History of Chinese Literature*. Columbia University Press, 2001.

Majumdar, S.B. 'Kashmir Smast'. *Proceedings of the Indian History Congress*, vol. 66, 2005–2006.

Mitchiner, J.E. *Traditions of the Seven Ṛṣis*. Motilal Banarsidass, 2000.

Mukherji, P.D. *The Citrasūtra of the Viṣṇudharmottara Purāṇa*. IGNCA, 2001.

Nair, S. *The Natyashastra and the Body in Performance*. McFarland, 2015.

Nakamura, H. *Indian Buddhism*. Motilal Banarsidass, 1980.

Nijenhuis, E. Te. *Indian Music: History and Structure*. Brill Academic, 1974.

Pal, P. *Bronzes of Kashmir*. Hacker, 1978.

———. *The Arts of Kashmir*. Asia Society, 2007.

———. A Painted Book Cover from Ancient Kashmir. *Asian Art*, 2008.

Pandit, K.N. *Baharistan-i-shahi: A Chronicle of Mediaeval Kashmir*. Srinagar: Gulshan Books, 2013.

Pasedach, P. *Bhagavatstutivarṇana or the Description of the Praise of the Divine: A Critical Edition of Text and Commentaries, and Annotated Translation of the Sixth Canto of Ratnākara's Haravijaya*. University of Hamburg, 2017.

Puri, B.N. *Buddhism in Central Asia*. Motilal Banarsidass, 1987.

Pushp, P.N. *Gurunātha Parāmarśa of Madhurāja*. Research and Publication Department, J&K Government, 1960.

Rangacharya, A. *Introduction to Bharata's Nāṭyaśāstra*. Munshiram Manoharlal Publishers, 1998.

Robinson, R.H. *Early Mādhyamika in China and India*. Madison: University of Wisconsin Press, 1967.

Ryder, A.W. *The Panchatantra*. Bombay: Jaico Publishing House, 1925, 1949.

Sharma, A. *Abhinavagupta Gitārtha Saṅgraha*. E.J. Brill, 1983.

Sharma, P.V. *Caraka-Saṃhitā: Agniveśa's Treatise Refined and Annotated by Caraka and Redacted by Dṛḍhabala*. Chaukhambha Prakashan, 1981–1994.

———. *History of Medicine in India*. Indian National Academy of Science, 1992.

Sharma, R. N. *Aṣṭādhyāyī of Pāṇini*. New Delhi: Munshiram Manoharlal, 2001.

Singh, J. *Śiva Sutras*. Motilal Banarsidass, 1979.

———. *Spanda-Kārikas*. Motilal Banarsidass, 1980.

———. *Pratyābhijñahṛdayam*. Motilal Banarsidass, 2008.

Siudmak, J. 'Early Stone and Terracotta Sculpture'. In P. Pal (ed.), *The Art and Architecture of Ancient Kashmir*. Mumbai: Marg, 1989.

Smith, D. *Ratnākara's Haravijaya*. Oxford University Press, 1985.

Stein, M.A. *Kalhaṇa's Rājataraṅginī: A Chronicle of the Kings of Kashmir*. Motilal Banarsidass, 1900.

Sureshananda, S. (tr.), *Yoga Vāsiṣṭha Sāra*. Ramana Ashram, 1973.

Tawney, C. H. *The Kathā-sarit-sāgara or Ocean of the Streams of Story* by Somadeva Bhatta. Calcutta: Baptist Mission Press, 1880.

Vatsyayan, K. *Aesthetic Theories and Forms in Indian Tradition.* Munshiram Manoharlal, 2008.

Venkatesananda, S. *Vasiṣṭha's Yoga.* State University of New York Press, 1993.

Widdess, R. *The Ragas of Early Indian Music.* Oxford University Press, 1996.

Widdess, R., and R. Sanyal, *Dhrupad. Tradition and Performance in Indian Music.* Farnham, 2004.

Wink, A. *Al-Hind: The Making of the Indo-Islamic World.* Brill, 2002.

Xuanzang, *Record of the Western Regions.* Translated by Samuel Beal, 1884.

About the Author

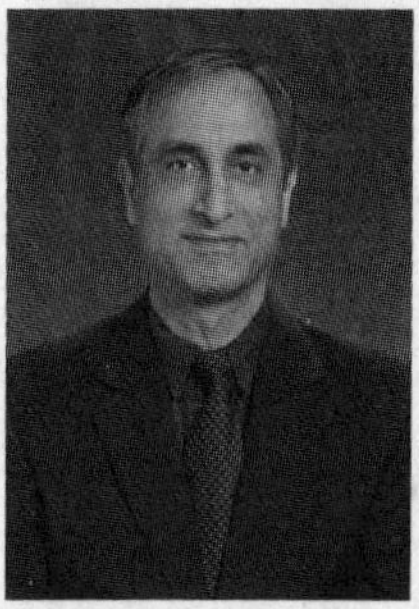

Subhash Kak is a scientist and historian. He teaches at the Oklahoma State University, Stillwater. He has held visiting appointments in Britain and Australia. His areas of research are history and philosophy of science. He has translated several Sanskrit texts, including Kaṇāda's *Vaiśeṣika Sūtra*, which is the earliest book on physics from India. Kak's work has been showcased in the popular media such as Discovery and History channels, PBS, Public TV in Europe, and in several documentaries on science and art. He is the author of 30 books, the most recent two being *The Idea of India: Bharat as a Civilisation* and *Eternal Bharat: Truth, Meaning, and Beauty*. He is a member of the Prime Minister's Science, Technology and Innovation Advisory Council (PM-STIAC). He was born in Srinagar and educated in Kashmir and Delhi.